BESTSELLING BOOK SERIES

MCSE Networking Essentials For Dummies®, 2nd Edition

IEEE 802 specifications

Specification	Description
802.3	CSMA/CD (Ethernet)
802.4	Token-passing bus network
802.5	Token-passing ring network
802.12	Demand Priority Access network

Maximum cable distances

Cable media	Maximum distance per segment
Fiber optic	2,000 meters
10Base5 (thicknet)	500 meters
10Base2 (thinnet)	185 meters
10BaseT (twisted pair)	100 meters

Maximum nodes

Network	Maximum number of nodes
10Base5	100
10Base2	30
10BaseT	1024

Network speeds

Network	Speed
Ethernet	10 Mbps
Fast Ethernet	100 Mbps
Token Ring	4 and 16 Mbps
FDDI	100 Mbps

Network devices

Device	Layer
Bridge	Data Link
Repeater	Physical
Router	Network
Gateway	Upper four

Coaxial cable types

Specification	Description
RG-58 /U	Solid copper wire
RG-58 A/U	Stranded copper wire
RG-58 C/U	Military RG-58 A/U specification
RG-59	Television coaxial cable
RG-62	ARCnet

The OSI model

Physical layer: Puts all the data on the network, which has to do with the electrical, mechanical, or optical interface used.

Data Link layer: Provides the physical interconnection between two devices. Includes hardware (MAC) addresses.

Network layer: Concerned with addressing, routing, and traffic problems.

Transport layer: Breaks the messages into frames. This layer has to figure out the right frame size to break the messages into. Based upon physical (Data Link) layer protocol, ethernet packets are approximately 1514 (from 72 to 1526) bytes in length, and token-ring packets are approximately 4K in length.

Session layer: Concerned with starting, using, and ending a connection, or session. This layer must make sure both computers know who transmits and for how long.

Presentation layer: Translates the information between the two computers. It can also make use of encryption. Compression can also be used at this level.

Application layer: Directly supports applications for file transfer, messaging, and database access.

Definitions

Baseband uses a single frequency and transmits digital signals, whereas *broadband* transmission uses a range of frequencies and transmits analog signals.

Share-level security enables you to assign passwords to resources; only users with valid passwords are allowed access. *User-level security* authenticates the user with a list of authorized users for that particular resource.

CSMA/CD uses collision detection to listen on the network for an opportunity to transmit. *CSMA/CA* uses collision avoidance by broadcasting its intent to transmit on the network before actually transmitting.

MCSE Networking Essentials For Dummies®, 2nd Edition

Cheat Sheet

Network diagnostic tools

Time domain reflectometer (TDR)	Uses sonarlike pulses on the network media to detect shorts and breaks
Network monitor	Captures and analyzes packets on the network
Protocol analyzer and congestion	Uses software only or a combination of hardware and software that monitors traffic on a network
Oscilloscope	Measures signal voltage on the network media
Digital volt meter (DVM)	Measures signal voltage through resistance

Remembering the layers of the OSI model

All	Application layer
People	Presentation layer
Seem	Session layer
To	Transport layer
Need	Network layer
Data	Data Link layer
Processing	Physical layer

Default Interrupt Request Lines (IRQs)

IRQ	Typical Use
1	Keyboard
2	Video card
3	Com 2, Com 4
4	Com 1, Com 3
6	Floppy disk controller
7	Parallel port (LPT1)
9	Cascaded IRQ 2
12	PS/2 mouse
14	Hard disk controller

On test day . . .

Before the test begins, quickly write down as much as you can remember concerning the following topics:

- IRQs
- Layers of the OSI model
- Where network devices lie in the OSI model
- Network cable specifications (maximum length, name, type, speed)

The IDG Books Worldwide logo is a registered trademark under exclusive license to IDG Books Worldwide, Inc., from International Data Group, Inc. The ...For Dummies logo is a trademark, and For Dummies and ...For Dummies are registered trademarks of IDG Books Worldwide, Inc. All other trademarks are the property of their respective owners.

...For Dummies®: Bestselling Book Series

™

BESTSELLING BOOK SERIES

Certification for the Rest of Us! ™

Are you intimidated and confused by computers? Do you find that traditional manuals are overloaded with technical details you'll never use? Do your friends and family always call you to fix simple problems on their PCs? Then the *...For Dummies*® computer book series from IDG Books Worldwide is for you.

...For Dummies books are written for those frustrated computer users who know they aren't really dumb but find that PC hardware, software, and indeed the unique vocabulary of computing make them feel helpless. *...For Dummies* books use a lighthearted approach, a down-to-earth style, and even cartoons and humorous icons to dispel computer novices' fears and build their confidence. Lighthearted but not lightweight, these books are a perfect survival guide for anyone forced to use a computer.

> *"I like my copy so much I told friends; now they bought copies."*
>
> — **Irene C., Orwell, Ohio**

> *"Quick, concise, nontechnical, and humorous."*
>
> — **Jay A., Elburn, Illinois**

> *"Thanks, I needed this book. Now I can sleep at night."*
>
> — **Robin F., British Columbia, Canada**

Already, millions of satisfied readers agree. They have made *...For Dummies* books the #1 introductory level computer book series and have written asking for more. So, if you're looking for the most fun and easy way to learn about computers, look to *...For Dummies* books to give you a helping hand.

IDG BOOKS WORLDWIDE ®

MCSE
NETWORKING
ESSENTIALS
FOR
DUMMIES®

2ND EDITION

MCSE
NETWORKING
ESSENTIALS
FOR
DUMMIES®

2ND EDITION

by Robert Aschermann

Foreword by Eckhart Boehme

IDG
BOOKS
WORLDWIDE

IDG Books Worldwide, Inc.
An International Data Group Company

Foster City, CA ♦ Chicago, IL ♦ Indianapolis, IN ♦ New York, NY

MCSE Networking Essentials For Dummies®, 2nd Edition

Published by
IDG Books Worldwide, Inc.
An International Data Group Company
919 E. Hillsdale Blvd.
Suite 400
Foster City, CA 94404
www.idgbooks.com (IDG Books Worldwide Web site)
www.dummies.com (Dummies Press Web site)

Library of Congress Catalog Card No.: 98-85839

ISBN: 0-7645-0614-5

Printed in the United States of America

10 9 8 7 6 5 4 3 2

2O/RQ/QY/ZZ/IN

Distributed in the United States by IDG Books Worldwide, Inc.

Distributed by CDG Books Canada Inc. for Canada; by Transworld Publishers Limited in the United Kingdom; by IDG Norge Books for Norway; by IDG Sweden Books for Sweden; by IDG Books Australia Publishing Corporation Pty. Ltd. for Australia and New Zealand; by TransQuest Publishers Pte Ltd. for Singapore, Malaysia, Thailand, Indonesia, and Hong Kong; by Gotop Information Inc. for Taiwan; by ICG Muse, Inc. for Japan; by Norma Comunicaciones S.A. for Colombia; by Intersoft for South Africa; by Eyrolles for France; by International Thomson Publishing for Germany, Austria and Switzerland; by Distribuidora Cuspide for Argentina; by Livraria Cultura for Brazil; by Ediciones ZETA S.C.R. Ltda. for Peru; by WS Computer Publishing Corporation, Inc., for the Philippines; by Contemporanea de Ediciones for Venezuela; by Express Computer Distributors for the Caribbean and West Indies; by Micronesia Media Distributor, Inc. for Micronesia; by Grupo Editorial Norma S.A. for Guatemala; by Chips Computadoras S.A. de C.V. for Mexico; by Editorial Norma de Panama S.A. for Panama; by American Bookshops for Finland. Authorized Sales Agent: Anthony Rudkin Associates for the Middle East and North Africa.

For general information on IDG Books Worldwide's books in the U.S., please call our Consumer Customer Service department at 800-762-2974. For reseller information, including discounts and premium sales, please call our Reseller Customer Service department at 800-434-3422.

For information on where to purchase IDG Books Worldwide's books outside the U.S., please contact our International Sales department at 317-596-5530 or fax 317-596-5692.

For consumer information on foreign language translations, please contact our Customer Service department at 1-800-434-3422, fax 317-596-5692, or e-mail rights@idgbooks.com.

For information on licensing foreign or domestic rights, please phone +1-650-655-3109.

For sales inquiries and special prices for bulk quantities, please contact our Sales department at 650-655-3200 or write to the address above.

For information on using IDG Books Worldwide's books in the classroom or for ordering examination copies, please contact our Educational Sales department at 800-434-2086 or fax 317-596-5499.

For press review copies, author interviews, or other publicity information, please contact our Public Relations department at 650-655-3000 or fax 650-655-3299.

For authorization to photocopy items for corporate, personal, or educational use, please contact Copyright Clearance Center, 222 Rosewood Drive, Danvers, MA 01923, or fax 978-750-4470.

About the Authors

Robert Aschermann (MCP, MCSE, MCT, MBA) has been involved with networking as an IS professional for nearly ten years. During his career, he has worked in technical support, systems design, consulting, and training. Robert has been an MCSE for almost three years and has passed 15 Microsoft certification exams. By the time this book reaches print, he should be one of the first to obtain the new Microsoft certification, Microsoft Certified Systems Engineer + Internet (MCSE+I). Currently, Robert works as a trainer and consultant for Empower Trainers and Consultants, Inc., one of Microsoft's oldest and largest Authorized Technical Education Centers (ATEC). Courses that he leads include Networking Essentials, TCP/IP, SNA Server, Windows NT Administration, Windows NT Core Technologies, and Windows NT in the Enterprise. He is also a Certified Sylvan-Prometric Test Administrator.

While working with Empower Trainers and Consultants, Robert has worked in almost every major line of business the company offers, including Systems Integration, Application Development, and Project Management, as well as Technical Training. As a project manager, he has led large Microsoft Windows NT and Windows 95 operating systems migrations and deployments as well as many small networking infrastructure upgrades.

Syngress Media creates books and software for information technology professionals seeking skill enhancement and career advancement. Its products are designed to comply with vendor and industry-standard course curricula and are optimized for certification exam preparation.

About the Contributors

Todd Shanaberger works for DataNet, a systems integrator and Microsoft Solutions Provider located in Raleigh, North Carolina. He is a Microsoft Certified Systems Engineer and a Certified Netware Administrator. Todd lives in Raleigh with his wife Cathelene and can be contacted at rtshanab@intrex.net.

Kyle L. Rhynerson (MCSE, MCP+I, MCT, MBA) has focused his interest and talents in the IS profession toward the areas of training and Internet/intranet development. While working at Kansas City–based Sprint and later Sprint PCS, he was able to build his expertise in each of these fields. He created content for both the companies' intranets and facilitated training classes for Sprint PCS. He has also created Web sites for several commercial businesses and a local university. Currently, Kyle is a technical trainer for Empower Trainers and Consultants, Inc. Some of the courses that Kyle's certifications and experience have prepared him to instruct include Internet Information Server, Networking Essentials, Windows NT Administration, Windows NT Core Technologies, and Windows NT in the Enterprise.

Paul Shields is a Microsoft Certified Systems Engineer. He has installed and administered Macintosh and Windows networks for the last five years. He has been a key implementor of integration technologies for Macintosh, Windows, and UNIX platforms. He is currently working as advisor for Desktop Computing and Support Strategies at a major telecommunications firm.

Tom Gugliotta lives in Albuquerque, New Mexico, with his wife, Joan, and baby son, Daniel. He holds a BS degree in Geology from the University of New Mexico and works at a major research laboratory in Albuquerque. Tom obtained his MCSE certification in 1997 entirely through self-study. When Tom is not studying for another Microsoft exam, he can be found hiking, biking, reading, gardening, and playing with his new son.

ABOUT IDG BOOKS WORLDWIDE

Welcome to the world of IDG Books Worldwide.

IDG Books Worldwide, Inc., is a subsidiary of International Data Group, the world's largest publisher of computer-related information and the leading global provider of information services on information technology. IDG was founded more than 30 years ago by Patrick J. McGovern and now employs more than 9,000 people worldwide. IDG publishes more than 290 computer publications in over 75 countries. More than 90 million people read one or more IDG publications each month.

Launched in 1990, IDG Books Worldwide is today the #1 publisher of best-selling computer books in the United States. We are proud to have received eight awards from the Computer Press Association in recognition of editorial excellence and three from Computer Currents' First Annual Readers' Choice Awards. Our best-selling ...*For Dummies*® series has more than 50 million copies in print with translations in 31 languages. IDG Books Worldwide, through a joint venture with IDG's Hi-Tech Beijing, became the first U.S. publisher to publish a computer book in the People's Republic of China. In record time, IDG Books Worldwide has become the first choice for millions of readers around the world who want to learn how to better manage their businesses.

Our mission is simple: Every one of our books is designed to bring extra value and skill-building instructions to the reader. Our books are written by experts who understand and care about our readers. The knowledge base of our editorial staff comes from years of experience in publishing, education, and journalism — experience we use to produce books to carry us into the new millennium. In short, we care about books, so we attract the best people. We devote special attention to details such as audience, interior design, use of icons, and illustrations. And because we use an efficient process of authoring, editing, and desktop publishing our books electronically, we can spend more time ensuring superior content and less time on the technicalities of making books.

You can count on our commitment to deliver high-quality books at competitive prices on topics you want to read about. At IDG Books Worldwide, we continue in the IDG tradition of delivering quality for more than 30 years. You'll find no better book on a subject than one from IDG Books Worldwide.

 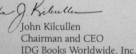

John Kilcullen
Chairman and CEO
IDG Books Worldwide, Inc.

Steven Berkowitz
President and Publisher
IDG Books Worldwide, Inc.

Eighth Annual
Computer Press
Awards ≥1992

Ninth Annual
Computer Press
Awards ≥1993

Tenth Annual
Computer Press
Awards ≥1994

Eleventh Annual
Computer Press
Awards ≥1995

IDG is the world's leading IT media, research and exposition company. Founded in 1964, IDG had 1997 revenues of $2.05 billion and has more than 9,000 employees worldwide. IDG offers the widest range of media options that reach IT buyers in 75 countries representing 95% of worldwide IT spending. IDG's diverse product and services portfolio spans six key areas including print publishing, online publishing, expositions and conferences, market research, education and training, and global marketing services. More than 90 million people read one or more of IDG's 290 magazines and newspapers, including IDG's leading global brands — Computerworld, PC World, Network World, Macworld and the Channel World family of publications. IDG Books Worldwide is one of the fastest-growing computer book publishers in the world, with more than 700 titles in 36 languages. The "...For Dummies®" series alone has more than 50 million copies in print. IDG offers online users the largest network of technology-specific Web sites around the world through IDG.net (http://www.idg.net), which comprises more than 225 targeted Web sites in 55 countries worldwide. International Data Corporation (IDC) is the world's largest provider of information technology data, analysis and consulting, with research centers in over 41 countries and more than 400 research analysts worldwide. IDG World Expo is a leading producer of more than 168 globally branded conferences and expositions in 35 countries including E3 (Electronic Entertainment Expo), Macworld Expo, ComNet, Windows World Expo, ICE (Internet Commerce Expo), Agenda, DEMO, and Spotlight. IDG's training subsidiary, ExecuTrain, is the world's largest computer training company, with more than 230 locations worldwide and 785 training courses. IDG Marketing Services helps industry-leading IT companies build international brand recognition by developing global integrated marketing programs via IDG's print, online and exposition products worldwide. Further information about the company can be found at www.idg.com. 1/24/99

Dedication

To my loving wife Rebecca, a constant source of support and inspiration.

Acknowledgments

I would like to thank the people at IDG Books who worked to bring this book to market, especially Diane Steele, Jill Pisoni, Mary Corder, Mary Bednarek, Susan Pink, and Suzanne Thomas.

Publisher's Acknowledgments

We're proud of this book; please register your comments through our IDG Books Worldwide Online Registration Form located at http://my2cents.dummies.com.

Some of the people who helped bring this book to market include the following:

Acquisitions, Editorial, and Media Development

Project Editors: Kelly Ewing, Susan Pink

Acquisitions Editors: Joyce Pepple, Jill Pisoni

Technical Editor: Greg Frankenfield

CD-ROM Exam Reviewers: Joe Wagner, MCSE, Systems Engineer, ST Labs, Inc.; Steven A. Frare, MCP, Network Engineer, ST Labs, Inc.

Media Development Editor: Joell Smith

Associate Permissions Editor: Carmen Krikorian

Media Development Coordinator: Megan Roney

Editorial Managers: Leah Cameron, Rev Mengle

Media Development Manager: Heather Heath Dismore

Editorial Assistants: Paul E. Kuzmic, Jamila Pree, Beth Parlon

Production

Project Coordinator: Tom Missler

Layout and Graphics: Kelly Hardesty, Angela F. Hunckler, Brent Savage, Jacque Schneider, Brian Torwelle

Proofreaders: Christine Berman, Marianne Santy, Janet M. Withers

Indexer: Sherry Massey

Special Help
Pat O'Brien; Gwenette Gaddis; Barry Pruett; Suzanne Thomas; Prime Synergy: Development of the QuickLearn Game by André LaMothe of Xtreme Games, LLC; CD-ROM Exam authored by Raul A. Jimenez, MCSE, MCT

General and Administrative

IDG Books Worldwide, Inc.: John Kilcullen, CEO; Steven Berkowitz, President and Publisher

IDG Books Technology Publishing Group: Richard Swadley, Senior Vice President and Publisher; Walter Bruce III, Vice President and Associate Publisher; Steven Sayre, Associate Publisher; Joseph Wikert, Associate Publisher; Mary Bednarek, Branded Product Development Director; Mary Corder, Editorial Director

IDG Books Consumer Publishing Group: Roland Elgey, Senior Vice President and Publisher; Kathleen A. Welton, Vice President and Publisher; Kevin Thornton, Acquisitions Manager; Kristin A. Cocks, Editorial Director

IDG Books Internet Publishing Group: Brenda McLaughlin, Senior Vice President and Publisher; Diane Graves Steele, Vice President and Associate Publisher; Sofia Marchant, Online Marketing Manager

IDG Books Production for Dummies Press: Michael R. Britton, Vice President of Production; Debbie Stailey, Associate Director of Production; Cindy L. Phipps, Manager of Project Coordination, Production Proofreading, and Indexing; Shelley Lea, Supervisor of Graphics and Design; Debbie J. Gates, Production Systems Specialist; Robert Springer, Supervisor of Proofreading; Laura Carpenter, Production Control Manager; Tony Augsburger, Supervisor of Reprints and Bluelines

Dummies Packaging and Book Design: Patty Page, Manager, Promotions Marketing

♦

The publisher would like to give special thanks to Patrick J. McGovern, without whom this book would not have been possible.

♦

Contents at a Glance

Table of Contents

Foreword

C ertification makes computer professionals stand out. Technical managers recognize the Microsoft Certified Professional (MCP) designation as a mark of quality — one that ensures that an employee or consultant has proven experience with and meets the high technical proficiency standards of Microsoft products. The ...*For Dummies* series from IDG Books Worldwide, Inc., really stands out in the marketplace and can help you achieve your goal of certification.

The ...*For Dummies* series of MCP Approved Study Guides is based on the exam's objectives — and designed to help you meet them. By partnering with Microsoft, IDG Books has develop the MCSE series to ensure that every subject on the exam is covered. Every Microsoft Approved Study Guide is reviewed and approved by an independent third party.

And certification will help you stand out from the crowd as one of the best in your industry. Microsoft training and certification let you maximize the potential of Microsoft Windows desktop operating systems; server technologies, such as the Internet Information Server, Microsoft Windows NT, and Microsoft BackOffice; and Microsoft development tools. In short, Microsoft training and certification provide you with the knowledge and skills necessary to become an expert on Microsoft products and technologies — and to provide the key competitive advantage that every business is seeking.

Research shows that MCP training and certification also provide these other benefits to businesses:

- ✔ A standard method for determining training needs and measuring results – an excellent return on training and certification investments

- ✔ Increased customer satisfaction and decreased support costs through improved service, increased productivity, and greater technical self-sufficiency

- ✔ A reliable benchmark for hiring, promoting, and career planning

- ✔ Recognition and rewards for productive employees by validating their expertise

- ✔ Retraining options for existing employees so that they can work effectively with new technologies

- ✔ Assurance of quality when outsourcing computer services

As an MCP, you'll also receive many other benefits, including direct access to technical information from Microsoft; the official MCP logo and other materials to identify your status to colleagues and clients; invitations to Microsoft conferences, technical training sessions and special events; and exclusive publications with news about the MCP program.

The challenges — both for individuals and for the industry — are out there. Microsoft training and certification will help prepare you to face them. Let this book be your guide.

— Eckhart Boehme, Marketing Manager Certification and Skills Assessment, Microsoft, Inc.

Introduction

• •

So you think you need a little help passing the Microsoft Networking Essentials (70-058) certification test? You've come to the right place. This book was written for people just like you.

I'm a Microsoft Certified Trainer (MCT), and one of the classes I teach is Networking Essentials. I classify my students into one of two categories. The first category are those who think the information may help them in their job or who want to know how something works. The second group, by far the larger of the two, are those planning to take the certification test. This second group is more challenging because these students have a goal and expect me to help them attain it. I assume you're in the second group and hungry for certification!

As soon as you attain a certification in one area, Microsoft puts out a new product, and your certification in a different area becomes out of date. As a veteran of 15 certification tests, all related to networking, Microsoft operating systems, or Microsoft BackOffice products, I've developed a guerrilla warfare approach to certification. The only way to get ahead is to minimize study time and maximize test-taking skills. To do this, you may have to adjust your perception of product knowledge.

Some people feel that product knowledge requires mastery of a product. I disagree. You don't have time to master a product these days. Instead, my definition of product knowledge requires you to be only productive with a product. This level of knowledge will get you through the certification test. Being certified will get you opportunities to work with the product. Working with the product will help you master it. I don't believe you can master a product by sitting through a class or reading a book.

With this in mind, *MCSE Networking Essentials For Dummies,* 2nd Edition will help you gain the product knowledge you need while pointing out some land mines and booby-traps you might run into on the test. This book is an MCSE study guide, not a networking basics reference book. Plenty of the latter are available, and I highly recommend that you purchase one to use during your Networking Essentials studying. Use this book as your outline.

Already certified as a Novell or Banyan CNE? Consider taking another MCP exam instead of Networking Essentials. Your current certification covers the requirements of the Networking Essentials exam, so you're entitled to free credit for Networking Essentials if you pass any other MCP exam. Take another MCP exam and then apply to Microsoft for your credit. After Microsoft has verified your certification, your official transcript will show credit for the Networking Essentials exam.

How This Book Is Organized

Each chapter in the book contains all the tools you need to study for and to pass the exam. Here's how it works. Every chapter starts with a preview of what's to come, usually in the form of a list of exam objectives covered in the chapter.

Next, for those chapters that address exam objectives, you are presented with a Quick Assessment quiz that assesses what you already know about the objectives. The questions are grouped by objective, and the answers tell you which section to review in the chapter. If you're in a hurry, study only the sections pertaining to the questions you miss. If you answer all the questions correctly, skip to the end of the chapter and have a shot at the Prep Test.

The Prep Test poses questions as you'll find them on the exam. Each question gauges your understanding of a chapter's topic. If you miss a question, the answer tells you which section of the chapter to review. Also like the exam, Prep Test questions have circles to mark when only one answer is correct. When questions could have more than one answer, the answers have squares to mark.

In addition to chapter divisions, the book is divided also into parts. The following sections describe the different parts of _MCSE Networking Essentials For Dummies,_ 2nd Edition.

Part I: A Journey of a Thousand Miles

Part I is where it all begins. You find out about exam-specific information and are introduced to the certification roadmap. The technical information in this section may not be specifically testable, but it is necessary as a foundation for the material that is testable. The certification roadmap is your guidebook to achieving the coveted MCSE certification. If you periodically review the roadmap, it will help you stay focused on your journey and keep you from making a wrong turn.

Part II: Networking Standards and Deployment

Part II is one of the most important parts in the book. Many of the test questions directly test your knowledge of standards, terminology, and the different limitations of each standard. Other questions are scenario based and test the same material from an application standpoint. In this part, you concentrate on popular networking standards including Ethernet, token ring, ATM, and FDDI. You also review terminology such as bridging, routing, and gateways. This part reviews the OSI model to provide a framework for organizing protocols and various LAN and WAN technologies. Microsoft Remote Access Service and methods for expanding networks are also discussed in Part II.

Part III: Selecting, Installing, and Troubleshooting Hardware and Media

Part III prepares you for questions on the fundamentals of planning and deploying different types of networks. Special attention is given to choosing the appropriate topology, media access method, and physical media. The many pages describing decision-making criteria, such as cost, security, flexibility, and growth potential, reflect the relative importance of these topics on the exam.

When it comes to planning, it's likely that you'll encounter scenario questions on the exam. I present information in this part in a way that should help you effectively analyze these types of questions. In Part III, you also find a chapter on installing network adapters and a chapter on troubleshooting network adapters; both topics constitute a large portion of the exam. Part III also covers installing cables and connections, and finishes with a discussion of client systems.

Part IV: Installing and Troubleshooting Network Clients and Servers

In Part IV, you concentrate on making the distinction between clients and servers; this skill is necessary for analyzing some scenario-based questions on the exam. I also discuss the most important tasks that a network administrator performs. Generally accepted concepts of network administration are tested throughout the Networking Essentials exam.

Part V: The Part of Tens

Part V contains some top ten lists and is a great way to reinforce key points in the book. You'll probably have the first chapter in this part open on the passenger seat next to you as you drive to the exam. Don't spill! The second chapter discusses some online resources to tap before the exam.

Part VI: Appendixes

Appendixes A and B are complete practice exams that show you whether you're ready for test day! Appendix C is an overview of the Microsoft certification process and how the Networking Essentials exam fits into the various available certifications. Appendix D explains what's on the CD-ROM, which is full of powerful study aids and valuable resources.

Icons in This Book

Helps you manage and save time while taking the exam or studying.

Identifies correct and incorrect exam answers at a glance.

Highlights the important capabilities and advantages of the technology.

Points out problems and limitations of the technology that may appear on the exam.

Where to Go from Here

MCSE Networking Essentials For Dummies, 2nd Edition is all you need to prepare for the Networking Essentials exam. So don't waste time: Turn the page and get started!

Part I
A Journey of a Thousand Miles

The 5th Wave   By Rich Tennant

Rev. Mark

"Miss Lamont, I'm filing the congregation under 'SOULS', my sermons under 'GRACE', and the financial contributions under 'AMEN'."

In this part . . .

Some say the purpose of a journey is not the arrival but the journey itself. That's great if you're looking for spiritual healing, but you're trying to pass a certification test! Your purpose is most definitely to arrive.

Before you start studying, it's imperative that you understand the domain of knowledge the test covers so that you can make the most efficient use of your time. In this part, you find out about what is — and is not — on the test. In that way, you can figure out what you must do to successfully complete the certification test.

I'll never forget the first certification test I scored really well on: 980 out of 1,000. When I showed my mentor my test results, he asked what score I needed to pass. I told him 750. He shook his head and said, "You over-studied by 230 points. You could have passed almost two certification tests in the time it took you to pass this one." He had a good point. The Networking Essentials test is a pass-or-fail test, so you should study for it as such. The rest of this book is organized to help you do just that.

Chapter 1

The Networking Essentials Exam

*T*he Networking Essentials exam (70-058) is usually the first or the last Microsoft certification exam that most certified professional candidates take. That's not to say that it's a make-or-break test. It just seems that people either look forward to or dread this test. I think it has to do with the amount of networking experience they've had before studying for the exam. The comments I hear are either "That was the easiest test I've taken," or "That test was a killer!" People who find the test difficult usually cite the fact that the test covers such a wide range of information: from Ethernet standard specifications to developing a backup procedure and performing data recovery. At least with such a broad area of knowledge being tested, the shallower the testing is in any one area.

The Exam

The Microsoft preparation guide on the Networking Essentials exam states the following:

> This certification exam measures your ability to implement, administer, and troubleshoot information systems that incorporate Microsoft Windows 95, and any products in the Microsoft BackOffice family. The exam covers only the networking knowledge and skills common to both Windows 95 and BackOffice products.

The items you will be tested on are shown in the following bullet lists.

Standards and terminology:

- ✔ Define common networking terms for LANs and WANs.
- ✔ Compare a file-and-print server with an application server.
- ✔ Compare user-level security with access permissions to a shared directory on a server.
- ✔ Compare a client/server network with a peer-to-peer network.
- ✔ Compare the implications of using connection-oriented communications with connectionless communications.
- ✔ Distinguish whether SLIP or PPP is used as the communications protocol for various situations.
- ✔ Define the communications devices that communicate at each level of the OSI model.
- ✔ Describe the characteristics and purpose of the media used in IEEE 802.3 and IEEE 802.5 standards.
- ✔ Explain the purpose of NDIS and Novell ODI network standards.

Planning:

- ✔ Select the appropriate media for various situations. Media choices include:

  Twisted-pair cable

  Coaxial cable

  Fiber-optic cable

  Wireless

  Situational elements include:

  Cost

  Distance limitations

  Number of nodes

- ✔ Select the appropriate topology for various token-ring and Ethernet networks.

✔ Select the appropriate network and transport protocol of protocols for various token-ring and Ethernet networks. Protocol choices include:

  DLC

  AppleTalk

  IPX

  TCP/IP

  NFS

  SMB

✔ Select the appropriate connectivity devices for various token-ring and Ethernet networks. Connectivity devices include:

  Repeaters

  Bridges

  Routers

  Brouters

  Gateways

✔ List the characteristics, requirements, and appropriate situations for WAN connection services. WAN connection services include:

  X.25

  ISDN

  Frame relay

  ATM

Implementation:

✔ Choose an administrative plan to meet specified needs including performance management, account management, and security.

✔ Choose a disaster recovery plan for various situations.

✔ Given the manufacturer's documentation for the network adapter, install, configure, and resolve hardware conflicts for multiple adapters in a token-ring or Ethernet network.

✔ Implement a NetBIOS naming scheme for all computers on a given network.

✔ Select the appropriate hardware and software tools to monitor trends in the network.

Troubleshooting:

- ✔ Identify common errors associated with components required for communications.
- ✔ Diagnose and resolve common connectivity problems with cards, cables, and related hardware.
- ✔ Resolve broadcast storms.
- ✔ Identify and resolve network performance problems.

Number of questions

You will be given 30 minutes to answer 15 to 40 test questions. How many questions you're asked depends on how well you do on the previous question. For example, if you answer one question correctly, the next question is a little harder; if you answer a question incorrectly, the next question is easier. If you answer every question correctly, you will receive only 15 questions. (Good for you!) The more questions you miss, the more you receive. If you receive all 40 test questions, you fail.

I suppose that you're probably wondering what I scored on the test. (It wasn't adaptive then.) Well, you did buy the book, so it's only fair to tell you. On a scale of 1,000 points with a passing score of 793, I scored a 948. My section scores were 100 percent on standards and terminology, 93 percent on planning, 100 percent on implementation, and 86 percent on troubleshooting.

I still can't figure out what happened in the troubleshooting area. Either there were fewer questions or my previous experience worked against me. Believe it or not, people with little or no networking background have an advantage over the pros in the troubleshooting section.

You get credit for knowing only the Microsoft way of doing things. Remember that. Those of us who have been networking for a while know half a dozen ways to test something, and some of them are better than the Microsoft way. It doesn't matter though. Why? *You get credit for knowing only the Microsoft way of doing things!*

How questions are structured

Some questions have multiple correct answers, so read through all the possible answers. Questions that allow you to choose multiple answers are accompanied by check boxes instead of radio buttons, which allow you to select only one answer at a time. The existence of a check box, however, doesn't necessarily mean the question has more than one correct answer.

One aspect of the Networking Essentials test that I like is that most questions are short — a small paragraph or a single sentence. The answers are equally short. The only exception is the situational-type question, which involves more reading because it consists of a setup paragraph, a paragraph defining objectives, a paragraph defining the proposed solution, and finally the multiple-choice answer.

Study Strategy

This section details my approach to test taking. Although I've validated this approach on more than 15 certification exams, it isn't for everybody. You must develop your own approach if you plan on becoming and remaining a Microsoft Certified Professional. Testing is a fact of life. Accept it and excel at it.

If my approach doesn't work for you, seek out someone who has passed a number of exams and is similar to you in personality, age, educational background, and so on. Find out his or her methodology and try to adapt it to your characteristics. The more people you talk to, the more ideas you will have to work with.

Unfortunately, some information you need to know for the exam has to be memorized. Let's face it — you can't use deductive reasoning to determine what the maximum cable distance is for 10BaseT using Category 5 twisted-pair wire. Throughout the book, tables contain information you need to memorize. This format enables you to see all the information at a glance and aids in retention because the information is presented in a logical structure.

Part of my personal study routine for certification exams is to mark all the pages containing tables, charts, and diagrams in the books that I use. If I'm struggling with information in a book and it doesn't have an accompanying graphic, I create my own. This improves my understanding and gives me something to study later.

I always schedule at least an hour before the test as cram time. I take my books, notes, and graphics and lock myself in a quiet room. I spend a minute or two clearing my mind and concentrating on the task at hand. Then I dive in. I quickly review everything I have marked at least twice and memorize the things that have to be memorized.

When I'm finally in the testing room, I go through all the test questions looking for the ones that require regurgitated information, such as the standards and terminology section. After answering those questions, I clear my mind of that information and concentrate on the questions that require deductive reasoning, such as the planning, implementation, and trouble-shooting questions. The human mind isn't great at handling multiple modes of operation at the same time. The mind is best at recall when that's all it has to do, and it's best at deductive reasoning when a lot of recall isn't involved.

How long should I study?

You can study for the certification exam in many ways. The first exam you take is always the hardest because you don't have your studying methodology defined yet. After the second or third test, studying is much less stressful and time consuming because you have a good feel for what you must do to prepare.

On the first certification exam you take, you will probably find that you have studied either too much or not enough. You'll likely go back and forth between too much and not enough for the next few exams until you settle on the right amount. At $100 a pop, erring on the side of too much studying is easier on your wallet.

A mentor once told me that certification exams give back exactly what you give them. If you don't give them the proper respect, you won't receive any in return. The Networking Essentials exam is no exception. I've known seasoned networking professionals who have failed because they didn't study, and I know networking novices that passed on the first try because they gave the certification test healthy respect and studied accordingly.

How much study is enough? The simple answer is that it depends on the individual. Here's a piece of information I dug out of a chapter on learning from an undergraduate psychology book. According to the text, when you feel comfortable with the material or can pass a basic skills assessment test, that represents 100 percent of the required studying needed to master the subject. Studies have shown that overstudying by 50 percent ensures long-term retention. For example, if it takes you two hours to master the OSI model, you would need to study the model for one more hour to ensure that you will remember enough information to pass the test in the next few weeks. (For all you psychology majors out there, forgive me if I oversimplified that.)

Another way to determine how long to study is to use vendor practice tests. I've used the Transcender series and find that it is an excellent set of tests. Transcender states that if you can consistently score 80 percent on all the tests it provides for a Microsoft certification test, it will guarantee that you will pass the Microsoft test. Transcender offers to pay for your Microsoft test if you fail. My guess is that it doesn't pay for many tests. Most of the time, I find the Transcender series of tests more difficult than the actual certification tests.

Where do I begin?

Where do you begin? You're off to a great start just by purchasing this study guide! However, you might want to acquire some additional resources. The Preparation Guide objectives are listed at the beginning of this chapter, but you may find it beneficial to explore the links leading from the Preparation Guide for Exam 70-058, Networking Essentials, at `http://www.microsoft.com/Mcp/exam/stat/SP70 058.htm`.

Studying advice

Following is the advice I give all my Networking Essentials students:

- Microsoft has been known to include questions that cover material not listed in the exam objectives, so be prepared to see some questions that seem to emphasize Windows 95 or Windows NT.

- Complete all chapter review questions, the appendix practice tests, vendor practice tests, and Microsoft roadmap or PEP tests. You can't take too many practice tests.

- Review the exam objectives periodically as you are studying. This will help reinforce the key areas and help you focus on them while you're studying.

- Watch out for incorrect answers on practice tests. Don't study purely from practice tests because even the Microsoft practice tests have some incorrect answers. If you think you've found an incorrect answer, research it and understand why it is incorrect.

- Remember that the main objective is to understand the material — not to pass the exam. If you understand the material, the exam is an afterthought. Some exam questions can't be answered unless you understand the technology behind the question.

The final piece of advice that I give my students on the last day of class may be the most important. Choose a date to take the test and register in advance. Draw a line in the sand and tell yourself, "I am taking the exam on. . . ." Then build a study plan working backward from your test date. Set some simple objectives and follow your plan. I've known too many students who have paid to take a class but have never taken the certification test because they haven't been able to set a deadline for themselves. If you break your certification into a series of small steps, your road to certification will be a challenging, yet rewarding, trip instead of an arduous trek.

Registering for the Exam

So, are you ready to schedule your test? Some people schedule a week or two ahead of time; others wait until a few days before. The exam fee is $100, well worth every penny when you pass!

You can register for the exam by contacting either of the following two companies:

- ✔ Sylvan Prometric at 1-800-755-EXAM, or you can register online at www.sylvanprometric.com.
- ✔ Virtual University Enterprises at 1-888-837-8618, or online at www.vue.com.

Chapter 2

Exam Prep Roadmap

● ●

In This Chapter

▶ Comparing LANs and WANs

▶ Sharing hardware and software

▶ Keeping data safe

▶ Finding out about clients and servers

▶ Discovering the different types of servers

▶ Reviewing the different types of network topologies

▶ Assessing the advantages and disadvantages of different types of media

▶ Beginning your network plan

● ●

*T*he types of networks and networking concepts form the foundation for all questions on the Networking Essentials exam.

The Networking Essentials exam is adaptive and consists of 15 to 40 questions. Expect to see questions like the following:

✔ **When is the best time to use a client/server network or a peer-to-peer network?** You need to know the differences between these networks and the situations that are best for each.

✔ **How do shared resources work?** You need to know how to share a resource, who assigns access to the resource, and where the access is given. You should know how resources are shared on both client/server and peer-to-peer networks.

The Networking Essentials exam is unique among the Microsoft certification exams. No other exam covers the breadth of material that the Networking Essentials exam does. That shouldn't scare you; just be prepared to study a wide variety of concepts and technologies.

In the next few sections, you examine some fundamentals of networking. This chapter is designed to help you get comfortable with the material in the rest of the book by giving you a sneak peek of what's to come.

Network Types

A local area network (LAN) connects a number of computers located geographically close to one another. For example, two computers directly connected to each other can be considered a LAN. A corporate network that services multiple adjacent buildings and links several hundred machines, however, can also be considered a LAN. Figure 2-1 shows a local area network.

A wide area network (WAN) ties together computers in locations that could be distributed throughout the country or even overseas. Most WANs comprise a number of LANs connected by long-distance, high-speed data links. A wide area network is shown in Figure 2-2.

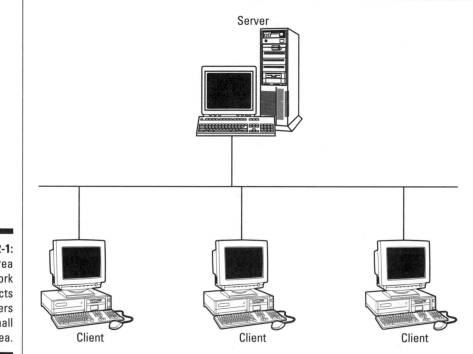

Figure 2-1:
A local area network connects computers in a small area.

Server

Client   Client   Client

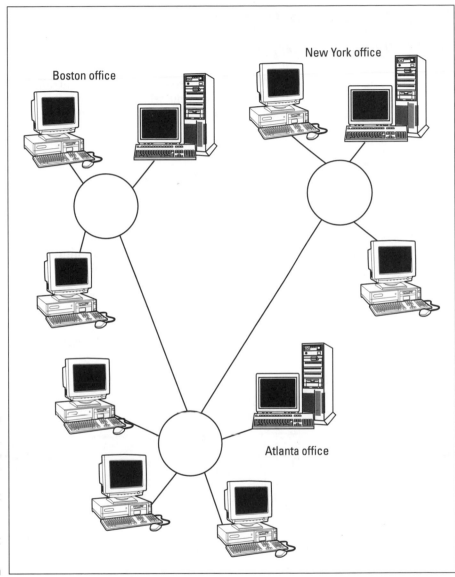

Figure 2-2:
A wide area
network
connects
LANs that
could be
located in
different
cities.

Sharing Hardware and Software Resources

The purpose of a network is to share resources in a controlled manner. You're probably familiar with sharing printers on a network, but you can share almost any hardware device, such as the following:

- CD-ROMs
- Tape backup drives
- Fax modems
- Hard drive storage

Some devices, such as certain types of printers, can be attached directly to the network and do not need to be attached to a computer. Figure 2-3 shows how you can connect devices to your network so that everyone can use them.

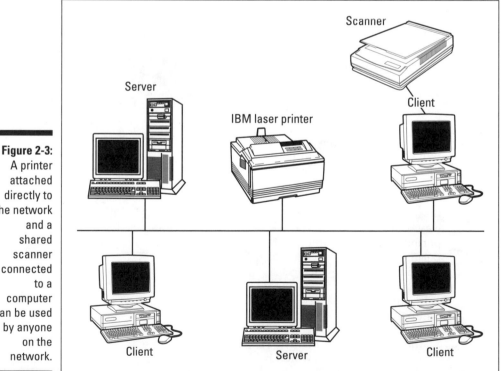

Figure 2-3:
A printer attached directly to the network and a shared scanner connected to a computer can be used by anyone on the network.

In addition to sharing hardware resources, networks can share software resources. The usual databases, spreadsheets, and other documents and data can be accessed from multiple computers. In addition, some applications can be installed on a single server, and multiple users (with the appropriate site or client licenses) can run the applications from that server. Creating a network share is accomplished through a process called *sharing*.

You need to know who *assigns* the share (does the sharing): Does the network administrator or the user who has the resource at his or her desk make the assignment?

You need to know also who has *access* to the resource: Is everyone allowed to use it, or will you set up a password to control access? If you are sharing a printer, for example, you might need to restrict access to it — you wouldn't want everyone sending their favorite JPEG files to your expensive color laser printer! Or perhaps the type of shared resource is data, rather than hardware. People in an accounting department, for example, need to be able to exchange data on corporate earnings, but that information must not be available to other employees (at least, not until the quarterly report comes out).

Preserving and Protecting Information

Security and permissions are covered in more detail in Chapter 13. Here are some basics. How can you keep people from looking at information they shouldn't see, such as the personnel records of other employees? How do you make sure information is not lost if something happens to your network? A network can take care of both these jobs.

A network uses passwords to secure your data. You give each user on your network a user name and a password. This information must be entered every time a user logs on to the network. Only then will the network allow the user to access any information. You also set up access permissions so that users are allowed to work with only certain information and in only the way they are allowed to work with it. For example, one user might be permitted to read from and write to a file, whereas another user might be permitted to only read that file. What a user is allowed to do with information depends on the access permissions granted to the user's user account for that resource.

A network also allows you to back up information to a central location. If you do not have a backup and your system goes down, all the information on the system could be lost. You can back up all the information on your network to one place, which is usually a tape backup device on your network's server.

Clients and Servers

You will definitely see exam questions on the types of networks and their purposes. All computers on a network act either as a client or a server. A *server computer* shares resources, which can be files, printers, modems, or any other item on the network, with network users. A *client computer* uses the shared resources provided by the server.

In some networks, computers can act as both a client and a server. The computer is a server, for example, when it shares its attached printer with the other computers and the network. The computer is also a client when it accesses data shared on another computer. This type of computer on the network is known as a *peer,* and a network designed in this manner is a *peer-to-peer network.*

Client/server networks and domains

A client/server network provides for centralized control of network resources. One or more computers, called *servers,* share the resources on the network. All other computers, called *clients,* use these resources. Figure 2-4 shows the role of both servers and clients in a network.

A computer used as a server is usually not used also as a general office use computer. It is used solely to provide access to network resources, commonly used files and printers. User accounts and passwords are validated by a server with an accounts database. After users have been validated, they can access any resources they have been granted permissions to.

In a Windows NT network, users can be grouped in a domain, and their logons are handled by a domain controller, which is one of the servers on the network. The domain controller makes sure that this user is supposed to be on the network and then assigns the user access to the resources. The system administrator is responsible for assigning access rights to users based on what they need to do. Because these access rights are assigned in a central location, account administration is simplified.

Servers also centrally locate your data, making it easy to manage — access rights and backup procedures are all performed on a single machine, rather than distributed across a number of computers.

Client/server networks, however, can be relatively expensive, especially for a small workgroup, because the server is typically one of the most expensive computers on the network and all it does is share resources. The network operating system software can also be expensive. Another disadvantage of client/server networks involves resource availability and single point of failure. If the server goes down, no one can access any resources shared on that server until it is repaired.

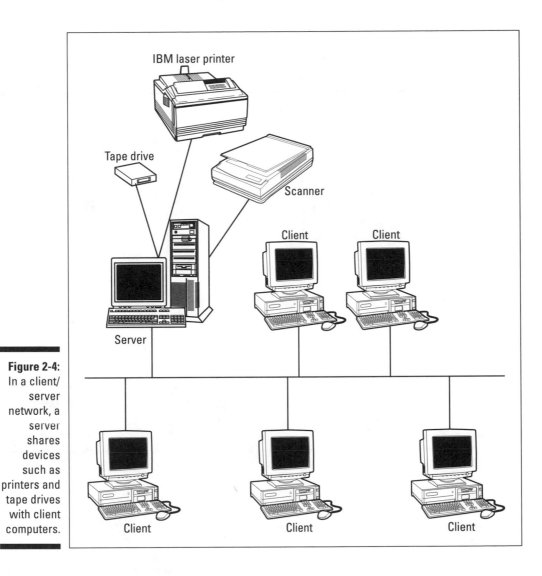

Figure 2-4:
In a client/
server
network, a
server
shares
devices
such as
printers and
tape drives
with client
computers.

Peer-to-peer networks

A peer-to-peer network has no centralized administration and no computers acting solely as servers. Each computer on the network can act as either a server, by sharing resources, or a client, by using a shared resource on another computer. Figure 2-5 shows a peer-to-peer network.

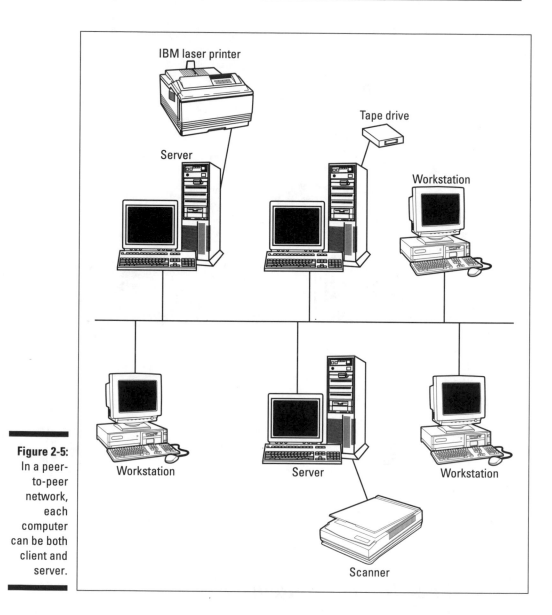

Figure 2-5:
In a peer-
to-peer
network,
each
computer
can be both
client and
server.

Any peer computer with a shared resource will experience a performance degradation when that resource is accessed. For example, if a peer computer is sharing a printer, that computer might slow down when someone prints. In addition, because shared resources are distributed around the network, it can be difficult to find which computer has the resource you need. An even more vexing problem is how to deal with access rights. Each user has to assign access rights to his or her shared resources.

Peer-to-peer networks do have advantages. They are much cheaper and easier to set up than a client/server network. In a small office in which users need to share some data files and printers, a peer-to-peer network is a good way to start. In addition, if one computer goes down, it will not affect the rest of the network except that the resource on that computer will be unavailable.

Here are a few tips on when you should use a peer-to-peer network. These questions may help answer a question on your exam. Presented with a scenario, ask yourself the following:

✔ Does the network have less than ten users?

✔ Is the business not very concerned with security?

✔ Are all users in the same general area?

✔ Is the organization not planning to grow rapidly soon?

If you can answer yes to all these questions, a peer-to-peer network might be a good solution.

Table 2-1 shows a side-by-side comparison of peer-to-peer and client/server networks.

Table 2-1	Network Consideration	
Issue	*Peer-to-Peer*	*Client/Server*
Size	Works well for up to ten users	Limited only by hardware and software
Cost	Inexpensive	Can become very expensive depending on the network size
Security	Maintained by each user	Maintained by an administrator
Administrator	Each user maintains his or her own computer	One administrator maintains all computers
Backups	Each user is responsible for backing up his or her data	One central system backs up everything

On the exam, you will see questions trying to confuse you with the incorrect use of a peer-to-peer or client/server network. You will see also several questions about which type of network to use in a given situation, so study Table 2-1 and be prepared.

Hybrid networks

Many of today's networks use various good features of both client/server and peer-to-peer networks. This creates a hybrid, or combination, network. A *hybrid network* usually has a network server running a network operating system such as Microsoft Windows NT that is used for central file storage, user logon authentication, and backup resources. Client computers on the network can access these resources in a client/server role. These computers can act also like peers and share resources such as a printer or data on their local hard disk. Although this type of network is useful, it can be difficult to set up and maintain. Figure 2-6 shows how you can combine client/server and peer-to-peer networks to create a hybrid network.

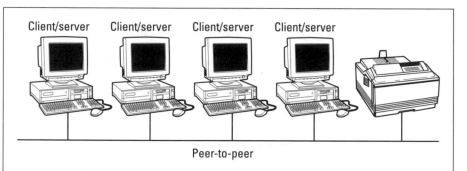

Figure 2-6:
Servers and
clients both
share
resources
on a hybrid
network.

Peer security versus server security

Security is a major issue in a network and therefore a probable topic for exam questions. This section is a basic review.

With very sensitive data, a client/server network is almost a must. All security is handled at the server, where logons are processed. This security is set up and maintained by a person or a team of people who should be well trained in network security. In a peer-to-peer network, security is maintained by each user for his or her computer. Because users have varying levels of expertise — and varying levels of concern — a peer-to-peer network is less secure than a client/server configuration.

No matter which network system is used, passwords are the keys to the network. If someone knows your password, he or she can access your data just as you can. You — and users on the network — need to follow some important rules about passwords:

✔ Change passwords frequently. Most network operating systems have a setting that enables you to force users to change their passwords at a set interval, such as every 45 days.

✔ Require unique passwords. In this way, a user cannot change his or her password and then immediately change it back to what it was originally.

Server Types

Several types of servers will be presented in exam questions, so this section offers a refresher course. A server can fulfill many different needs. For example, a server may be used primarily to share disk resources and printers, or it may be used primarily to share server-based applications. Some servers are used for special purposes such as network fax servers or communications gateways.

After you establish what type of servers you need in your environment, you should think about and plan for network growth. You want to be able to implement new servers as your network grows without having to inconvenience your users. Figure 2-7 shows a network that utilizes many types of servers.

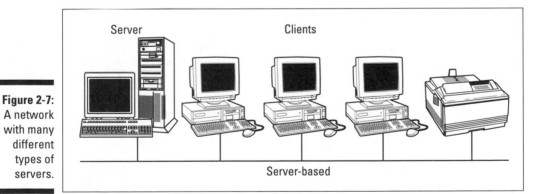

Figure 2-7: A network with many different types of servers.

Server   Clients

Server-based

File servers

Almost every network has at least one file server. This is where users store data files such as word-processing documents, spreadsheets, and graphics files. File servers provide a centralized storage area for data. This central storage area also makes it easier to do backups — you back up only the file server rather than every computer that has data stored on it.

Print servers

In a small, peer-to-peer network, simply sharing a printer on a computer and letting everyone else print to it works fine. When a network becomes larger, the computer connected to the printer would slow down to the point where it could not work efficiently. In this case, you can set up a print server to handle printer sharing.

A print server makes printers available to users over a network. Each printer defined on the server accepts print jobs from users and holds those jobs until a print device is available. The print server handles the slow communications to the printer so users can return to their program faster than if they were printing directly to a print device.

In addition to being faster, printing to a queue can also be cheaper. One printer can be used by many people instead of having a separate printer for each person. The printer can also be located in a central area for the use of all users instead of in someone's office as a shared printer would be in a peer-to-peer network.

Communications servers

You can set up a communications mail server to handle your network communications, including the following tasks:

- **Electronic mail.** An e-mail server can handle your office e-mail and take care of all the e-mail you need to send to and receive from the Internet. A separate server just to handle e-mail can be set up if the volume of messages is large.

- **Fax.** A fax server can handle all faxing needs. This server can share fax modems and allow many users to have access to faxing capabilities while using only a small number of fax modems.

- **Internet.** Everyone wants to surf the Internet. In addition, many companies use the Internet to do business. Your company may want to set up an Internet server to handle its Web pages and Internet services.

Application servers

Question: Your network has several hundred users running Microsoft Office 95, which is installed on their hard drives. Your company decides you need to upgrade all the users to Microsoft Office 97. What do you do?

With an application server, you wouldn't have to run a setup program on every computer. Instead, if a network version of Office 95 is installed on an application server, you simply upgrade this version to Office 97. All users would be updated automatically. They access the software from the application server and load it into their computer's memory to run it.

Another benefit to using an application server is that you can make sure everyone is using the same version of software. You don't have different versions floating around that have to be maintained and supported. It's also easy to back up these applications because they are all on one server.

Note that your application server should not be the same as your file server. Otherwise, if many users are accessing programs and files at the same time, network performance will suffer.

If you decide to use an application server, you probably won't be able to just install the software on the server and let everyone run it. Usually you have to buy a network version of the software, which allows multiple users to access the program at the same time.

Database servers

Database servers can provide a network with a way to handle a large database application, which can contain several gigabytes of data and would not run efficiently on a regular computer. The server handles all data storage, database management, and query requests. The computers run the client end of the application and send requests for data to the server. Distributed databases can be spanned across several servers to increase processing power and storage, while still appearing to be in one place to the client computers.

Network Topology

Topology is a picture of how computers, printers, and other components on the network are physically connected. This is the design used to lay out the network before cable is run. The type of topology affects what type of network adapters are in each computer, the way the network can expand, and how the cables will be run to each computer.

The three basic types of topology are

- ✔ **Bus:** The computers are connected in a row on the cable.
- ✔ **Star:** Each computer has its own cable segment and all cable segments run back to a central location, or a *hub*.
- ✔ **Ring:** The cable forms a closed circle, with all computers attached to that circular cable.

Most networks are made up of combinations of these three. The two most common combinations are star-bus and star-ring.

Topology is another main topic on the exam, taking up probably four or five questions. Study the topology diagrams and know what each looks like. You will usually be given a description of how the network is set up and asked what type of topology is being used. The description on the test will usually let you visualize how the topology looks, and you should be able to match that to the correct name.

Network Media

The network *media* is the device that physically carries the data from computer to computer. The three major types of network media are

- Copper cable
- Fiber-optic cable
- Wireless

Figure 2-8 shows different media that you can use in your network.

Copper cable

Copper cable is the most common type of network media used today. The data is carried over the copper cable in the form of electrical signals from computer to computer. The disadvantage of sending data over a copper wire is that the farther the signal travels, the weaker it becomes. Copper is, however, the easiest, quickest, and cheapest form of network media to install. (Remember that — it may help answer an exam question!) Most of today's local area networks use copper cable.

Fiber-optic cable

Fiber-optic cable uses glass strands to transmit data at the speed of light. The data is carried over these glass strands in the form of light beams. These beams of light can carry signals a much greater distance at a much higher speed than copper cable. These signals are not as subject to degradation or electronic interference as is the case with copper.

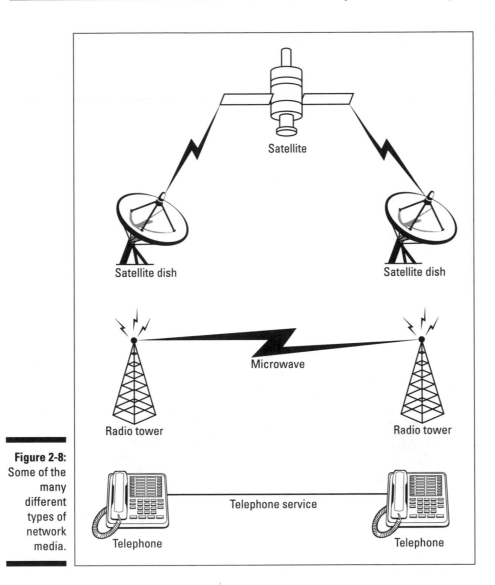

Figure 2-8:
Some of the
many
different
types of
network
media.

The disadvantage of fiber-optic cable is that it is very expensive and difficult to install and maintain. The equipment, such as network adapters and hubs, is also more expensive than the equipment used for copper-cabled networks. Because of the expense and difficulty of installing fiber optic, it is normally used only in places with the potential for a lot of electronic interference, or as a backbone that connects several networks.

Wireless networks

As you can see in Figure 2-9, the main advantage that wireless networks have over copper and fiber optic is that you don't have to run and connect cables to the computers. The three major types of wireless networks today are infrared, microwave, and radio.

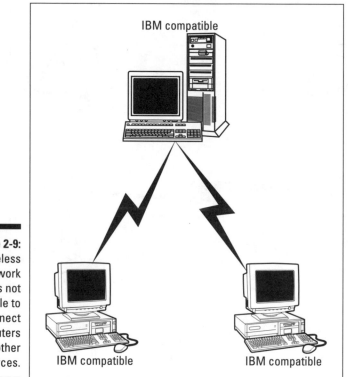

Figure 2-9:
A wireless network does not use cable to connect computers and other resources.

Infrared networks

Infrared networks are normally used in small areas where you don't have to transmit a signal very far, such as an infrared port to connect a laptop to a network. The problem with infrared networks is that they are line-of-sight, which means the port on the computer has to be able to see the network port. Other disadvantages are their expensive cost and slow speed. Most of today's copper networks operate at 10 to 100 Mbps. Most infrared adapters can operate from only .3 to 4 Mbps. All these disadvantages keep infrared from becoming widely used in today's networking environments.

Microwave networks

Microwave networks are normally used to transmit data over a long distance where cables cannot be used. Microwave also requires line-of-sight, but it can carry data longer distances. Microwave networks use a string of towers to carry data along the ground, or satellites to carry data across large bodies of water or other long distances. The disadvantage of microwave is that rain or fog can degrade the signal to the point where it is unreadable.

Radio-frequency (RF) networks

Radio-frequency (RF) networks are becoming more popular. Radio waves can go through walls and can be installed where it would be difficult to install cable. With all the satellites in orbit, radio waves can reach almost anywhere on Earth. Radio is more reliable than microwave because it is unaffected by weather.

The problem with radio is that a limited number of frequencies can be used. Changes are occurring, however, that will open up more frequencies so that the number of radio networks can continue to grow.

Networking Choices

Now you can begin to plan your network. The technical information is covered in the next few chapters, but you can use what you've found out here to begin to get an idea of how a network functions and to discover more information for the exam.

You first need to decide whether your network should be peer-to-peer or client/server. Use a peer-to-peer network if

- ✔ You have less than ten users
- ✔ Users can administer their computers' resources
- ✔ No one is assigned to be a network administrator
- ✔ Funds are not available for a dedicated file server
- ✔ You don't have to worry about secure information
- ✔ The company isn't planning to expand soon

Use a client/server network if

- ✔ You have more than ten users
- ✔ A knowledgeable network administrator will set network policies
- ✔ Data must be secure from unwanted intrusions and must be backed up often

If you are using a client/server network, you need to decide which type of servers you will use:

- If your company has many users, you might want separate servers for different functions.

- If your company has departments (such as accounting, human resources, and data processing), you might want a file server in each department and one central communications server for company e-mail.

If you are using a client/server network, you need to decide the power of the computers you are using as servers:

- A fast computer with a lot of memory can handle more functions.

- Most people start with a few servers and add more as needed.

To choose the right topology, consider the following factors:

- Cost

- Distance

- Ease of installation and expansion

Here are a few hints for choosing the right topology:

- For a small, inexpensive network, use a bus or star network.

- For a network that can quickly expand as necessary, use a star network.

- For a busy network in which you want everyone to have the same chance of sending data over the network, use a *mesh* network. A mesh network is a network in which every node/device is connected to each other. For example, A is connected to B, C, and D with individual cables; B is connected to A, C, and D with individual cables; and so on.

When determining the type of media to use, consider the following:

- Copper is the least expensive and most commonly used option.

- Fiber-optic cable is a good choice for a heavily used network or as a backbone between local area networks.

- Wireless networks using microwave transmissions or satellite relays are often used to build wide area networks.

Part II
Networking Standards and Deployment

The 5th Wave   By Rich Tennant

WE'RE HERE TO SERVICE YOUR LOCAL-AREA-NETWORK.

In this part . . .

The certification test does a good job of measuring your knowledge of standards and terminology, so pay close attention to the discussions of the OSI model in this part. Local area networking and wide area networking are also major components of the test; concentrate on associating the right terms with the right technologies. You have to understand the terminology to be able to understand and successfully answer some questions.

Standards are a different matter. Your knowledge of standards is tested repeatedly with multiple-choice questions as well as scenario questions, so you must have a firm grasp of the standards discussed in this part. Luckily, the test does not focus on arcane or obscure networking standards or terminology. Specifically, concentrate on the Ethernet standards and the cabling requirements for 10Base2, 10Base5, and 10BaseT.

Expanding networks is another large portion of the test. Networks can be expanded using a number of different devices and technologies. When you try to organize all these devices and technologies, use the OSI model as your framework. For the test, you'll need to be able to associate a device or a technology with a particular layer of the OSI model.

Chapter 3
Protocols and the OSI Model

● ●

Exam Objectives

▶ Comparing the implications of using connection-oriented communications with connectionless communications

▶ Explaining the purpose of NDIS and Novell ODI networks

▶ Selecting the appropriate network and transport protocol or protocols for various token-ring and Ethernet networks

● ●

*I*n this chapter, you examine two networking models: the OSI model and the Project 802 model. Both models set standards for how data flows from an application, through the network, and then to an application on another computer. You also examine network protocols and how they package and transmit data.

One of the objectives of this chapter is to differentiate between connection-oriented and connectionless communications. The implication of which communications type you choose has a significant effect on another chapter objective: selecting the appropriate network and transport protocols for various networks.

This chapter focuses primarily on network protocols and other software-related issues. You spend some time with common protocol stacks such as TCP/IP and IPX/SPX and look at some of the common protocols included with those stacks such as NFS, FTP, and SMTP.

I also discuss the NDIS and ODI standards. You will need to remember where each of these standards is used and what benefits they offer.

One thing that you can do to make studying this chapter a little easier is to keep track of the acronyms. Keep a pencil and paper handy and write definitions for each acronym you come across. Knowing the acronyms will give you a big advantage on the test because many test questions fail to spell out acronyms.

Quick Assessment

Select the appropriate network and transport protocol or protocols for various token-ring and Ethernet networks

1   The _____ layer of the OSI model ensures error-free delivery of data.

2   The Session layer can communicate in three modes: _____, _____, and _____.

3   The _____ sublayer connects the computer's network adapter to the network media.

4   The two most significant Project 802 standards are _____ and _____.

5   The three portions of a network packet are _____, _____, and _____.

6   The amount of data in a packet is typically _____ bytes to _____ bytes.

7   Name the four common networking protocols: _____, _____, _____, _____.

8   NWLink supports the _____ protocol.

9   _____ is best for small, non-routed networks.

Explain the purpose of NDIS and Novell ODI networks

10   The _____ driver is used on Novell NetWare networks.

Compare connection-oriented with connectionless communications

11   A(n) _____ protocol does not require an acknowledgment that data has been delivered.

Answers

1   *Transport.* Review Table 3-1.

2   *Simplex; half duplex; full duplex.* Review "Session layer."

3   *Media Access Control.* Review "802 enhancements to the OSI model" for information about the two sublayers of the OSI model.

4   *802.3 Ethernet; 802.5 token ring.* Check out Table 3-2.

5   *Header; data; trailer.* See "Packets and packet structure" for more information.

6   *72; 1526.* Review "Packets and packet structure."

7   *TCP/IP; IPX/SPX; NWLink; NetBEUI.* You should also know whether or not each one is routable. Review "Common Networking Protocols."

8   *IPX/SPX.* Review the "IPX/SPX" section.

9   *NetBEUI.* Review the "NetBEUI" section.

10   *ODI.* Review "Network Driver Standards."

11   *Connectionless.* Review "Connection versus connectionless communications."

Networking Models

Networking encompasses a huge body of knowledge. Consequently, I need to organize this knowledge in a way that allows us to deal with just one small piece of it at a time. One of the tools that allows us to do just that is called a *networking model*. In this section, I describe a few popular networking models that have developed over the years, and how communications are accomplished between computers using these different models.

The OSI model

In 1978, the International Standards Organization (ISO) released a set of specifications for connecting devices on a network. In 1984, the ISO updated these specifications and called it the Open Systems Interconnection (OSI) model. This model has become an international standard for networking. It describes how network hardware and software work together to communicate. The OSI model contains seven layers and shows how information on the source computer travels down through each layer, across the network media, and back up through the layers on the destination computer. Figure 3-1 shows the seven layers of the OSI model. Table 3-1 is a brief overview of each layer.

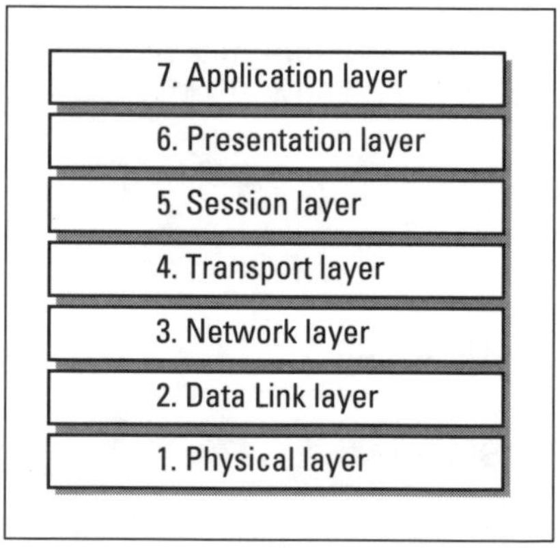

Figure 3-1:
The seven layers of the OSI model.

| 7. Application layer |
| 6. Presentation layer |
| 5. Session layer |
| 4. Transport layer |
| 3. Network layer |
| 2. Data Link layer |
| 1. Physical layer |

Table 3-1	The OSI Model
OSI Layer	*Function*
Application	Interfaces between your application and the network
Presentation	Negotiates the formats for data exchange
Session	Establishes connections using easy-to-remember names

OSI Layer	Function
Transport	Provides reliable, error-free data delivery between computers
Network	Routes data through large networks
Data Link	Grants access to the network media
Physical	Converts data into bits that are transmitted over the network

Do you want an easy way to remember the seven layers of the OSI model for the exam? The first letter of each of the following words represents a layer of the OSI model:

Please **D**o **N**ot **T**hrow **S**ausage **P**izza **A**way

Next, you take a more detailed look at each of these layers, starting with the Application layer and proceeding down through the model to the Physical layer. This is the path that data would take from an application sending data to another system. The data would travel from the Physical layer up to the Application layer on the receiving system.

Application layer

The *Application layer,* the seventh and topmost layer, is the link between your application and the network. It allows user applications to send e-mail, access a network database, and transfer files across the network. The Application layer is not your actual application, just a support layer used by an application to perform network functions.

Presentation layer

The Presentation layer determines the format used to transfer data between network computers. When data is transmitted between different types of computer systems, the Presentation layer negotiates and manages the way data is represented and encoded. For example, the Presentation layer provides a common denominator between ASCII and EBCDIC machines as well as between different floating point and binary formats. The Presentation layer is also responsible for compressing and encrypting the data.

Session layer

The *Session layer* allows applications on different computers to establish and use a connection called a *session.* The Session layer provides the network address of each computer as well as other functions, such as security, so that the two computers can talk to each other. The Session layer also inserts checkpoints in the data to make sure all data is sent. That way, if there is a problem on the network, only the data since the last checkpoint has to be retransmitted.

Sessions can be set up to communicate in three ways:

- ✔ **Simplex communications** are simple, one-way communications, such as radio or television transmissions.

- ✔ **Half-duplex communications** allow only one device to transmit at a time. The second device cannot transmit until the first is finished. This is similar to using a CB or shortwave radio. If both parties key the mike at the same time, neither party is able to receive information.

- ✔ **Full-duplex communications** allow transmissions in both directions at the same time, such as a telephone conversation.

The Session layer communicates directly with its support layer, known as the Transport layer.

Transport layer

The *Transport layer* makes sure all data is delivered without errors and in the correct order. The Transport layer separates the data from the Session layer into packets that can be sent over the network easily. The receiving computer reassembles these packets into their original form — and into the correct order, if necessary — and then sends an acknowledgment that all data was received. The sending computer does not send the next piece of data until it receives the acknowledgment. If it does not receive this acknowledgment in a specified amount of time, the data is resent. This is called *flow control.*

Network layer

The *Network layer* addresses messages and determines the best route for getting your message to the correct computer. It is responsible for establishing, maintaining, and terminating the network connection between two users and for transferring data along those connections. Only one network connection can exist between two users, although many communication sessions, or conversations, can exist between two users who use the same network connection. The primary responsibility of the Network layer is to choose the most efficient route through the network to use for a connection.

Data can be sent between computers in two ways. If the computers are on the same network, the data is sent directly between the computers. If the computers are on different networks, the data is sent to one or more routers, which then pass the data over to the other network.

Data Link layer

The *Data Link layer* packs the data sent from the upper layer into data frames, adding a *cyclical redundancy check,* or CRC. (A *CRC* is a number calculated by running the data to be sent through a numerical process at the sending computer. When the data is received, the receiving computer runs the data through the same process and should come up with the same number. If it does, the data is accepted. If not, the receiving computer tells the sender to retransmit the data.)

The Data Link layer on the receiving end is in charge of identifying your computer on the network. It receives the information, rebuilds the frames, runs its CRC, and if everything is okay, sends back an acknowledgment. The sending computer waits for this okay before it sends the next set of information.

The Data Link layer is also in charge of who can transmit on the network at any given time so that each computer knows when it can transmit and when it needs to receive data.

Physical layer

The bottom layer of the OSI model is the *Physical layer.* The Physical layer converts the data into a raw bit stream and transmits it over the network medium, such as copper or fiber-optic cable. When the bit stream is received at the other end, the signal is reconstructed into data frames.

This layer specifies the bit synchronization that ensures that when the sending computer sends a 1, the receiving computer receives a 1 and not a 0. The Physical layer also identifies the adapter interface used to attach the network cable to the network adapter. Common network card interfaces include BNC, RJ-45, and AUI. The specification also defines how many pins the network cable has and what each pin does.

Peer-layer communications

For two systems to be able to communicate, they must use the same communications model and protocols. Most network models are made of distinct layers that provide different services. Each layer in the model is responsible for sending data to a layer above or below itself. The same layers, in the same sequence, exist on each system. The layers are set up so that it seems as if they are communicating with the same layer on the other computer. This is like a virtual connection between peer layers on the two computers. Figure 3-2 shows these virtual connections. Although the data is really moved up through the layers, it seems to pass between peer layers. For example, the Network layer on the sending computer appears to communicate with the Network layer on the receiving computer.

Peer-layer communications is a key concept that you will see repeated over and over again in almost all network models, including the OSI and IEEE 802 models.

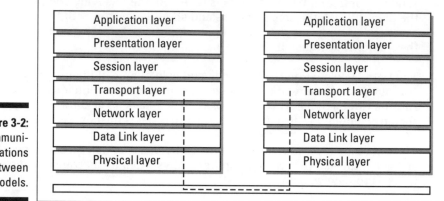

Figure 3-2:
Communi-
cations
between
OSI models.

The IEEE 802 model

The Institute of Electrical and Electronics Engineers (IEEE) developed
standards called *Project 802* for the physical connection of network adapters. The 802 standards, listed in Table 3-2 and described in Table 3-3, define
the way data is placed on the physical network media by network adapters.

Twelve 802 standards are described in this section, but for the exam you
need to concentrate on the 802.3 standard (for Ethernet) and the 802.5
standard (for token ring). The other standards may be mentioned, but you
won't need the details of their implementations. You need the details only
for token ring and Ethernet.

Table 3-2	Project 802 Standards
Number	*Category*
802.1	Internetworking
802.2	Logical Link Control
802.3	Ethernet
802.4	Token Bus
802.5	Token Ring
802.6	Metropolitan Area Network (MAN)
802.7	Broadband Technology
802.8	Fiber-Optic Technology
802.9	Integrated Voice and Data

Number	Category
802.10	Network Security
802.11	Wireless Networks
802.12	100BaseVG-AnyLAN

Table 3-3   IEEE 802 Model Standards and Functions

Standard	Defines
802.1	Transparent bridging
802.2	The LLC sublayer of the Data Link layer
802.3	CSMA/CD (Carrier-Sense Multiple Access with Collision Detection) for Ethernet networks
802.4	Networks that use token-passing bus, a rarely used type of network
802.5	IBM's token-ring network
802.6	A network with two physical channels, or a Metropolitan Area Network (MAN)
802.7	The Broadband Technical Advisory Group
802.8	The Fiber-Optic Technical Advisory Group
802.9	Integrated Voice and Data Networks
802.10	Network security issues
802.11	A standard still under development that will address the problems of wireless networks
802.12	The new standard for 100-Mbps LANs developed by Hewlett-Packard

802 enhancements to the OSI model

During the development of the OSI model and the 802 standards, the IEEE thought that the Data Link layer of the OSI model needed more detail, so it divided the Data Link layer into two sublevels:

- ✓ **Logical Link Control** layer is for error and flow control
- ✓ **Media Access Control** layer is for access control

Figure 3-3 shows where these enhancements fit into the OSI model.

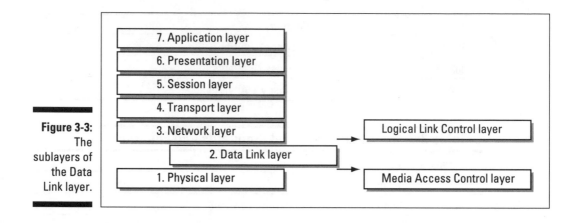

Figure 3-3:
The
sublayers of
the Data
Link layer.

Logical Link Control sublayer

The Logical Link Control (LLC) sublayer is responsible for maintaining the data link connection between two computers while the computers send data over the network. The LLC establishes a series of checkpoints called Service Access Points (SAPs) that other computers use to transfer information to the upper layers of the OSI model. It can transfer data in two ways:

- **Unacknowledged connectionless service** is the fastest way to transmit data at this level. It is also the most unreliable, however, because the packet of data is unacknowledged. This service is still the most commonly used because layers higher up in the OSI model handle their own error checking.

- **Connection-oriented service** uses acknowledgments to make sure data is delivered error free. This service is slower than unacknowledged connectionless service.

Because not all network computers run at the same speed, one computer must control the amount of data it sends so that the other computer can keep up. The LLC sublayer handles this process, called *flow control,* in two ways:

- **Sliding window.** This method allows the two computers to decide how many frames of data can be sent before an acknowledgment is needed.

- **Stop and wait.** When the receiving device runs out of the memory it uses to store information, it tells the sending computer to stop sending. When the receiver has processed the information and freed up its memory, it tells the sender to begin sending again.

The LLC performs error correction using cyclic redundancy checks (CRCs).

Media Access Control sublayer

The Media Access Control (MAC) sublayer is responsible for physically connecting the computer network adapter to the network media and for delivering error-free data between two computers on the network. The MAC sublayer controls the physical address of the devices on the network. Every network adapter contains a physically encoded address, which is called the *MAC address* of the computer on the network. Only one device may transmit on the network at a time, to avoid messing up a signal from another device. The MAC sublayer controls which computer can transmit data over the network.

Network Driver Standards

Several pieces must come together in the OSI model for a network to function correctly. Drivers and protocols are among these things.

A driver for your network adapter card allows the adapter to communicate with the operating system in your computer. Examples of network operating systems include Microsoft Windows NT and Novell NetWare. Each has a driver for each network adapter card that might be installed on your computer. You must have the right driver before you can access the network.

The driver for your network adapter card works at the Media Access Control (MAC) sublayer of the Data Link layer. (This is why the network adapter address is called its MAC address.) The MAC sublayer provides the network adapter with access to the Physical layer, allowing the computer to communicate with the rest of the network.

Another set of standards must also be considered when discussing network adapter cards and network adapter drivers. These standards, called NDIS and ODI, seek to simplify and document the programming interfaces between the hardware adapter and the software driver. They allow multiple software vendors (such as Microsoft and Novell) to write different drivers for the same network adapter card. These standards — Network Drive Interface Specification (NDIS) and Open Data-link Interface (ODI) driver standards — were developed to allow more than one protocol to be bound to a single network adapter. ODI was developed by Novell and is used mainly on Novell NetWare networks. NDIS was developed by Microsoft and is used mainly with Microsoft's networking products.

Introduction to Protocols

Before beginning the tour of networking protocols, you need to be familiar with two basic concepts. The first was introduced previously in the "Peer-layer communications" section. As a quick review, when the discussion turns to the OSI model and the IEEE 802 model (or any model for that matter), you will see that a model is just a collection of layers. These layers work with each other to provide network communications. The second thing you need to remember is that various protocols are often combined to provide a suite, or stack of protocols. For example, TCP/IP is not just one protocol. It is a collection of protocols that work together, much like the way layers of a model work together.

Connection versus connectionless communications

When you need to communicate with a large group of people, you have a few choices. One, you could call each person. This method would take a long time but would also guarantee that everyone received the message. Or, two, you could make an announcement over the local intercom system. This would be much faster, but you wouldn't have a guarantee that everyone heard the message. In networking terminology, calling everyone is connection-oriented communications, and the intercom example is connectionless communications. Understanding the implications of the two types of communications is a requirement for the Networking Essentials exam.

Sometimes data needs to be sent to several computers at a time, and sometimes it needs to be sent to a single computer. A *connectionless protocol* sends the data without waiting for an acknowledgment that the receiving computer received the data. Consequently, the data can be sent to multiple computers very quickly. Unfortunately, with connectionless communications, data is not guaranteed to reach any of its destinations. As a matter of fact, there's no way of telling whether data reached any destinations at all.

A *connection-oriented protocol* establishes a connection between two computers, transmits a packet, waits for an acknowledgment, and sends the next packet. If no acknowledgment is received or the data has an error, the packet is resent. This is a very safe way to transmit data, but it is much slower than connectionless transmissions.

Routable versus non-routable protocols

Most networks are connected with other networks to form LANs using a device called a *router,* which routes information from one network to another. Protocols that can be used across these networks are called *routable protocols.* Routable protocols are more complex and require more overhead than non-routable protocols due to the information needed in the packet to handle the routing functions. Non-routable protocols were developed before networks grew into the larger LANs in use today. Some of these non-routable protocols are still used today because they are faster and require less overhead.

Table 3-4 lists the protocols you will need to be familiar with for the exam and whether or not they are routable. These protocols are often referred to as *common transport protocols.*

Table 3-4   Routable and Non-Routable Transport Protocols

	Routable	*Non-Routable*
AppleTalk	X	
DLC		X
IPX/SPX	X	
NetBEUI		X
SNA	X	
TCP/IP	X	

Packets and packet structure

A computer sending data onto the network first breaks the data into smaller sections called *packets,* because the file containing the data is usually too large to be transmitted across the network all at once. The data is broken down into packets also for error control. If the transmission has an error, only the one small section — not the entire file — must be resent. Using packets makes data transmission quicker and makes it easier to correct transmission errors.

The receiving computer collects and reassembles the packets in the proper order to form the original data. The network operating system adds special information to each packet to allow the data to be tracked and reassembled in the correct order. This information also allows the data to be checked for errors after it has been put back together.

All packets contain certain components that help them on their journey through the network:

- ✔ Address of the sending computer

- ✔ Data being transmitted

- ✔ Destination address of the receiving computer

- ✔ Directions telling the network how to get the data to the receiving computer

- ✔ Information telling the receiving computer how to put the information in the packets back together in the correct order to get the complete data

- ✔ Error-checking information that makes sure the data is correct

These components are broken into three groups: header information, the data, and trailer information:

- ✔ The **header** information includes the source address of the computer sending the data, the destination address of the computer that will receive the data, and timing information to help synchronize the transmission.

- ✔ The **data** information is the actual data being transmitted. The size of the data in the packet can vary depending on the type of network and how the network was configured during setup. Data size typically ranges from 72 bytes to 4K. Because most data files are much larger than 4K, the data must be broken down into packets to be transmitted.

- ✔ The information in the **trailer** varies depending on the type of communications method, or protocol, being used. Most protocols contain at least the error-checking function, normally in the form of a CRC, cyclical redundancy check.

Assembling packets

The creation of packets begins at the top of the OSI model at the Application layer, where data is generated. As the data is passed from the Application layer to the Presentation layer, header information is added. When this information is passed to the Session layer, it does not distinguish the data from the header information. It sees only data. This process continues, with each layer adding its own header information. After the receiving computer receives the data, each layer reads the information passed to it and removes the header information created by the corresponding layer on the sending computer.

The header information is simply control information that each layer uses to identify data and options at that layer. The header information placed in a packet on the sending system is stripped off and processed by the same layer on the receiving system. Without the header information, the receiving layer wouldn't know what to do with the data.

The data is broken into packets at the Transport layer. The Transport layer also adds sequencing information to the data to help the receiving computer put the data back together in the correct order.

Most packets are sent out onto the network to only one computer. Every computer on the network sees every data packet sent out, but only the computer that sees its own MAC (or hardware) address on the packet receives it. Some packets may be sent out in broadcast; every computer on the network will read these packets. A broadcast is analogous to a mass mailing, in which everyone receives a letter, versus addressing a letter for an intended recipient.

Network components use the addressing information on the packets to route them to the correct receiving computer. Network components direct packets in two ways:

 ✔ In **packet forwarding,** each component sends the packet to the next appropriate network component based on the address in the packet's header.

 ✔ In **packet filtering,** some network components will look for only packets with specific addresses and select these packets to receive.

Protocol stacks

A *protocol* is a language computers use to talk to each other. Just as computers use protocols to talk to each other, the OSI model uses protocols to send data between layers. Each layer of the OSI model has different protocols that define how information travels. The way the different protocols in the OSI model work together is called a *protocol stack*.

Protocol stacks and bindings

To use a certain protocol with a network computer, the protocol must be bound to the network adapter. Two protocols (such as TCP/IP and IPX/SPX) can be bound to one card. In addition, you can have two network adapters in a computer, with a different protocol bound to each adapter.

The order that protocols are bound to an adapter determines the order in which the operating system will use them to try to connect to the network. For example, if IPX/SPX is bound to a card first, the computer tries to connect to the network with IPX/SPX. If that fails and the second protocol in the binding order is TCP/IP, the computer will then try to connect using TCP/IP.

Standard protocol stacks

The computer industry has designated several standard protocol stacks. The most important ones are

- Internet Protocol Suite, TCP/IP
- Novell NetWare's Protocol Suite, IPX/SPX
- IBM's Systems Network Architecture, SNA
- ISO/OSI Protocol Suite
- Digital's DECnet
- Apple's AppleTalk

These are all discussed later in this chapter.

Each stack has different protocols that operate at different layers of the OSI model and are grouped into three categories:

- **Application protocols** work in the upper level of the OSI model providing support for application-to-application interaction and data exchange.
- **Transport protocols** establish communications sessions between computers and ensure that data is transmitted without errors to the correct destination.
- **Network protocols** handle addressing, routing information, and error checking, and also define rules for communicating in different network environments.

Figure 3-4 shows the layers of the OSI model associated with each type of protocol.

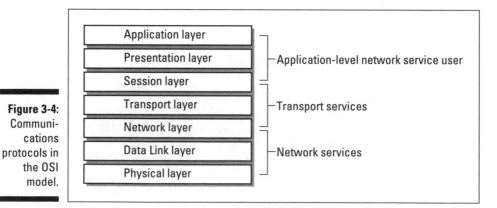

Figure 3-4:
Communi-
cations
protocols in
the OSI
model.

Common Networking Protocols

For network communications to exist, computers have to share a common protocol. Over the years, several protocols developed to handle various aspects of the communications process.

The protocols you should concentrate on for the exam are TCP/IP, IPX/SPX, NWLink, and NetBEUI. For each one, you should know its function and whether or not it is routable.

Server Message Block (SMB)

Server Message Block (SMB) is a Presentation layer, Microsoft network protocol that computers on a Microsoft network use for communications between the network redirector and the server. The network redirector is the software that allows a user's computer to see network resources as if they were local resources. The redirector could give a user an F drive, for instance, that could be a data drive on the network. The user could copy data back and forth between C and F drives and use the F drive in the same way as the user's other drives.

Suppose a user wants to use Windows Explorer to view files on the Microsoft server. First a network connection would be established between the user's computer and the server using a network protocol, such as NetBEUI or TCP/IP. Then a session would be created between the redirector and the server process software on the server. Finally, the two computers would transmit SMB packets back and forth so that the user could view the files. You will most likely see the Server Message Block protocol on the exam.

TCP/IP

Transmission Control Protocol/Internet Protocol (TCP/IP) is a suite of industry-standard protocols. TCP/IP, also known as the *Internet protocol,* is a routable network protocol that also provides access to the Internet. TCP/IP has become the most common protocol for internetworking because of its capability to be used with almost any network operating system and equipment.

Network classes

Computers on your network need an address so that other computers can get information to them. Every computer on a network, therefore, has a unique IP address. This address is divided into four parts, or octets, of numbers ranging from 0 to 255. (An *octet* is a unit of data that is 8 bits in length.) A period separates each octet, 88.51.1.172, for example. If a computer is on an internal network that does not connect to the Internet, the system administrator can assign IP addresses that are unique to the network. If the computer attaches to the Internet, however, an IP address must be obtained from the Internet service provider.

IP addresses are divided into classes. When an organization requests a range of IP addresses, they are assigned an address class based on the size of the organization, as follows:

- ✔ **Class A addresses** are for extremely large networks and use only the first octet of the address to identify the network. The remaining three octets are used to address each device, or host, on the network. (A *host* is a computer, or a printer, or any other network device.) A Class A network can have over 16 million hosts. Class A addresses always have the first octet between 1 and 126. An example of a Class A address is 101.45.36.110, where the network address is 101 and 45.36.110 is the host address.

- ✔ **Class B addresses** are for medium-sized networks. These addresses use the first two octets to identify the network and the last two to identify the host on the network. Class B networks can have over 65,000 hosts per network. The first octet of a Class B address is always between 128 and 191. An example of a Class B address is 145.1.110.2, where the network address is 145.1 and the host address is 110.2.

- ✔ **Class C addresses** are the most common and are used for smaller networks. Class C networks use the first three octets for the network address and the last octet for the host address. These networks can have up to 254 hosts per network. The first octet of a Class C network is always between 192 and 223. An example of a Class C address is 202.75.64.107, where 202.75.64 is the network address and 107 is the host address.

Addresses that begin with 127 and 224 through 255 are used for testing and are not available for public use.

Subnet mask

A computer on a TCP/IP network uses a *subnet mask* to determine whether a computer that it needs to send data to is located on a local network or on a remote network. For example, a Class C network uses a subnet mask of 255.255.255.0 to identify the network and host portions of the computer's IP address. The three octets containing 255 indicate that the network address is contained in the first three octets, and the octet that contains 0 indicates that the host portion of the computer's IP address is located in the last octet.

The computer compares the first three octets of the destination address with the first three octets of its own IP address to see whether the octets are the same. If they are, the destination computer is on a local network and the sending computer can send the data directly to the destination computer. If the first three octets are not the same, the destination computer is on a remote network and the sending computer must send the data to an intermediate router for delivery to the destination computer. Table 3-5 shows the three most common subnet masks.

Table 3-5	Most Common Subnet Masks
Subnet Mask	*IP Address Class*
255.0.0.0	Class A
255.255.0.0	Class B
255.255.255.0	Class C

TCP/IP is made up of two protocols, TCP and IP. The TCP/IP suite, however, contains a number of other protocols that might pop up on the exam. The following sections will cover the TCP and IP protocols as well as some of the other protocols in the suite.

Transmission Control Protocol (TCP)

Transmission Control Protocol, TCP, is a connection-oriented protocol that functions on the Transport layer of the OSI model. When two computers on a network need to communicate, TCP opens a connection between the computers. When the data packet is ready to be sent, TCP adds to the packet header information that contains flow control and error checking.

A computer may have more than one connection at a time. To make sure that the data goes to the right place, each connection is assigned a port number. The header on the data packet contains the port number to which the data needs to be delivered on the receiving computer. When the data arrives, the receiving computer delivers the data to the appropriate port, where an application is "listening" and ready to process the data.

Internet Protocol (IP)

The Internet Protocol, IP, is a connectionless protocol that operates at the Network layer of the OSI model. When data packets are sent over the network, IP is responsible for addressing the packets and routing them through the network. Attached to each packet is an IP header that contains the sending address and the receiving address. If data is transmitted across networks that do not have the same packet size, the packets may be split up during transmission. If this happens, a new IP header is added to each part of the split packet. When the packets reach their final destination, the IP puts all the packets together again in the correct order.

User Datagram Protocol (UDP)

The User Datagram Protocol (UDP) provides a datagram service. Datagram service is a way of sending messages with a minimum of overhead. Delivery is not guaranteed. No checking for missing or out-of-sequence packets is performed, and no acknowledgments are sent.

Routing Information Protocol (RIP) and Open Shortest Path First (OSPF)

The Routing Information Protocol (RIP) and Open Shortest Path First (OSPF) protocol determine the best path for a packet to take to reach its destination. RIP counts the number of routers *(hops)* it has to go through to get from the source computer to the destination computer. OSPF uses not only the number of hops, but also the speed of the network between hops and the amount of traffic between each hop to figure out the best way to send packets. These protocols deal with routing, so they are Network layer protocols.

Address Resolution Protocol (ARP)

For a computer to send data to another computer on a network, the sending computer must know the MAC address of the destination computer. The Address Resolution Protocol (ARP) sends to every computer on the network a *discovery packet,* looking for the TCP/IP address. When the computer that has this TCP/IP address receives the discovery packet, it replies to the sending computer and sends its MAC address. When the sending computer gets this message, it knows where to send the data. ARP keeps a list of matching MAC and TCP/IP addresses and checks this list for the requested MAC address first before sending out a discovery packet.

File Transfer Protocol (FTP)

File Transfer Protocol, or FTP, is used for file sharing between computers that use TCP/IP to communicate. FTP allows users to log on to a remote computer on a network and see what files are on the computer. It allows users to also upload and download files between the two computers. FTP is a widely used Application layer protocol because an FTP service exists for almost every operating system.

Simple Mail Transfer Protocol (SMTP)

Simple Mail Transfer Protocol (SMTP) makes sure that e-mail is delivered from the sender's server to the intended recipient's e-mail server. It does not handle the delivery to the final e-mail desktop location. SMTP is an Application layer protocol.

Telnet

Telnet enables a user to log on to a computer remotely and run applications. All processing occurs on the remote computer. The user's computer is nothing but a dumb terminal used for display. Telnet is available for most operating systems and is included with Windows 95 and Windows NT. Telnet is an Application layer protocol.

Network File System (NFS)

Network File System (NFS), developed by Sun Microsystems, is a newer way to share files and drives. It's a combination of FTP and Telnet that lets a user use files and disk drives on a remote computer as if they were located on the user's own system. NFS is becoming very popular because of its flexibility and ease of use. NFS is an Application layer protocol.

IPX/SPX

Internetwork Packet Exchange/Sequenced Packet Exchange, IPX/SPX, is a routable protocol suite designed by Novell, Inc., and used by Novell's NetWare. Unlike TCP/IP, which was developed for use in peer-to-peer networks, IPX/SPX was developed for Novell's server-based networks. It enables a user to tell the difference between resources on the server and resources located on the user's local computer. IPX/SPX is also easy to administrate. Addressing is performed on the Novell server, which simply chooses a network address that is not found on any other connected Novell server and passes the address to the requesting computer. Like TCP/IP, IPX/SPX has many protocols, not just the two main ones. The following descriptions discuss the different protocols in the IPX/SPX suite and where they function in the OSI model.

Multiple Link Interface Driver (MLID)

The Multiple Link Interface Driver (MLID) protocol works on the MAC sublayer of the Data Link layer of the OSI model and decides how your system will access the network media. MLID is the network adapter driver specification. Each network card requires its own MLID driver. Novell created a driver specification called Open Data-link Interface, or ODI, that allows third-party network adapter vendors to create network adapters that work with Novell's network operating system.

Link Support Layer (LSL)

The Link Support Layer, LSL, also operates at the Data Link layer and is the interface between MLID and the upper OSI model layer protocols. The Link Support Layer makes sure that the data goes to the correct upper-layer protocol if you are using more than one protocol stack.

Internetwork Packet Exchange (IPX)

The Internetwork Packet Exchange (IPX) protocol works on the Network layer of the OSI model and is responsible for connectionless data service. It routes data across an internetwork and takes care of network addressing. The IPX address of a computer is made up of the network adapter's MAC address and an assigned network address. Most network data transfers in a Novell network are handled by IPX. If the data must cross a router, however, SPX is used.

Sequenced Packet Exchange (SPX)

Sequenced Packet Exchange, SPX, takes care of the possible problems that could arise from the use of IPX. IPX is a connectionless protocol, so no check is performed to make sure that the data arrives without errors. SPX is a connection-oriented protocol and handles sequencing and error control to make sure the data is error free. SPX works with IPX to make sure no data is lost and that the data goes to the correct place. SPX is used when the data goes across a router in an internetwork and uses acknowledgments to make sure the data arrives in the right place. SPX is a Transport layer protocol.

Routing Information Protocol (RIP)

IPX can use different protocols to decide the best way to send data through an internetwork. One of these is the Routing Information Protocol (RIP), a simple routing protocol that counts the number of routers, or hops, the data must pass through to get to its destination. The route with the fewest hops is chosen to send the data. The problem, however, is that not only the number of hops but also the speed of the network and the amount of traffic contribute to the fastest way to send packets. A path with more hops but over a faster network might be a faster way to transmit data, but would not be chosen over a path with fewer hops but a slower link. This is the same RIP protocol used with TCP/IP and is a Network layer protocol.

NetWare Link Services Protocol (NLSP)

NetWare Link Services Protocol (NLSP) is another routing protocol that IPX can use to send data over the internetwork. Hence, it is a Network layer protocol. NLSP uses more than a hop count to determine the best way to send the data. The speed of the links between routes and the amount of traffic using the links is also considered. This makes NLSP a more efficient routing protocol.

NetWare Control Protocol (NCP)

NetWare Control Protocol (NCP) operates on four layers of the OSI model:

- ✔ Transport layer — connection-oriented services for error control, flow control, and sequencing
- ✔ Session layer — session control

> ✓ Presentation layer — translation of data characters
>
> ✓ Application layer — application programming interface

NCP takes care of most networking functions including file transfers and printing. NCP is the language that the Novell client computer uses to talk to the server. NCP is used to make requests and send replies between the client and server.

Service Access Protocol (SAP)

Service Access Protocol (SAP) is used to set up and configure servers on a network. Each computer on the network that shares a resource with other computers on the network sends out a SAP message with information about that resource, including its location. This allows resources to be shared without manually configuring each one. Packets are sent out at a regular interval and can easily take up a lot of bandwidth on a large network unless the interval is set to a level proportional to your network size. SAP is an Application layer protocol.

NWLink

NWLink is a routable, Transport layer protocol that is Microsoft's implementation of IPX/SPX. NWLink provides support for NetBIOS names as well. NetBIOS is covered in detail in Chapter 12.

NetBEUI

NetBEUI, a Microsoft network protocol, is a low-overhead, non-routable protocol used on small Microsoft networks and by IBM in its LAN Manager and OS/2 products. NetBEUI is fast and easy to configure because you need to know only the computer names of the other computers on your network. Because NetBEUI is not routable, it will not work with a larger network that uses routers. If you are using only NetBEUI, you can't communicate with other computers on the other side of the router. NetBEUI is a Transport layer protocol.

AppleTalk

AppleTalk is Apple Computer's proprietary protocol stack that enables Apple Macintosh computers to share files and printers in a networked system. The protocols of the AppleTalk suite follow:

> ✓ **AppleShare** provides Application layer services.
>
> ✓ **AppleTalk Filing Protocol (AFP)** manages file sharing.

   ✔ **AppleTalk Transaction Protocol (ATP)** provides a Transport layer connection between two computers.

   ✔ **Datagram Delivery Protocol (DDP)** provides Network layer transportation of packets across a network.

Data Link Control (DLC)

Data Link Control is a non-routable data transfer protocol that operates in the Data Link layer of the OSI model. It was designed to connect IBM mainframes and Hewlett-Packard network printers. DLC needs to be installed only on the computer that is used as the print server and is communicating directly with the printer. DLC doesn't need to be installed on client computers printing to the printer. It cannot be used for data communications.

DLC is a commonly used choice on the exam for answers about protocols. If you get a question about using DLC, remember that it is not a full protocol suite and therefore cannot be used to do many normal networking functions such as file transfers between servers and network computers. For this reason, DLC is not commonly used with network PCs.

Systems Network Architecture (SNA)

It is unlikely that the answer to a question on the certification exam will be SNA, IBM's Systems Network Architecture. You might, however, see SNA listed as a choice, so you should at least know what it is. *SNA* is a suite of protocols used with IBM mainframes and AS/400 computers. The two main protocols used with SNA are Advanced Program-to-Program Communications (APPC), which provides Transport and Session layer services to allow peer-to-peer communications, and Advanced Peer-to-Peer Networking (APPN), which provides Network and Transport layer connections between computers.

When you think you are finished reviewing for the exam, return to this chapter for a quick review. Look at the figures and read the tables; you should be able to get through the tables in 20 minutes. Check out all the network protocols, especially DLC, AppleTalk, IPX, TCP/IP, NFS, and SMB.

Prep Test

1 Which layer of the OSI model is responsible for transmitting raw data on the network?

A ○ Network

B ○ Application

C ○ Transport

D ○ Physical

2 Which OSI layer separates data into packets?

A ○ Transport

B ○ Physical

C ○ Session

D ○ Application

3 Which OSI layer determines the format of the data that will be transmitted?

A ○ Presentation

B ○ Application

C ○ Network

D ○ Session

4 The 802.3 standards define which type of network?

A ○ Token ring

B ○ Token bus

C ○ Ethernet

5 The Logical Link Control sublayer and the Media Access Control sublayer are in which layer of the OSI model?

A ○ Transport

B ○ Data Link

C ○ Physical

D ○ Network

6 What is data broken down into to be transmitted over the network?

A ○ Protocols

B ○ Packets

C ○ Stacks

D ○ Adapters

7 Which communications protocol provides error checking of the data?

A ○ Connectionless

B ○ Routing

C ○ Connection-oriented

D ○ Stacking

8 Which of the following are contained in packets? Select all that apply.

A ❑ Destination address

B ❑ Data

C ❑ Source address

D ❑ Error-checking information

9 Which of the following is a TCP/IP Class B network address?

A ❑ 130.0.34.7

B ❑ www.microsoft.com

C ❑ 97.65.123.200

D ❑ 152.1.110.2

10 What is Microsoft's version of the IPX/SPX protocol?

A ○ NetBIOS

B ○ SMB

C ○ NWLink

D ○ NetBEUI

11 If you want to print to Hewlett-Packard network printers from your IBM mainframe, you need to have what installed?

A ○ RIP

B ○ SNA

C ○ DLC

D ○ NetBIOS

Answers

1 *D.* The Physical layer of the OSI model transmits raw data onto the network. *Review "Physical layer."*

2 *A.* The Transport layer of the OSI model separates the data into packets. *Review "Transport layer."*

3 *A.* The Presentation layer of the OSI model determines the format of the data to be transmitted. *Review "Presentation layer."*

4 *C.* The 802.3 standard defines Ethernet networks. *Review "The IEEE 802 model."*

5 *B.* The LLC sublayer and MAC sublayer exist on the Data Link layer of the OSI model. *Review "802 enhancements to the OSI model."*

6 *B.* Data is broken down into packets that are transmitted over the network. *Review "Assembling packets."*

7 *C.* Connection-oriented communications provide for error checking. *Review "Connection versus connectionless communications."*

8 *A, B, C,* and *D.* The destination address, data, source address, and error-checking information are all contained in packets. *Review "Assembling packets."*

9 *A.* This is a Class B address. C is a Class A address. *Review "Network classes" in the "TCP/IP" section.*

10 *C.* NWLink is Microsoft's version of IPX/SPX. *Review "IPX/SPX."*

11 *C.* DLC allows IBM mainframes to print to Hewlett-Packard network printers. *Review "Data Link Control (DLC)."*

Chapter 4

Local Area Networks

● ●

Exam Objectives

▶ Describing the characteristics and purpose of the media used in IEEE 802.3 and IEEE 802.5 standards

▶ Selecting the appropriate media (twisted-pair cable, coaxial cable, fiber-optic cable, or wireless) for various situations

▶ Selecting the appropriate topology for various token-ring and Ethernet networks

▶ Selecting the appropriate network and transport protocol or protocols for various token-ring and Ethernet networks

● ●

*T*he Networking Essentials test — unlike the other certification tests, which require Microsoft product-specific knowledge — is designed to test your basic knowledge of a subject. One aspect of networking that you will be tested on is your understanding of networking standards. Trying to keep all the various standards straight for the test is a tall order, but you *can* do it. To help you, I provide a set of tables that summarizes and compares various standards at a glance.

The first objective in this chapter is to help you become familiar with the characteristics and purpose of the media that can be used with two important IEEE (Institute of Electrical and Electronic Engineers) standards: the 802.3 (Ethernet) standard and the 802.5 (token ring) standard. These standards define network functions as well as different media that can be used to create the physical connections for the network.

After you are familiar with the standards, you must be able to choose which network to use for a given situation. The choice of network also affects the type of network design, or topology, that will need to be implemented. Each standard has a unique set of characteristics that make it better suited for some situations and less suited for others. Additional information about media choices and characteristics is covered in Chapter 10.

Another objective of this chapter is to choose the right type of media for the right type of network. Finally, after you've decided on the network standard, topology, and media types, you need to select the right communications protocol. This chapter builds on the protocol definitions found in Chapter 3.

Quick Assessment

Describe the charac-teristics and purpose of the media used in IEEE 802.3 and IEEE 802.5 standards

1 The three Ethernet cable standards for copper wire are _____, _____, and _____.

2 A(n) _____ is used to prevent signal bounce on a bus network. On an Ethernet bus network, the resistance rating for this device is _____ ohm.

3 A(n) _____ completes the ring in an IBM token-ring environment.

Select the appropriate media for various situations

4 The best Ethernet cable standard to use for connecting two 10BaseT networks that are a little less than a mile apart is _____.

5 The maximum number of nodes that can be attached to a 10Base2 network (by definition) is _____.

6 _____ is often referred to as thinnet, and _____ is often referred to as thicknet.

7 RJ-45 connectors are used with the _____ Ethernet cable standard. Standard BNC connectors are used with the _____ Ethernet cable standard.

Select the appropriate topology for various token-ring and Ethernet networks

8 A Standard Ethernet network transmits data at _____ Mbps. IBM token-ring networks transmit data at either _____ or _____ Mbps.

9 Fast Ethernet transmits data at _____ Mbps.

10 CSMA/CD, demand priority, and token passing are three examples of _____ _____ control. They determine how and when a computer is allowed to transmit a signal on the network.

Answers

1 *10Base2; 10Base5; 10BaseT*. Review the "Ethernet" section.

2 *Terminator; 50 ohm*. Review the "Ethernet" section.

3 *MAU*. Review the "Token ring" section

4 *10BaseFL*. Review the "Ethernet" section.

5 *30.* See the "Ethernet" section.

6 *10Base2; 10Base5*. Review "Ethernet."

7 *10BaseT; 10Base2*. Review the "Ethernet" section.

8 *10; 16; 4.* Review the "Ethernet" and "Token ring" sections.

9 *100.* Review the "Fast Ethernet" section.

10 *Media access*. Review the "Classifying Networks" section.

Classifying Networks

To organize and compare all the different networking standards, you need to establish a set of criteria for describing and categorizing them.

When talking to people who had taken the Networking Essentials test, I noticed that they all gave the same piece of advice: Memorize the characteristics of the different standards and media types.

General characteristics

Networks are classified based on many criteria. Following are four of the most important:

- **The number of computers on the network.** More important than the actual number of computers are the different types of computers and the different configurations on the network. Supporting ten computers is not that different from supporting a hundred if they are all the same make and model and have the same configuration.

- **The cost of the network.** You need to determine how much of the Information Technologies (IT) department budget is allocated to support and the purchase of hardware and software. A new concept, Total Cost of Ownership (TCO) of PCs, is a Microsoft initiative to make the Microsoft/Intel platform more attractive. Studies have shown that only 20 percent of the total cost of owning a PC is hardware and software. The rest is support and maintenance.

- **The type of operating systems and software on the network.** A network administrator's responsibility is to match the appropriate NOS (network operating system) to the needs of the organization. Some take a single-vendor approach and select whichever vendor supports the majority of their requirements. This reduces support costs but limits functionality. Others take a best-of-breed approach and select the best NOS for each requirement or situation. This results in higher support costs but more flexibility.

To reduce TCO, companies are standardizing on a single 32-bit NOS that provides adequate security and scalability. Companies also are rewriting their legacy applications to 32-bit client/server applications to run on these network operating systems.

- **The supported topologies of the network.** Some networks, such as Ethernet, can support a variety of topologies, including bus, star, and star-bus. Other networks, such as token ring, can support only a ring or star-ring configuration. I talk more about topologies later in the chapter.

Logical Link Control characteristics

Another common way of classifying networks is by examining what is happening at the Logical Link Control layer (LLC). The LLC is where many of the network's properties are defined. Data frame size and format, media access control, and transmission speed are just a few of these properties. Media Access Control is particularly important.

Following are the most common forms of Media Access Control:

- ✔ **CSMA/CD.** Carrier Sense Multiple Access with Collision Detection. This method of media access control detects two systems trying to transmit data on a network at the same time. When a collision is detected, both systems wait a random amount of time and then attempt to retransmit their data. Ethernet networks use CSMA/CD.

- ✔ **CSMA/CA.** Carrier Sense Multiple Access with Collision Avoidance. A computer using this method of media access control transmits a special signal to the entire network indicating its intention to transmit data. All other computers hear that signal and wait for the first computer to transmit its data before trying to send data of their own. Thus, collisions are avoided.

- ✔ **Demand polling.** Demand polling requires a very intelligent hub. The hub questions each computer connected to it looking for a computer that has data to send. If the hub finds a computer with data to send, the hub opens a connection for that computer, and no other computers are allowed to transmit.

- ✔ **Token passing.** Systems employing a token-passing scheme use a special signal called a *token* to determine who can transmit data on the network. The network has only one token, and a computer must have the token before it is allowed to transmit.

Many general networking questions concerning standards and capabilities will come from the information in the next few pages.

LAN Topologies

Many networking topologies are in use. For the test, however, you should be familiar with three topologies in particular:

- ✔ Bus
- ✔ Star
- ✔ Ring

If all computers are connected in a row on a cable, the topology is a bus topology. If each computer has its own cable segment and all cable segments run back to a central location, or *hub*, the topology is a star topology. If the cable forms a closed circle, with all computers attached to that circular cable, the topology is a ring topology.

Bus topology

I begin with the bus topology because it's the simplest. In a *bus network,* all computers are connected in a line, as shown in Figure 4-1. The network cable, called the *backbone*, runs from one computer to the next all the way to the last computer on the network.

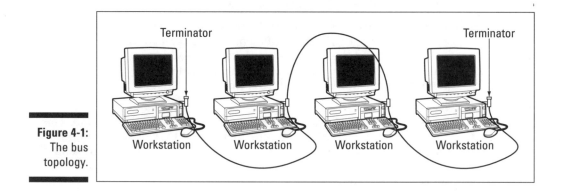

Figure 4-1:
The bus
topology.

You need to know about three concepts relating to a bus network:

- ✔ Signal transmission
- ✔ Signal bounce
- ✔ Termination

Only one computer at a time can transmit a signal. While one computer is transmitting, the others are listening. The data is transmitted from the sending computer down the backbone. Each computer that the data passes looks at the data to see whether it is addressed to its network address. If it is, that computer receives the data and processes the request. The signal, even though it's been received by its intended target, remains on the line and continues down the backbone. All other nodes will simply discard the signal after determining that the address is not intended for them, and finally the signal will be cleared off the backbone once it reaches the terminator. Because the computers only look at the data, rather than amplify the signal, the bus is a *passive network.*

Network performance is affected by the number of computers on the network. The more computers on the network, the more computers will be waiting to send data and the slower the network.

Signal bounce is what happens when an electrical signal reaches the end of a wire and is reflected back into the wire. On a bus network, computers send their signals to the entire network, so the signal travels the length of the bus. If the signal were allowed to continue uninterrupted, it would bounce back and forth along the wire, preventing other computers from transmitting.

The transmission must be stopped, or absorbed, at the end of each cable segment. A *terminator,* which is nothing more than a resistor placed at the end of a cable, absorbs the signal. Any open cable end — that is, a cable without a terminator — or a broken cable segment causes the entire network to malfunction as a result of signal bounce. If one computer (not the cable) fails, however, it does not affect the rest of the network.

To form a longer cable segment, multiple cable segments can be combined, usually with a BNC (British Naval Connector) barrel connector. If greater distances are needed, you can use a networking device called a *repeater.* The repeater takes a weak signal from one cable segment and regenerates it before transmitting it on another segment. The signal boost allows the signal to travel a longer distance.

On the certification test, you may see a question referring to attenuation. *Attenuation* is the tendency for a signal to become weaker as it travels greater distances. Repeaters are the devices used to counteract attenuation.

Star topology

In a star topology, each computer has its own network segment that links the computer back to a central location called a hub, as shown in Figure 4-2. The *hub* provides centralized network management capabilities. Each computer sends signals to the hub, and the hub sends the signals to the other computers on the network.

You can choose between two types of hubs. A *passive hub* sends the data out to all computers connected to it. These are used in small networks in which the computers are close together. If the distance between the computers and the hub is longer, an *active hub* is used to amplify the signal so that it can travel farther.

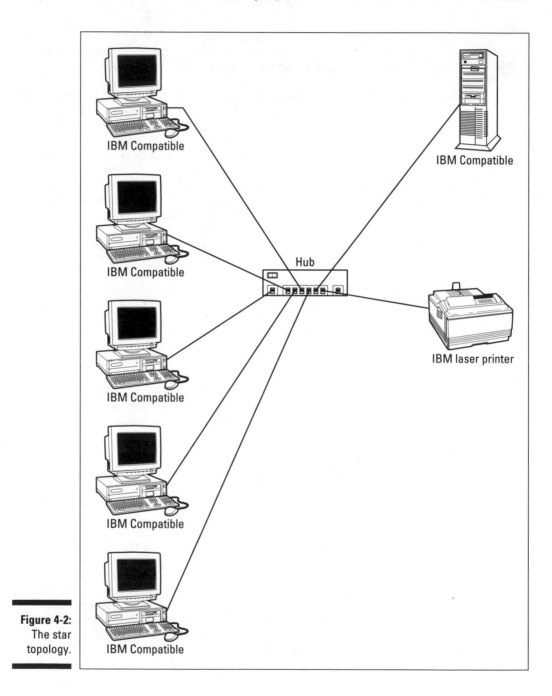

Figure 4-2:
The star
topology.

Star networks are like bus networks in that only one computer can transmit at a time and every computer on the network looks at the data to see whether it belongs to them. In a star network, however, a break in the cable affects only the computer attached to that cable. All other computers will still be able to communicate. Ironically, the device that makes that possible — the hub — is the biggest disadvantage of the star topology. If the hub fails, the entire network fails. Keep in mind that star networks cost a little more because of the need to have a hub.

Ring topology

The ring topology is easy to recognize because all computers are connected on a cable that forms a closed circle, or ring. In a ring network, the cable has no beginning and no end, just like a circle, as shown in Figure 4-3. With no cable ends, cable termination is unnecessary. Signals travel the wire in one direction from computer to computer until they reach their destination.

Unlike the bus topology, the ring topology is an active topology. So when a computer receives a signal, it regenerates the signal before sending it down the wire. Each computer is responsible for receiving signals and passing them on. The signals travel the wire in one direction from computer to computer until they return to the sending computer.

Only one computer at a time can send data. A *token* is passed from computer to computer until it gets to one that has data to send. The sending computer attaches the data to the token and sends the frame (containing the token and the data) around the network to the receiving computer. After the data is received, the token is sent back to the original sending computer with a message saying that the data was received. The sending computer then puts the token back out onto the network.

In a pure ring topology, the failure of a single computer or any piece of cable will cause an interruption in the signal. One interruption causes the entire network to fail. This is one reason why few, if any, networks are implemented as a pure ring topology. Another reason is that this type of network costs more than twice as much as other networks.

Mixed topologies

In practice, networking is rarely implemented as purely one topology or the other. Ethernet running on 10Base2 (thinnet) or 10Base5 (thicknet) cable is one of the few examples of a pure topology — in this case a pure bus topology. You are much more likely to see networks implemented as one of the following mixed topologies:

- Star-bus
- Star-ring

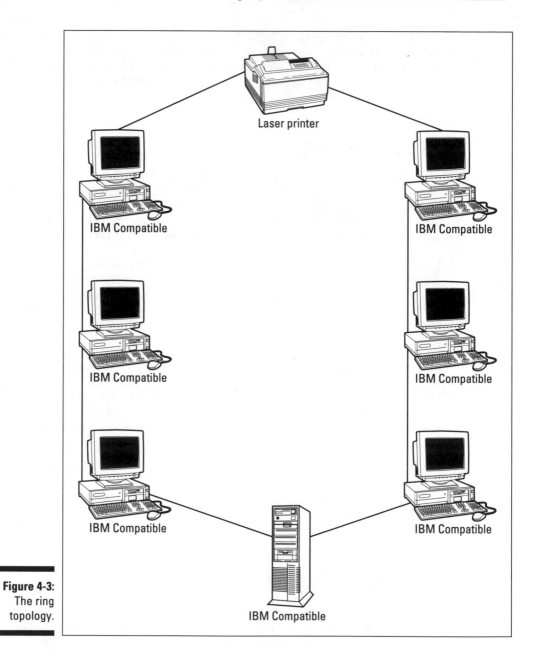

Laser printer

IBM Compatible

IBM Compatible

IBM Compatible

IBM Compatible

IBM Compatible

IBM Compatible

Figure 4-3:
The ring
topology.

Star-bus topology

The *star-bus topology* is simply several star networks connected by a bus network. When the first hub is full, a second hub is added and the two hubs are connected with a cable. Hubs can continue to be added as the network grows.

When a computer transmits a signal, it is propagated first to the other computers located on the same hub as the sending computer, and then to the computers on other hubs. If one of the links between the hubs is broken, a computer will be able to communicate only with other computers on the same hub or computers on hubs still physically connected to the sending computer's hub. Figure 4-4 illustrates a star-bus network.

This type of network works well in an office on several floors. Each floor has a hub to connect the computers on that floor. A bus network cable runs between floors and connects each hub.

Star-ring topology

In a *star-ring topology*, the computers are connected by a hub as in a star network. The hubs, however, are wired internally to form a ring network, as shown in Figure 4-5. In this way, if one computer goes down, the rest of the network will still function. By using token passing, as in a ring network, each computer in a star-ring topology has an equal chance of communicating.

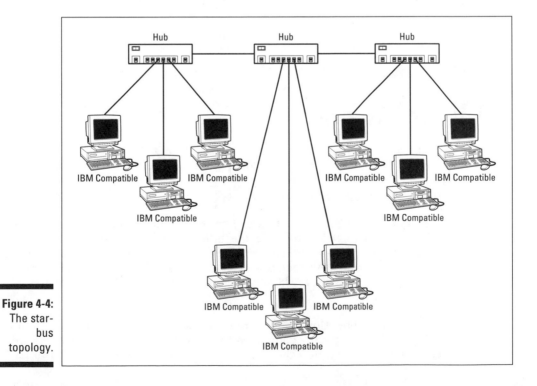

Figure 4-4:
The star-
bus
topology.

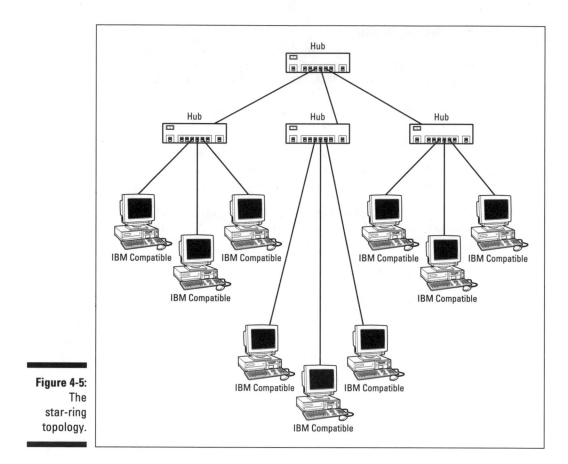

Figure 4-5:
The
star-ring
topology.

LAN Technologies

In this chapter, I take the approach that all local area network (LAN) standards have a few things in common. All are designed to accommodate many computers connected directly to the media, and all are designed to operate within a small geographic area.

A common rule to follow is that any network contained in a radius of one mile is a LAN. Anything between one mile and ten miles is a metropolitan area network (MAN), and anything beyond ten miles is a wide area network (WAN). MAN and WAN technologies are discussed in Chapter 6. For now, concern yourself with LAN technologies and the myriad of options for creating LANs.

The type of connection also determines whether the network is a LAN or a WAN. LANs are typically connected by a token ring or Ethernet. WANs are typically connected by a third-party connection — for example, T-1 or ISDN.

Ethernet

The IEEE designation for the Ethernet standard is 802.3. Remember the OSI seven-layer model? The 802.3 Ethernet standard defines the functions of the Logical Link layer (LLC) for Ethernet networks. The Ethernet standard defines the most popular network architecture used today. The 802.3 Ethernet standard defines also the network operations of the Physical and Data Link layers.

Ethernet basics

Ethernet is the most popular form of local area network. The Ethernet standard defines all characteristics of the network, including cable types, access methods, and frame formats. Ethernet networks are implemented as a bus, star, or star-bus topology. Although Ethernet networks are not the fastest network, they offer the best price performance. Ethernet networks are capable of transmitting data at 10 Mbps using CSMA/CD media access. Ethernet is a passive topology, which means power is drawn from the computers on the network.

The Ethernet standard has evolved considerably since the mid-1970s when it was first presented, but the basics remain the same and are presented in Table 4-1.

Table 4-1	Ethernet Basics
Characteristics	*Description*
Specification	IEEE 802.3
Traditional topology	Linear bus
Other topologies	Star bus
Architecture	Baseband
Access method	CSMA/CD
Transfer speed	10 Mbps
Cable types	Thicknet, thinnet, UTP
Frame size	Between 72 and 1526 bytes

Now that you have the basics, the next thing you need to look at to understand the Ethernet standard is the Ethernet frame format.

Ethernet frame format

The *frame* is the basic unit of transmission on an Ethernet network. Part of the 802.3 standard is a format for an Ethernet frame. Table 4-2 lists the fields that make up an Ethernet frame.

Table 4-2	Ethernet Frame Format
Field	*Description*
Preamble	Start of the frame
Destination	Hardware address of receiving computer
Source	Hardware address of sending computer
Type	Network layer protocol (IP or IPX)
Data	Application data
Frame check	Cyclic redundancy check (CRC) to detect corruption

The Ethernet frame size can be set between 64 bytes and 1518 bytes. The entire frame does not represent data, however, because 18 bytes of overhead for header and trailer information are associated with each frame. The header and trailer are used to ensure proper delivery of the data. The actual amount of data sent in each frame can range between 46 bytes and 1500 bytes.

Don't be surprised if you see some reference books listing the maximum transmission unit (MTU) for Ethernet at 1500 bytes rather than 1518. They've simply taken out the 18 bytes of overhead for you.

Note in Table 4-2 that an Ethernet frame starts with a preamble. Token-ring frames, on the other hand, use a start delimiter Although the names are different, both provide the same function — identifying where a frame starts. You'll need to remember the different names for the test.

Now that you are familiar with the basic unit of transmission, you need to consider the physical media used to create the connections between machines. The different types of media are referred to as cable types.

Ethernet cable types

Although many types of cable are available, the certification test stresses only Ethernet cabling standards. A number of questions on the certification test ask you to choose the appropriate cable type for a job. Most of those questions can be answered using Table 4-3.

Table 4-3	Cable Types and Selection Criteria			
Characteristic	*10Base2 (Thinnet)*	*10Base5 (Thicknet)*	*10BaseT (Twisted pair)*	*Fiber optic*
Cost	More than twisted pair	More than thinnet	Least expensive	Most expensive
Flexibility	Flexible	Least flexible	Most flexible	Flexible but delicate

Characteristic	10Base2 (Thinnet)	10Base5 (Thicknet)	10BaseT (Twisted pair)	Fiber optic
Installation	Easy	Easy	Very easy	Difficult
Interference features	Good resistance	Good resistance	Susceptible	Immune
Features	Electronic components less expensive than twisted pair	Electronic components less expensive than twisted pair	Same as telephone wire and often preinstalled	Supports voice, data, and video
Uses	Medium to large sites with security needs	Backbone segments between wiring closets	UTP: small sites on a budget; STP: token ring	Any site needing high speed and high security
Maximum cable distance	185M	500M	100M	2Km

Table 4-3 is everything you need to know about the Ethernet cable standards for the test. If you want to assure some quick, easy answers, memorize this table.

It is possible to run 10 Mbps Ethernet over fiber-optic cable. The standard is called 10BaseFL. If the test presents a situation where you need to connect two LANs running Ethernet, and fiber-optic cable exists between the two LANs; the best solution is to use fiber-optic cable and the 10BaseFL standard to provide the connection.

Now that you are familiar with the different cabling types, you need to be able to associate what additional hardware components are used with each type to join physical segments to form a larger network. The type of connectors you use depends on the type of cable you use.

Ethernet hardware

Ethernet hardware can be categorized into two general categories. The first is coaxial hardware for 10Base2 and 10Base5 networks. The second general type of hardware is twisted pair (TP) or RJ-45 hardware components for 10BaseT networks.

After you have that down, the only other thing to remember to classify hardware is that 10Base5 connectors are referred to as BNC N-series connectors. BNC N-series connectors are a little bigger than standard BNC connectors because the 10Base5 cable itself is a little larger in diameter.

Following are the important connectors for each cable type, starting with 10Base2 (thinnet) hardware. While reviewing this list, refer also to Figure 4-6:

- ✓ **Network adapter card with a BNC connection**. All network adapter cards must have a BNC connector or an AUI port connected to a transceiver that provides a BNC connection.

- ✓ **BNC barrel connector.** Splices two pieces of coaxial cable together to create a longer run of cable. The BNC barrel connector is simply inserted and locked into place between the BNC connectors on the cable ends.

- ✓ **BNC T connector.** Attaches to the network card and allows the computer to be inserted between two pieces of coaxial cable.

- ✓ **BNC terminator.** Eliminates signal bounce on the network. The BNC terminator is a 50-ohm resistor. A terminator may also provide a grounding wire. At least one terminator on every network trunk segment should be grounded.

- ✓ **Repeater.** Regenerates weak signals by retransmitting them. Repeaters are often used to connect long cable segments.

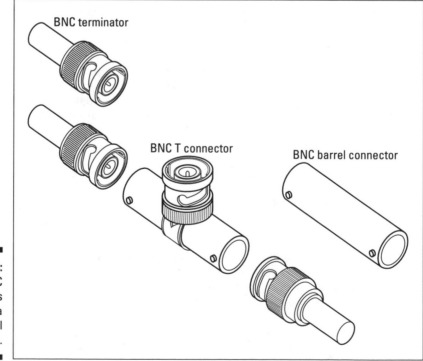

Figure 4-6:
The BNC connectors for a coaxial cable.

When using repeaters, the *5-4-3 rule* applies. No more than 5 network segments can be connected together. To connect the 5 segments, you are allowed to use 4 repeaters. Only 3 of these network segments can have computers attached to them. The other segments are used only to connect the repeaters and are referred to as *interrepeater links.* Refer to Figure 4-7.

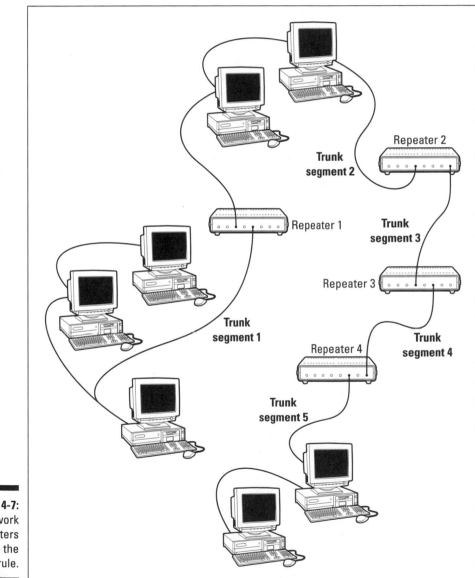

Figure 4-7:
Network repeaters and the 5-4-3 rule.

Following are the important connectors for 10Base5 (thicknet) hardware. See also Figure 4-8.

- ✔ **Transceiver.** Converts the parallel signals on the computer's bus to serial signals that can be transmitted on a network. All network adapters have a transceiver. Transceivers are usually located on the network adapter board. In the thicknet scheme, however, the transceiver is attached to a *vampire tap,* which pierces the cable to provide the physical connection between the transceiver and the thicknet cable.

- ✔ **Transceiver cable.** Connects a transceiver cable or network drop from the transceiver to the network adapter in the computer. The transceiver cable, which is sometimes referred to as a drop cable, connects to the AUI port on the adapter card. The AUI port is a 15-pin D-shell connector.

- ✔ **N-series BNC barrel connector.** Splices 2 pieces of coaxial cable together to create a longer run of cable. The N-series BNC barrel connector is simply inserted and locked into place between the BNC connectors on the cable ends.

- ✔ **N-series BNC terminator.** Eliminates signal bounce on the network. The N-series BNC terminator is a 50-ohm resistor. Terminators may also provide a grounding wire. At least one terminator on every network trunk segment should be grounded.

- ✔ **Repeater.** Regenerates weak signals by retransmitting them. Repeaters are often used to connect long cable segments.

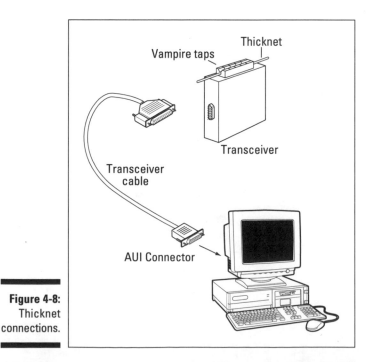

Figure 4-8:
Thicknet
connections.

Following are the important connectors for 10BaseT (twisted-pair) hardware. Refer also to Figure 4-9.

- ✔ **RJ-45 connector.** Connects twisted-pair cables to a computer. After the category of cable has been chosen (Category 3 or 5), RJ-45 connectors are placed on either end of the cable. The connector may be a male or a female connector. The female connector is often referred to as a wall jack.

- ✔ **Hub.** Provides a central connection for all computers in the network. This is true for both active and passive hubs. In addition, an active hub also monitors network performance, detects collisions, and regenerates weak signals. Most hubs with a power source are active hubs. Almost all hubs manufactured today are active hubs with different levels of intelligence.

You must be very careful when terminating 10BaseT cables (putting the RJ-45 connectors on each end) because the standard defines how much untwisted wire is allowed at each end of the cable. Twisted-pair cables contain 4 pairs of wires that are twisted in such a way that the electrical signals on one pair of wires do not interfere with the electrical signals on another pair of wires. Too much untwisted wire on either end could result in so much interference that the cable might be unreliable for transmitting network traffic.

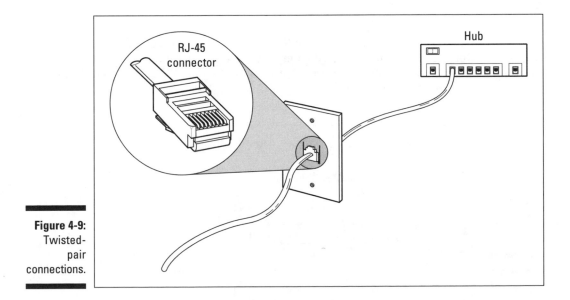

Figure 4-9:
Twisted-
pair
connections.

Ethernet topologies

Ethernet is rarely implemented as a linear bus (10Base2 or 10Base5) for any large installations. Because twisted-pair cable may already exist at a site and twisted-pair cable is easier to work with and less expensive than 10Base2 or 10Base5 cable, most companies choose to implement the 10BaseT (twisted-pair) standard.

A 10BaseT network is usually anchored with an active hub, making it an active topology. No single computer failure (unless it's the only server on the network) will affect the network, but a hub failure will interrupt service. The physical layout appears as a star, or as a star-bus if multiple hubs are joined together.

Fast Ethernet

Since the original Ethernet standard was defined, a lot of effort has gone into expanding its throughput capabilities. Fast Ethernet is the result, but with competing standards. Fast Ethernet is a general term that can be used in reference to any of the following 100-Mbps Ethernet standards:

- 100VG-AnyLAN, 100BaseVG, VG, or AnyLAN (all the same standard)
- 100BaseX Ethernet

100VG-AnyLAN

The *VG* in the 100BaseVG specification stands for voice grade. The 100BaseVG standard is still emerging, so it hasn't caught on as much as 100BaseX Ethernet. The specifications for 100BaseVG are listed in Table 4-4. Refer also to Figure 4-10.

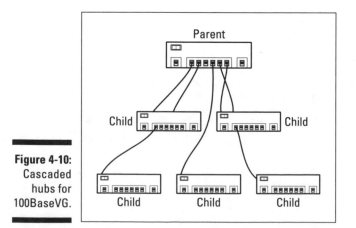

Figure 4-10: Cascaded hubs for 100BaseVG.

Table 4-4	100BaseVG (802.12) Specifications
Specification	*Requirement*
Data rate	Minimum 100 Mbps
Topology	Star with cascaded hubs
Supported media	Category 3, 4, 5 twisted-pair and fiber-optic cable
Media access	Demand priority with a low and high priority
Security	Capability to filter frames at the hub for privacy
Additional	Support for Ethernet frames and token-ring packets

The disadvantages to the 100BaseVG specification are as follows:

✔ Cable distances are somewhat limited

✔ Special adapter cards and hubs are required to implement the specification

✔ The ultimate size of the LAN is limited because the hubs must be cascaded

The advantages include the following:

✔ Not contention based, so computers can't force their way onto the network

✔ Facilities for prioritizing traffic allow more important traffic to have a higher priority

100BaseX (Fast Ethernet)

When people talk about Fast Ethernet, they're probably referring to the 100BaseX standard, which is the most popular and widely implemented 100-Mbps Ethernet standard. It requires UTP Category 5 cable and uses a CSMA/CD media access method in a star-bus topology. The four media specifications associated with 100BaseX are listed in Table 4-5.

Table 4-5	100BaseX Media Specifications
Specification	*Requirements*
Data rate	Minimum 100 Mbps
Topology	Star or star-bus
Supported media	Category 5 twisted-pair and fiber-optic cable
Maximum cable distance	100M for 100BaseT4 (most common cable)

You will see the 100BaseX qualified in the following ways to denote the type of cable being used:

- 100BaseT4, 4-pair Category 5 UTP
- 100BaseTX, 2-pair Category 5 UTP or STP
- 100BaseFX, 2-strand fiber-optic cable

100BaseX Ethernet networks use one of two types of hubs. The first is a hub capable of 100-Mbps throughput using the same type of internal connections as a 10-Mbps hub. The hub looks similar to a 10-Mbps hub, and some of these hubs can even accommodate both 10-Mpbs and 100-Mbps transmissions. This type of hub is only a little more expensive than a standard 10-Mbps hub and results in a contention-based environment just like its 10-Mbps cousin. Computers can force their way onto the network just like on a 10BaseT network.

The second type of hub is much more complicated and expensive. If you really want to set a 100-Mbps Ethernet network on fire, instead of purchasing a standard 100-Mbps hub, purchase a 100-Mbps switching hub. A *switching hub* (or switch) provides the full 100-Mbps bandwidth of the network to a communications session.

A switching hub operates by using a switch to establish a physical connection between two computers. From the perspective of these two computers, they are the only two computers on the network, so they have the entire network bandwidth to themselves as long as the switch keeps the connection open. The systems do not share the bandwidth of the network or hub with any other systems during a conversation, so throughput is dramatically improved.

To accommodate all systems connected to the switch, the switch rapidly polls each computer to determine whether it has data to transmit. Only when a system has information to send does the switch establish a connection for the computer. This is a very efficient and fast way of managing network bandwidth. Also, because switching is not a contention-based access method, the network is not susceptible to computers forcing their way onto the network and usurping bandwidth.

Token ring

Token ring was introduced by IBM in 1984 as part of their networking solution. In 1985, the IEEE classified the specification as 802.5 and token ring became a networking standard.

Token-ring basics

Logically, the architecture of a token-ring network is truly a ring. Data travels from one computer to the next until it eventually returns to the sending computer. Physically, IBM token ring is implemented as a star-wired ring; the center of the star is a multiple access unit (MAU). A MAU acts very much like a hub in an Ethernet 10BaseT environment.

For the certification test, remember the token-ring characteristics listed in Table 4-6.

Table 4-6	Token-Ring Basics
Characteristic	*Description*
Specification	IEEE 802.5
Topology	Star-wired ring
Architecture	Baseband
Access method	Token passing
Transfer speed	4 Mbps or 16 Mbps
Cable types	STP and UTP cable (IBM Types 1, 2, and 3)
Frame size	Between 72 and 1526 bytes

The token-ring network is initialized when the first computer comes online and generates a special type of packet called a *token*. The token travels around the network polling each computer for data to be transmitted. A computer may not transmit unless it has the token.

When a computer that has data to send receives the token, the computer attaches a data frame to the token and retransmits the token. The token and frame travel around the ring from computer to computer until they reach the destination computer. The destination computer copies the frame, marks the frame as copied, and sends the token and frame on.

Eventually, the token with the data frame returns to the sending computer marked as copied. The sending computer then acknowledges a successful transmission, removes the frame from the network, and generates a new token.

Only one token can exist on the ring at a time, so a computer cannot force its way onto the network. The first computer to come online is also the token monitor and is responsible for regenerating a token if the token is lost or corrupted.

Now that you have an operational definition of an IBM token ring, it's time to look at some specifics. The first of these is the frame format.

Token-ring frame format

The token-ring frame format is considerably different than an Ethernet frame format. You don't need to know the details of the differences for the test, but you need to be able to identify which fields belong in which frame types. Review the token-ring frame format listed in Table 4-7, and then compare it with the Ethernet frame format shown in Table 4-2.

Table 4-7	Token-Ring Frame Format
Field	*Description*
Start delimiter	Start of the frame
Access control	Frame priority
Frame control	MAC information for all computers or single computer
Destination address	Hardware address of receiving computer
Source address	Hardware address of sending computer
Data	Application data
Frame check	CRC error-checking information
End delimiter	End of frame
Frame status	Whether or not the frame was copied

Now that you've seen the differences in frame formats between token-ring and Ethernet networks, you need to examine another key difference. Both these network types can use a star-type topology, which means they both use hubs. In an Ethernet network, a hub is called what it is — a hub. In a token-ring network, which was developed by IBM, the same device is called a multistation access unit (MAU). You can describe a token-ring network as a physical star-logical ring.

MAUs

The hardware used in a token-ring environment is different than the hardware used in an Ethernet environment. One important difference is cost. Token-ring hardware is much more expensive than Ethernet hardware.

Token-ring hubs, called MAUs or SMAUs, have ten ports. Eight of the ports may be used for computers; the other two are designated as Ring-In and Ring-Out ports. The ring ports connect MAUs to increase the size of the ring. The Ring-Out port on one MAU is connected to the Ring-In port on another MAU. To complete the ring, the Ring-Out port on the last MAU is connected to the Ring-In port on the first MAU. Up to 12 MAU devices can be connected together.

SMAUs (smart multiple access units) provide a simple form of fault tolerance. If a computer malfunctions, the SMAU detects the malfunction and disables the port that the computer is connected to. This prevents a single malfunctioning computer from adversely affecting the entire ring. MAUs do not have this capability. As a result, today almost everyone uses SMAUs instead of MAUs.

Now that you are familiar with the nerve center of the token-ring network, it's time to take a look at the actual nerves. IBM has its own set of cable standards that you should be familiar with for the certification test.

Token-ring cabling and connectors

The following cable types are part of the IBM cabling standard for token-ring networks:

- **Type 1** consists of a braided shield surrounding two twisted pairs of solid copper wire. This type is used to connect terminals and distribution panels or to connect wiring closets.

- **Type 2** consists of six twisted pairs. Two are shielded and used for networking; the other four are unshielded and used for telephone connections.

- **Type 3** is a lower grade of type 2 cable. It is less expensive, but can't be used for 16-Mbps token ring. It is used primarily for long, low-grade data transmissions within walls.

- **Type 5** is a fiber-optic cable that uses 100-micron or 140-micron optical fibers. This cable is used only for the main ring of a token-ring network.

- **Type 6** is the same as type 1, except the core wires are stranded instead of solid. The cable runs are shorter, but the cable is more flexible. Type 6 is used for patch and extension cables.

- **Type 8** uses a single shielded stranded core and is especially designed for use under carpets.

- **Type 9** is plenum-grade type 6 cable. It is fire resistant and designed for long runs in walls, ceilings, and floor spaces.

A number of connectors are associated with the token-ring standard:

- **Media interface connector (MIC) for type 1 and type 2 cable** is an androgynous connector because it is both male and female. Two connectors are combined by simply flipping one of them over.

- **RJ-45 (8-pin) for type 3 cable** houses eight cable connections that can be male or female connectors. Female connectors are often called wall jacks.

- **RJ-11 (4-pin) for type 3 cable** houses four cable connections that can be male or female connectors.

- **Media filters** connect the token-ring adapter card to RJ-11 or RJ-45 wall jacks.

I want you to know one more thing about token ring. It's a feature found in no other LAN technology: locally administered addresses (LAAs). Read the next section on addressing to find out more.

Token-ring card addressing

As with Ethernet cards, each token-ring card has a node address (hardware address) burned into the card by the manufacturer. Some token-ring cards allow you to override the address by specifying the hardware address you would like to use. This address is often referred to as the LAA (locally administered address).

The advantage of using an LAA is that an administrator can define a naming convention whereby he or she can determine information about a system such as its location, owner, or function simply by looking at the hardware address. This speeds up troubleshooting.

The biggest disadvantage to using an LAA is that it is easy to accidentally assign the same address to two or more systems. This will result in a variety of different problems depending on what the systems do and where they are located.

Jive AppleTalkin'

The AppleTalk protocol was developed by Apple Computer to provide networking services for its Macintosh line of PCs. Depending on the physical media used to create the network, AppleTalk may be referred to as LocalTalk, EtherTalk, or TokenTalk. The Apple file-sharing service is referred to as AppleShare. An AppleShare server is like a Windows NT Member Server that provides only file and print services.

LocalTalk

The LocalTalk specification includes components such as cables, connector modules, and cable extenders. The network is implemented in either a bus or a star topology. A LocalTalk segment supports a maximum of 32 devices. Figure 4-11 shows a variety of LocalTalk connectors.

The limitation of 32 devices on a segment is usually too severe for a LocalTalk network to be of much use to an organization. One alternative to the Apple standard is to use a different cabling scheme. For example, Farallon PhoneNet replaces Apple LocalTalk cable, giving an organization the capability to connect 254 devices to the network.

EtherTalk and TokenTalk

The EtherTalk and TokenTalk specifications extend the capabilities of the AppleTalk protocol by enabling the protocol to be run over networks that are more robust than LocalTalk. The underlying transport or physical media in this case is either a token-ring or an Ethernet network. Both are faster and more reliable than a LocalTalk network. TokenTalk and especially EtherTalk are implemented far more often than LocalTalk.

EtherTalk allows Macintosh computers to connect to an Ethernet coaxial cable — usually thinnet but sometimes thicknet. TokenTalk allows Macintosh computers to connect to an 802.5 token-ring network. Both EtherTalk and TokenTalk are compatible with the AppleTalk Phase 2 standard.

AppleShare

AppleShare is the file server on an AppleTalk network. AppleShare also provides a print server component for server-based print spooling. The client software for the AppleShare server is included with every copy of the Macintosh operating system.

AppleTalk Zones

To effectively implement an AppleTalk network, including AppleShare servers, *zones* are used to segment the network. Zones are used also to group small LocalTalk networks or workgroups into larger networks.

Each network or workgroup is identified by a zone name. Users in any zone can access resources in any other zone by simply selecting that zone. This is similar to Windows NT domains and workgroups. If the zones are properly implemented, the resources the user accesses most often will be in the same zone, and the user will not need to change zones to complete a task.

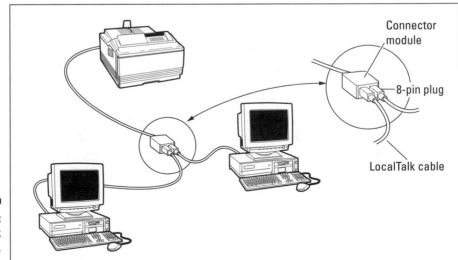

Figure 4-11:
LocalTalk connectors.

Zones do not have to map directly to the physical layout of the network. They can contain resources from all over a large network. If zones do closely map to the physical layout of the network, however, they have the benefit of confining network traffic to specific network segments, which improves network performance.

ARCnet

ARCnet (Attached Resource Computer network) was developed in the late 1970s. ARCnet is a simple, flexible, inexpensive network designed for small workgroups. An ARCnet can have a star-bus or a bus topology, but is typically implemented as a star-bus. A token-passing Media Access Control method provides transfer speeds of approximately 2.5 Mbps. A successor to the original standard, called ARCnet Plus, provides transfer speeds of about 20 Mbps.

ARCnet card addressing

A computer in an ARCnet can't transmit unless it has the token. Figure 4-12 illustrates how the token travels the network from computer to computer in an order based on the numerical number of the computer, regardless of how the computers are placed on the network. You might think that this would affect performance, especially on a bus network, but it doesn't. The token-passing scheme eliminates the potential for data collisions, which more than makes up for the less-than-optimal route the token takes.

Cabling for ARCnet

Every computer in an ARCnet is connected to a hub. The hub can be either an active or a passive hub. The standard cable is a 93-ohm RG-62 A/U coaxial cable. ARCnet also supports twisted-pair and fiber-optic cable.

Distances between computers vary with the type of cable used. With coaxial cable, BNC connectors, and an active hub (so it regenerates signals), the maximum cable distance between computer and hub is 610 meters (2000 feet). Without the hub providing a star topology, the maximum cable distance drops to 305 meters (1000 feet) for a single bus segment. Using UTP cable with RJ-11 or RJ-45 connectors, the maximum cable distance is 244 meters (800 feet) in both the star and bus implementations.

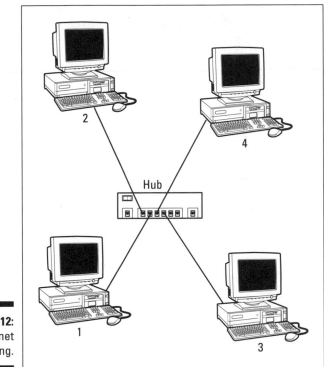

Figure 4-12:
ARCnet
addressing.

Prep Test

1 Which Ethernet standard is often referred to as thinnet?

A ○ 10Base2

B ○ 10Base5

C ○ 10BaseT

D ○ 10BaseFL

2 Which Ethernet standard is often referred to as thicknet?

A ○ 10Base2

B ○ 10Base5

C ○ 10BaseT

D ○ 10BaseFL

3 Which of the following is a method of signal transmission?

A ○ Token passing

B ○ CSMA/CD

C ○ Baseband

D ○ Demand priority

4 Which of the following is not a method of Media Access Control?

A ○ Token passing

B ○ CSMA/CD

C ○ Broadband

D ○ Demand priority

5 Which of the following is the most common Fast Ethernet standard?

A ○ 10BaseFL

B ○ 100BaseX

C ○ VG AnyLAN

D ○ SONET

6 Of the following logical grouping of systems, which is used in an AppleTalk network to segment the network?

A ○ Groups

B ○ Zones

C ○ Domains

D ○ Workgroups

7 Which of the following is the IEEE 802 model designation for token ring?

A ○ 802.2

B ○ 802.3

C ○ 802.5

D ○ 802.7

8 Which topologies suffer loss of availability when a single cable breaks? (Mark all that apply.)

A ❑ Star

B ❑ Bus

C ❑ Star-bus

D ❑ Ring

9 Which topology requires terminators?

A ○ Star

B ○ Bus

C ○ Star-bus

D ○ Ring

10 What is the most common topology for an Ethernet network?

A ○ Star

B ○ Bus

C ○ Star-bus

D ○ Ring

Answers

1 *A.* Thinnet and 10Base2 are synonymous. *Review "Ethernet."*

2 *B.* Thicknet and 10Base5 are synonymous. *Review "Ethernet."*

3 *C.* Baseband is a signaling method that uses discreet digital signals. Baseband is the most common form of signal transmission in LANs. *Review "Classifying Networks."*

4 *C.* Broadband is a signaling method that uses analog wave signals. Cable television is the most common example of a broadband transmission. Broadband is a unidirectional, analog transmission that uses amplifiers instead of repeaters to regenerate weak signals. *Review "Classifying Networks."*

5 *B.* Most companies implement 100BaseX when they want 100-Mbps Ethernet because they can make use of existing wiring if they already have a 10BaseT network. The hubs and adapter cards still need to be replaced, but 100BaseX hardware is much less expensive than 100VG-AnyLAN hardware. 100BaseX requires Category 5 cable. *Review "Fast Ethernet."*

6 *B.* An AppleTalk network uses AppleTalk zones to logically group systems by function or geographic area. The concept is similar to a workgroup in Microsoft networking. *Review "AppleTalk Zones."*

7 *C.* The IEEE 802 Project model designates the token ring network specification as IEEE 802.5. *Review "Token Ring."*

8 *B, D.* Any topology with a star configuration does not suffer when a single cable breaks because that cable was connecting only one computer to a central point. The other computers continue to operate. *Review "LAN Topologies."*

9 *B.* Bus topologies require terminators to eliminate signal bounce when a signal reaches the ends of the cable. *Review "LAN Topologies."*

10 *A.* The star bus topology using 10BaseT cable is the most popular implementation of Ethernet. *Review "Ethernet."*

Chapter 5

Remote Access Service

● ●

Exam Objective

▶ Distinguishing whether SLIP or PPP is used as the communications protocol for various situations

● ●

*O*ne of the most powerful and versatile technologies included with Microsoft's Windows NT Server is Remote Access Service (RAS). RAS was designed to make network resources available to remote clients through a variety of dial-up options including standard telephone lines, ISDN lines, and packet-switched networks such as X.25. Many configuration options are available, and RAS must be configured on the Services tab of the Network Control Panel (on the server) and through Dial-Up Networking (on the client). Also, if RAS is configured improperly, serious security consequences could result: An open door to the network could be created for any hackers with a little knowledge and too much time on their hands to exploit. To ensure that this doesn't happen and that the technology is implemented properly, Microsoft stresses your understanding of RAS configuration options and procedures on the certification test.

Remote Access Service (RAS) and Dial-Up Networking are among the most challenging portions of all Windows NT certification exams. The knowledge required to successfully negotiate the Networking Essentials exam centers on distinguishing between SLIP and PPP communications protocols for a given situation. Because Windows NT 4.0 supports only PPP communications, choosing the correct protocol isn't a tough decision in a Microsoft network! Because Microsoft hasn't completely taken over the computing world (yet), some networks may not be running Windows NT, which is why a choice between SLIP and PPP exists. Many Internet service providers are still using UNIX servers, which work with the SLIP communications protocol. As a result, the exam specifically tests your understanding of the benefits and drawbacks of using SLIP versus PPP to establish a connection to a remote network or to the Internet.

Quick Assessment

Distinguishing whether SLIP or PPP is used as the communications protocol for various situations

1 Two categories for classifying modems based on their transmission characteristics are _____ and _____.

2 The _____ RAS connection protocol is no longer supported under Windows NT 4.0 as a dial-in protocol.

3 On an external modem, the _____ connector connects the modem to the telephone system, and the _____ serial cable connects the modem to the computer.

4 Originally, modem transmission speeds were measured by _____ rate, but today _____ is the more accepted expression of throughput.

5 _____ allows more than one bit of data to be transmitted on a single-carrier wave oscillation.

6 _____ protocols ensure reliable transmission of data from one modem to another.

7 The RAS client on Windows NT and Windows 95 is called _____ _____.

8 The _____ RAS connection protocol supports TCP/IP as well as NWLink and NetBEUI.

9 UNIX systems typically use the _____ communications protocol to establish a connection to the Internet.

10 Public lines and leased lines are generally referred to as _____.

Answers

1   *Asynchronous; synchronous.* Review "Asynchronous versus synchronous modems."

2   *SLIP.* Review "SLIP Protocol versus PPP Protocol."

3   *RJ-11; RS-232.* Review the "Connections" section.

4   *Baud; bps.* See the "Transfer speed" section on modem transmission speeds.

5   *Compression.* Read more about modem compression techniques in the "Compression and error control" section.

6   *Error correction.* Read more about error correction techniques in the "Compression and error control" section.

7   *Dial-Up Networking.* Review "Installing RAS."

8   *PPP.* Review "SLIP Protocol versus PPP Protocol."

9   *SLIP.* Review "SLIP Protocol versus PPP Protocol."

10   *Carriers.* Review the "Carriers" section.

Modem Technology

Modems often provide the physical connections needed to link LANs together in a WAN. Modems enable computers to communicate over telephone lines. A modem converts the digital signals that travel a computer's bus to analog signals that can travel over standard telephone lines. Another modem, at the other end of the connection, then translates the analog telephone signals back into digital signals that can travel the computer's bus.

Connections

A modem uses a serial connection with a computer. Modems can be either internal or external devices. An *internal modem* looks like a circuit board with one or two RJ-11 telephone connectors in the front panel. An internal modem is installed in an expansion slot on the computer's bus.

An *external modem* has the same components as an internal modem, but they are housed in a separate case. The external modem attaches to one of the computer's serial ports with an RS-232 serial cable. External modems tend to be slightly more expensive than internal modems, but they offer additional features (such as diagnostic LEDs) that are not available on internal modems.

Regardless of whether the modem is external or internal, the connection to the telephone system is a 4-wire RJ-11C telephone plug, often referred to simply as RJ-11.

Don't confuse the RJ-11 telephone connector with the RJ-45 twisted-pair connector commonly used with 10BaseT Ethernet networks.

Transfer speed

Originally, a modem's speed was measured in bps (bits per second) or by baud rate. *Baud* refers to the speed of the oscillation of the sound wave on which a bit of data is carried. In the early days of modem technology, each oscillation represented one bit, so baud rate and bps were equivalent measures. Today, with modem compression, more than one bit of data can be transmitted with a single oscillation of the carrier wave. Therefore, bps rather than baud rate is a truer measure of throughput. Table 5-1 lists common modem standards and the throughput each represents.

Table 5-1	Modem Standards and Throughput	
Standard	*bps*	*Introduced*
V.22bis	2400	1984
V.32	9600	1984
V.32bis	14,400	1991
V.34	28,800	1994
V.42	57,600	1995

Compression and error control

As modem communications became more popular and bandwidth requirements increased, signal engineers found ways to compress and encode data so that each modulation of sound could carry more than one bit of data. Table 5-2 lists some standard protocols for data compression during modem transmissions.

Table 5-2	Modem Error Control and Compression Protocols
Modem Error Control Protocol	*Modem Compression Protocol*
MNP4	MNP5 (up to 2:1 compression)
V.42 w/ LAPM	V.42bis (up to 4:1 compression)

Error control and modem compression are optional features available with most modems. For reliable connections, the local and remote modem error control standards must be compatible. For improved throughput, their modem data and RAS data compression standards must be compatible as well.

A question on the certification exam involves modem protocols. V.42 with LAPM and MNP4 are two common error correction protocols. For a protocol to be used during a communications session, both modems must support it.

Asynchronous versus synchronous modems

Modems belong to one of two basic categories: asynchronous or synchronous. The term *Asynchronous communications* means that each byte is framed with a start and stop bit. RAS sends data asynchronously to the serial port, and the serial port sends data asynchronously to the modem.

This category of modem is the most common and least expensive type of modem communications. Asynchronous modems can operate on lower quality lines, so they are well suited for the public telephone network. Asynchronous modems also tend to interoperate with other models of asynchronous modems better than synchronous modems do because they are not as sensitive. They also tend to be easier to configure.

Synchronous modems receive a stream of characters from the computer and convert that stream into blocks of characters. The blocks are then sent synchronously to the other modem by using an error control protocol. The other modem disassembles the synchronous blocks to return a character stream to the receiving computer.

Synchronous communications use SYNC frames to make sure that modem clocks are synchronized. Then data is sent from one modem to the other with no start and stop bits. The receiving modem is able to correctly break the communications stream into characters based on the amount of time that has passed.

The main advantage to synchronous modems is higher throughput. Every start and stop frame that an asynchronous modem sends represents over-head and reduces the effective data throughput of the modem.

RAS supports X.25, ISDN, Null Modem, and asynchronous modem communications. RAS does not support synchronous communications and therefore cannot communicate with a synchronous serial port. Any RAS solution that proposes synchronous modems is not a valid answer.

Carriers

The *carrier* is the type of telephone network that exists between two modems in a dial-up connection. Many types of carriers are available, but for the certification test you need to be familiar with only two in particular: public lines and leased lines.

One of the many decisions that a network engineer must make when designing a network is which type of carrier to use. The three major criteria for choosing a carrier are

✔ Transmission speed

✔ Distance between sites

✔ Cost of using the carrier

Public lines

The public telephone network, also known as a Public Switched Telephone Network (PSTN), was designed as a voice network. Consequently, these public lines are usually slow and may be unreliable for data communications. Access, however, is simple and inexpensive. PSTN uses a series of switches (transparent to the user) to connect the end-to-end conversation. Each conversation is initiated by providing a phone number that acts as an address for a computer in the network.

Leased lines

Leased lines are often referred to as dedicated lines or dedicated circuits. Leased lines provide a full-time dedicated connection between sites. The quality of the line and the transmission speed are much greater than a PSTN because leased lines do not use a series of switches to make the connection. (Actually, most networking providers use switched circuits to provide the illusion of a dedicated leased line. Switches are present, but they are configured or reserved for a specific connection.)

Unfortunately, high quality and high throughput come with a high price. Full-time dedicated point-to-point leased lines are very expensive because the owner bears the full cost of the line as opposed to multiple owners (or users) sharing the cost of a PSTN.

SLIP Protocol versus PPP Protocol

SLIP and PPP are two communications protocols that allow a computer to connect to a remote network or to the Internet via a modem. SLIP and PPP are connection, or RAS, protocols. RAS supports networking protocols such as TCP/IP, NWLink, and NetBEUI by allowing a user to establish a communications session using one of the networking protocols over a dial-up connection. Although SLIP and PPP are similar in that they both establish a connection to a remote server, some key differences exist.

SLIP

Serial Line Internet Protocol (SLIP) is an older standard primarily developed to provide connectivity to the Internet for UNIX machines. I do not want to appear negative about older technology, but SLIP does have drawbacks. First, SLIP supports only the TCP/IP protocol, which is fine for dialing up to the Internet but can pose a problem if you need to dial into a remote network that utilizes other protocols. Second, to make a connection, you must supply a static IP address assigned to you by an Internet service provider (ISP). Third, you may need to configure such details as maximum transmission unit (MTU), maximum receive unit (MRU), and use of VJ compression header. You may be thinking, "All this just to dial into the Internet?" Although all these options can be confusing to set up, most ISPs are willing to provide dial-up scripts to automate the logon process.

PPP

Point-to-Point Protocol (PPP) is a newer technology that is quickly becoming the communications standard of choice because it is easier to configure, faster, and more reliable than SLIP. Another advantage of PPP is support for multiple protocols such as NetBEUI, IPX, and AppleTalk in addition to support for TCP/IP. Better yet, you can transport all these protocols at the same time on the same connection. Another advantage of PPP is the flexibility of dynamically obtaining an IP address from a predefined pool or from a DHCP server. This makes logging on to a remote network or the Internet easier because you don't have to provide a static IP address.

Deciding which protocol to use

Given a choice of using SLIP versus PPP, the answer will usually be PPP due to ease of configuration, dynamic IP address assignment, and support for multiple protocols. The time to utilize SLIP would be if an Internet service provider didn't support a PPP connection. For all other instances, the benefits of PPP make it the communications protocol of choice.

Whereas Windows NT 3.51 provided support for SLIP and PPP, Windows NT 4.0 supports only the PPP communications protocol. In comparing SLIP to PPP, the only possible advantage of SLIP is that it has less overhead associated with establishing a connection — because it doesn't do as much!

Remote Access Service

Configuring Remote Access Service, or RAS, is a two-step process. First, you must have a server with a modem and a connection to a LAN. Second, you must have client software that enables you to connect to the server and access LAN resources.

The server acts as a gateway to the LAN. Microsoft Windows NT Server 4.0 provides Remote Access Service as the server component. The Microsoft RAS server supports LAN connections with the TCP/IP, IPX, and NetBEUI protocols over the Point-to-Point Protocol (PPP) RAS protocol.

The Microsoft RAS server also provides security features. An administrator has the ability to turn off the gateway and routing functions for a particular LAN protocol. This, in effect, limits RAS clients to accessing resources provided by only the RAS server. Microsoft also provides the Point-to-Point Tunneling Protocol (PPTP), which allows users to connect to a local Internet service provider and establish a secure network connection with a Windows NT server.

Another benefit of the Remote Access Service is error reporting. RAS is tightly integrated with Windows NT features such as error logging. Any failed connection attempts or other RAS-related errors are written to the Windows NT system log, where they can be viewed through the Event Viewer.

If you are already familiar with RAS in the Windows NT 3.51 implementation, pay close attention to additional functionality available in the Windows NT 4.0 implementation, such as Multilink and Point-to-Point-Tunneling Protocol (PPTP).

Installing RAS

It is very unlikely that you will see RAS installation questions on the exam. Just remember that on Windows NT, RAS is installed as a networking service through the Network Control Panel application. Figure 5-1 shows RAS installed as a network service.

The RAS client on Windows NT and Windows 95 is called Dial-Up Networking. Client software is also available for Windows 3.1, Windows for Workgroups, and DOS, but you won't be tested for configurations for these older operating systems. Client knowledge is confined to the 32-bit Microsoft operating systems.

Administering RAS

The DialUp Monitor, shown in Figure 5-2, can be used to monitor RAS connections from the client. The tool of choice for administering RAS communications ports and connections on the server is the Remote Access Admin application.

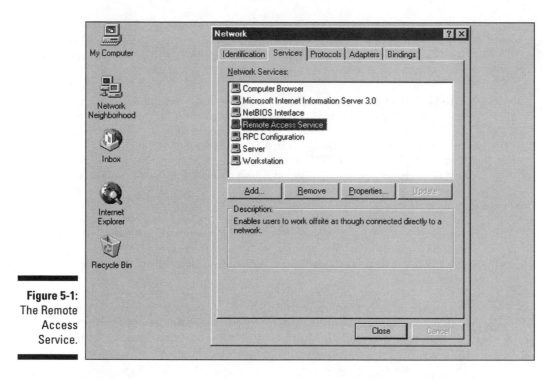

Figure 5-1:
The Remote
Access
Service.

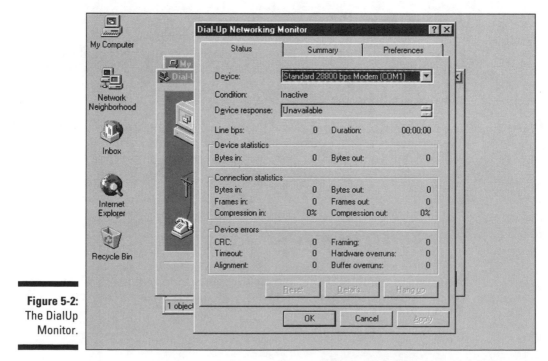

Figure 5-2:
The DialUp
Monitor.

One decision that must be made when configuring a RAS server is how the communications port will be used. Figure 5-3 shows the port configuration screen on the RAS server. Notice that a port can be restricted to either incoming or outgoing calls, or it can be used for both; you make this decision using the Services tab in the Network control panel.

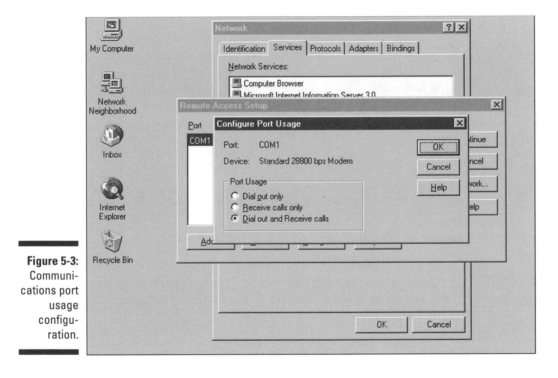

Figure 5-3: Communications port usage configuration.

Configuring

1 Which type of modem is not supported as a RAS communications device?

A ○ Synchronous

B ○ Asynchronous

C ○ Digital

D ○ Monochromatic

2 Which of the following is an error correction protocol commonly used in modem communications?

A ○ CRC

B ○ Parity

C ○ MNP4

D ○ Stop bits

3 Which standard defines modem communications as fast as 57,600 bps?

A ○ V.32

B ○ V.32bis

C ○ V.34

D ○ V.42

4 Which of the following is the telephone connector most commonly used to connect a modem to the telephone network?

A ○ RJ-45

B ○ RJ-11

C ○ 10BaseT

D ○ RS-232

5 What type of cable is used to connect an external modem to the serial port of a PC?

A ○ RJ-45

B ○ RS-232

C ○ RJ-11

D ○ 10BaseT

6 Which utility is most often used to administer RAS connections at the server?

A ○ Remote Access Admin

B ○ Event Viewer

C ○ Network Control Panel

D ○ User Manager

7 Which Windows NT utility is used to gain information about failed RAS connection attempts?

A ○ RAS Monitor

B ○ Event Viewer

C ○ Network Control Panel

D ○ User Manager

8 Which RAS dial-in protocol is supported by Windows NT 4.0 RAS servers?

A ○ SLIP

B ○ PPP

9 What is the most common measure of modem throughput?

A ○ Baud rate

B ○ bps

Answers

1 *A.* Synchronous modems are not supported as a RAS communications device. *Review the "Asynchronous versus synchronous modems" section of the chapter.*

2 *C.* Error correction protocols implemented within the modem and modem driver include V.42 with LAPM and MNP4 . *Review Table 5-2.*

3 *D.* V.42 is the only standard that supports modem communications at this transfer rate. *See Tables 5-1 and 5-2.*

4 *B.* Don't confuse the RJ-45 jack with the RJ-11 jack. They look similar, but the RJ-45 jack is used for 10BaseT networking, not telephone connections. *See "Connections."*

5 *B.* RS-232 is a serial standard that defines cable lengths and pin configurations for the connector. An external modem connects to a serial port on the PC with an RS-232 serial cable. *Review "Connections" for more information.*

6 *A.* Use the Remote Access Admin utility to administer the RAS ports and connections on a server. You can set the RAS dial-in permission through User Manager, but the preferred method is to use the Remote Access Admin utility. *See "Administering RAS" and Figure 5-2.*

7 *B.* All failed connection attempts are logged to the system log and can be viewed with Windows NT Event Viewer. This is the first place you should look to resolve a connection failure. *Review "Remote Access Service."*

8 *B.* SLIP is an older RAS protocol that is no longer supported by Windows NT 4.0 RAS as a dial-in option. PPP is faster, more flexible, and supports multiple LAN protocols. *See "Remote Access Service" and the Instant Answer in the section.*

9 *B.* Modem compression made baud rate obsolete as a measurement. Most people now express throughput in bps (bits per second). *See "Transfer speed."*

Chapter 6
Wide Area Networks

● ●

Exam Objectives

▶ Defining common networking terms for LANs and WANs

▶ Listing the characteristics, requirements, and appropriate situations for WAN connection services, including X.25, ISDN, frame relay, and ATM

● ●

*T*he focus of this chapter is wide area network (WAN) technologies. Wide area networks connect remote LANs to provide a seamless integration of data services across an organization. Wide area network technology is one of the fastest growing areas of networking. New providers are entering the market, and the capabilities of the technologies are advancing rapidly. An engineer must be familiar with dozens of networking standards — and competing standards for the same technology. Size, speed, cost, flexibility, and upgradeability are major concerns. The variety of options available to network engineers is staggering.

In this chapter, you examine the most common WAN connection services, which are also the services you need to be familiar with for the certification test. At a minimum, you must be able to identify the distinguishing features of each service. I describe line types, switching methods, high-capacity networks, and standards. If you are lucky enough to be in an organization that uses a WAN, try to identify what services your organization is using and relate those services back to the capabilities of the network as you see them from the user's perspective. If you are already a network guru, at certain places in this chapter you might say to yourself, "Hey that's not how that works!" Remember, my purpose is to prepare you for the certification test, and that includes informing you about standards as they existed when the certification test was written. Make sure that you focus on the exam objectives, noting that they specifically mention X.25, ISDN, frame relay, and ATM.

You will also examine SONET and FDDI, two cutting-edge technologies based on fiber optics. Because these technologies are not widely implemented or completely defined, they may not be on the test. This is a complicated chapter, but probably also the most fun!

Quick Assessment

Defining common networking terms for LANs and WANs

1 _____ is a fiber-optic-based technology that uses beaconing to identify the location of connectivity problems.

2 _____ is the process of combining multiple data sources into a single data stream before transmission.

3 _____ is the network provided by the telephone company that you can access by using a standard PC modem.

4 A(n) _____ is used to convert the digital signals used in a computer to the bipolar digital signals used for transmission on most digital leased lines.

Listing the characteristics, requirements, and appropriate situations for WAN connection services, including X.25, ISDN, frame relay, and ATM

5 _____ is a high-speed standard that uses a fixed-size cell that allows all networking equipment to be optimized for a fixed transmission unit, resulting in very high transfer rates.

6 A T1 line contains _____ data channel(s) and _____ link management channel(s), giving a subscriber an effective throughput of _____ Mbps.

7 T3 and T4 carriers require a high-frequency transmission, such as _____ or _____, because of their high throughput.

8 The most common implementation of a packet-switching network is known as _____.

9 _____ is a type of WAN that uses permanent virtual circuits (PVCs) and variable message lengths to provide very fast communications.

10 Networking equipment in an X.25 network is referred to as _____.

Answers

1 *FDDI*. Review the "Fiber Distributed Data Interface (FDDI)" section.

2 *Multiplexing*. Check out the " Asynchronous Transfer Mode (ATM)" section.

3 *PSTN*. Review the "Public Switched Telephone Network (PSTN)" section.

4 *CSU/DSU*. If you missed this one, review the "Digital lines" section.

5 *ATM*. Don't skip the "Asynchronous Transfer Mode (ATM)" section; you're going to need it!

6 *23; 1; 1.544*. Find out more about T1s in the "T-carrier" section.

7 *Microwave; fiber-optic*. Review the "T-carrier" section.

8 *X.25*. If you missed this one, it would be a good idea to review the "X.25 Packet-Switching Protocol" section before the test.

9 *Frame relay*. See the "Frame Relay" section.

10 *DTE/DCE*. Check out the "X.25 Packet-Switching Protocol" section.

Public Network Services

Public. There's a gray word. If you're like me, when someone says "public," the first thing you might think is "free." Well, nothing in this world is free — and that includes public network services. The two most common public network services that network engineers work with are Public Switched Telephone Network (PSTN) and the Internet.

Public Switched Telephone Network (PSTN)

PSTN is "Ma Bell," or at least what's left of her. PSTN includes local service providers and long-distance providers of telecommunications services. Read that as the telephone company. A large portion of the wiring for PSTN is the wiring running into and around your home. PSTN is characterized as having low- to medium-grade telephone lines, although some exceptions exist.

The biggest advantage in using PSTN is cost. You can make use of PSTN by simply plugging your telephone line into a modem. Unfortunately, you get what you pay for. Maximum throughput for a single connection is about 56 Kbps, with the average throughput closer to 28.8 Kbps. It's enough to browse the Internet, but a far cry from being a true WAN.

The Internet

The Internet is becoming more and more of an option for wide area networking, especially for smaller companies that can't afford leased lines or a full-time ISDN connection. In the past, the biggest drawback to using the Internet was lack of security, but that is changing.

Microsoft has released a product called Point-to-Point Tunneling protocol (PPTP) that allows secure, encrypted communications to occur over the Internet. (PPTP is covered in Chapter 5.) With security now not as much of an issue, the biggest issue with using the Internet is unpredictable network performance. For true WAN communications, including security, high throughput, and predictable performance, you must turn to one of the services discussed in the rest of this chapter, such as frame relay, ATM, or FDDI.

Switch Hitting

A variety of switching schemes exist. Some, such as circuit switching, are very low level and purely hardware based. Others, such as message switching, are mostly software based. For the certification test, be familiar with the methods in this section, especially the circumstances in which these schemes are most likely to be used.

Circuit switching

Circuit switching establishes a path through the network that remains fixed for the duration of the session. The same thing happens when you pick up your telephone and place a call. The disadvantages of circuit switching are unpredictable service, delays that result from having to set up the call at each switch in the route, and inefficient use of bandwidth within the network. Whenever a call is set up, the circuits used in the route are dedicated to that call and cannot be used on other calls. The resources are tied up regardless of whether data is being transmitted or not. The advantage is low cost, but you really do get what you pay for.

Message switching

Message-switching networks are often referred to as store-and-forward networks because each message is transferred in its entirety from one switch to another. The entire message is stored at the receiving switch before being forwarded to the next switch. Each message contains address and route information that the switches use to route the message. Routes are static; traffic from system A to system B always takes the same route through the network.

Message switching has a number of advantages:

- ✔ Data channels are shared among communication devices, so bandwidth is used efficiently.
- ✔ Switches can store messages until a channel becomes available, thereby reducing sensitivity to network congestion.
- ✔ Message priorities may be used.

The switches in the network are usually general computing devices that could include host systems, PCs, or UNIX workstations. They contain significant storage space, usually in the form of hard drives. Switches in a message-switching network are not the same as high-speed telecommunications relay switches like the ones used in circuit switching or packet switching.

Message switching is ideal for applications like e-mail in which a certain amount of delivery delay is acceptable. Message switching is not appropriate for real-time network operations.

Packet switching

Packet switching is a message delivery technique in which small units of information called *packets* are routed through a network from source to destination by using the best available route at a given time. The application data is broken into packets during a process known as packet assembly and recreated at the destination in a process called packet disassembly.

Packets may take different routes through the network. As a result, packets may arrive at the destination out of sequence. The receiving computer has the responsibility to reassemble the packets in the proper order to recreate the original data. The most common implementation of a packet-switching network is X.25.

Lines

The type of communication lines used in a WAN often determines the capabilities of the WAN in terms of throughput, security, and cost. A number of standards define both digital and analog lines. For the certification test, focus on the T-carrier series and the basic differences between dial-up and leased lines and the differences between digital and analog lines.

Dial-up lines

Associate *dial-up lines* with PSTN. Dial-up lines are inexpensive but slow and somewhat unreliable. The lines require modems at each end of the line to convert the computer signals to signals that can be transmitted over an analog network. Each time a connection is opened, circuit switches are assigned to maintain that connection. The connection is only as good as the switches and lines used to build the connection.

Telecommunications providers offer a variety of dial-up line types. The only difference between types is the quality of lines and switches used to make the connection. Types range from basic voice to application relays. The higher the quality, the more expensive the line is to install and maintain.

Analog dedicated lines

Analog dedicated lines are full-time communications links. The telecommunications provider assigns resources to maintain the links, and these resources are always available to only that link. Consequently, dedicated lines are expensive to purchase. The benefit is a higher quality transmission as a result of line conditioning.

Digital lines

As organizations grow, their WAN needs grow also, and they eventually exceed the capacity of their analog lines. When this happens, the organization can turn to a digital solution. With a digital line, transmission rates vary between 56 Kbps up to 622 Kbps, and data is transmitted 99 percent error free.

The forms of digital lines that you should be familiar with are

- T1
- T3
- Switched 56

Each is described in this section.

T-carrier

The *T-carrier* standard is a type of digital leased line. The most popular line in the series is T1, which uses two wire pairs. One pair sends data, and the other pair receives data. Therefore, communication on a T1 is full duplex. A T1 can be used to transmit voice, video, and data at speeds of 1.544 Mbps.

One of the benefits of the T-carrier series is that a subscriber does not need to purchase an entire, 24-channel line (23 lines are used for data, and 1 line is used for link management). For example, if a subscriber did not need a full T1, he or she could lease individual channels of the T1. In this instance, the line is referred to as a fractional T1 (FT-1).

Following are important T-carrier characteristics:

- Uses digital lines
- Channels can be divided for voice, video, and data
- Uses multiplexing to combine data sources over a single line

The T-carrier series uses a data rate standard known as the DS standard. Table 6-1 summarizes the T-carrier group and the DS rates associated with each member of the T-carrier series.

Table 6-1	T-Carrier Series and DS Data Rates			
Service	*Voice Channels*	*T1 Channels*	*Speed*	*Carrier*
DS0	1	N/A	64 Kbps	N/A
DS1	24	1	1.544 Mbps	T1
DS1C	48	2	3.152 Mbps	T1-C
DS2	96	4	6.312 Mbps	T2
DS3	672	28	44.736 Mbps	T3
DS4	4032	168	274.176 Mbps	T4

Copper wire will accommodate up to and including a T2 carrier. For the T3 and T4 carriers, a higher frequency medium, such as microwave or fiber optics, is required. The T3 is the second most popular carrier in the series. It, too, can be divided into fractional lines. Data rates for fractional T3 (FT-3) lines range from 6 Mbps to 45 Mbps.

Switched 56

The *switched-56 line* definition specifies a digital dial-up service that transmits data at 56 Kbps. It is often used for light LAN-to-LAN traffic. With the switched-56 line definition, each computer that uses the line contains a CSU/DSU that will dial up or establish a connection with a computer on the other end of the line. The main advantage of switched-56 lines is low cost. The connection is not full time or dedicated, so the lines do not need to be leased.

X.25 Packet-Switching Protocol

The X.25 standard is a set of protocols and equipment specifications that provides a link between two pieces of equipment referred to as DTEs. Examples of DTEs include the following:

- A host computer with an X.25 interface
- A packet assembler/disassembler (PAD)
- A gateway between a public data network (PDN) and a LAN

Figure 6-1 shows an example of how an X.25 network might be configured.

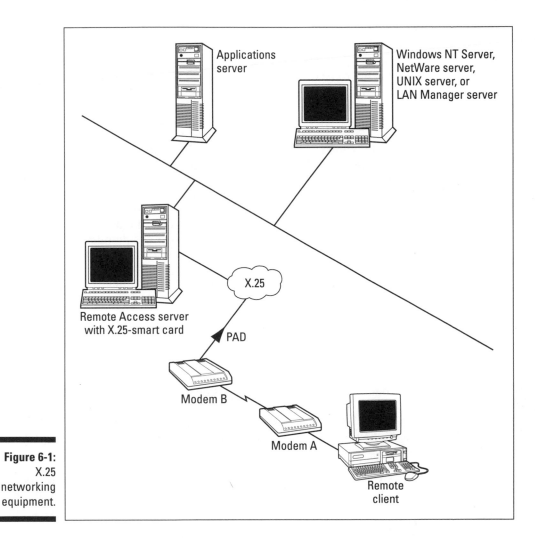

Figure 6-1:
X.25
networking
equipment.

The X.25 interface specification is broken down into two parts. The first is the data terminal equipment (DTE) device. DTE refers to a host computer or another device that acts as an endpoint for X.25 communications messages. The second part of the specification is the data communications equipment (DCE) device. The DCE acts as an entry point to the X.25 network for DTEs.

The X.25 network is sometimes referred to as a *public data network* (PDN) because the network is used by more than one organization at a time. The network, however, is not really public. X.25 networks are owned by long-distance telecommunications providers who charge for access to the network.

The first X.25 networks used standard telephone lines and switches. This was a very unreliable method of networking because of the quality of the lines and switches. Next, developers incorporated extensive error-checking and accounting routines, resulting in a network with a lot of overhead and slow transmission rates. At the time, however, it was a breakthrough in WAN technology. X.25 networks are still used today by many European organizations and a large part of the world's financial institutions.

For the certification test, remember that X.25 is a packet-switching network that uses circuits, switches, and routes to provide the best connection between two points at any given time. The routes change as conditions in the network change, so it is common for data packets to take multiple routes through the network during a communications session. Consequently, an X.25 network is pictured as a cloud. Data goes in and data comes out. What happens in between is a mystery. (Because network administrators don't have any control over what happens to X.25 traffic after it enters the X.25 provider's network, they simply represent the provider's X.25 network on their diagrams as a cloud, or an unknown.)

Frame Relay

As the world spun 'round, things began to improve for network engineers. Switches became faster, telephone lines became clearer and more reliable, and life became digital. All these evolutions made many of the error corrections, retransmissions, and accounting routines built into the original X.25 specification unnecessary. On top of that, engineers began to feel the need for speed. Thus, they invented frame relay.

Frame relay is an advanced packet-switching network that uses variable-length packets. Most of the overhead that shackled X.25 networks has been stripped away. Communications in a frame relay network are point-to-point using a *permanent virtual circuit* (PVC). Data travels from a LAN to a data switch over a digital leased line. After the data reaches the switch, it is sent into the frame relay network. Finally, the data arrives at the destination LAN. All data packets take the same route through the network during a given communications session unless a failure occurs somewhere in the network, requiring the data to be rerouted.

Frame relay networks are gaining popularity for two reasons. They are very fast, and they have the capability to provide subscribers with bandwidth on demand. This gives an organization the capability to pay for what it uses. Agreements between providers and subscribers often specify that a subscriber will be guaranteed a certain throughput at all times, and that the provider will ensure that a certain peak throughput level will be available. As an organization's needs change, they can purchase additional throughput from the provider.

Asynchronous Transfer Mode (ATM)

Asynchronous Transfer Mode (ATM) is a high-speed packet-switching technology that uses a fixed-size packet. An ATM packet, or data frame, is often referred to as a *cell.* Cells have a fixed size of 53 bytes, with 48 bytes representing application data and 5 bytes representing overhead. This is significantly different from most other networking technologies, which use a variable-length frame.

A unique feature of ATM is that it is equally adaptable to both broadband and baseband signaling, making ATM suitable for both LANs and WANs. With transfer speeds ranging between 155 Mbps and 622 Mbps, the popularity of ATM will certainly grow.

ATM networks require switches and use multiplexing technology to combine information from voice, video, and data sources into a single information stream. The most important part of the ATM network is the switch, which acts like a hub and router wrapped into one device. The switch, like a hub, provides a central point for all computers to connect to. The switch also recognizes cells destined for remote networks and forwards them appropriately. The switch contains a multiplexing technology that allows it to combine data from multiple sources onto a single transmission stream.

All hardware in an ATM network (including adapters, switches, and routers) is optimized for handling a fixed-length packet, which makes the hardware ultra efficient at moving data. Because all hardware in an ATM network must be ATM compatible, however, implementing this type of network requires the replacement of all existing networking hardware with new, very expensive ATM hardware. Figure 6-2 features an example of an ATM switch, the nerve center of the ATM network.

Currently, ATM relies on carriers, such as AT&T and US Sprint, for WAN implementations. Having the major ATM providers working together to develop a standard implementation will eliminate the problems of slow WANs by making ATM a robust and widely available WAN solution.

ATM networks can make use of coaxial or twisted-pair copper wire and fiber-optic cable. These types of media, however, do not support full ATM capability. The ATM forum has recommended the following physical interfaces as standard:

- ✔ FDDI (100 Mbps)
- ✔ Fiber channel (155 Mbps)
- ✔ OC3 SONET (155 Mbps)
- ✔ T3 (45 Mbps)

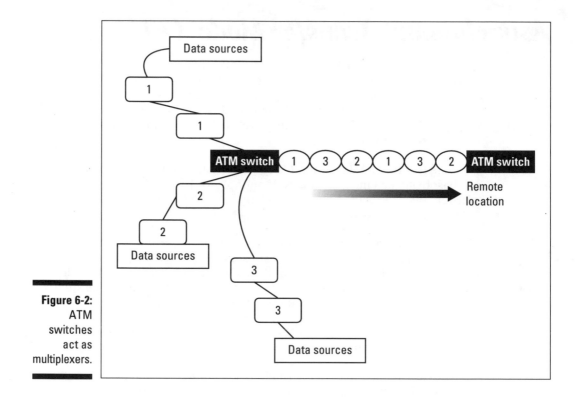

Figure 6-2:
ATM
switches
act as
multiplexers.

Frame relay and X.25 interfaces are also included in this list for now, but tend to be too slow to provide a good transport for ATM networks. Using X.25, with its overhead, eliminates any performance gains from using ATM.

Therefore, there is a good possibility that X.25 and frame relay will not be considered standard when the ATM specification is complete. They may not be included at all.

Integrated Services Digital Network (ISDN)

Integrated Services Digital Network (ISDN) is a digital communications specification that accommodates the following data sources:

- ✔ Data
- ✔ Video
- ✔ Voice

The specification was originally designed to replace the analog PSTN. The goal is to eventually run ISDN to every household and business in the world. Meanwhile, ISDN is being used primarily to link LANs.

ISDN comes in two flavors, basic (BRI) and primary (PRI). Table 6-2 lists the important differences between these two standards.

Table 6-2	ISDN BRI and PRI Specifications	
Characteristics	*Basic Rate (BRI)*	*Primary Rate (PRI)*
Data channels	2B+D	23B+D
Throughput	64 to 128 Kbps	64 Kbps to 1.5 Mbps
Carrier	PSTN (ISDN line)	T1
Primary use	RAS access; casual use not requiring high bandwidth	Full-time Internet or private WAN connection for voice, video, and data

Basic ISDN actually provides three communications channels. The first two channels, called B-channels, provide pathways for data. The third channel, the D-channel, provides link management. The two B-channels can be used independently, providing two 64 Kbps channels, or can be combined to provide one 128 Kbps channel.

Remember that ISDN is a dial-up standard. Therefore, each channel is associated with a telephone number. If the channels are used separately, the telephone numbers for the channels are different. If the channels are used together, there's only one telephone number. This is important to remember for both the RAS test questions and the ISDN test questions.

Primary ISDN is considerably different from basic ISDN. PRI ISDN uses the full capabilities of a T1 carrier. (A T1 carrier is a leased digital line broken into 24 64-Kbps channels.) ISDN uses 23 of the channels for data and one channel for link management. If all 23 channels are combined, primary ISDN can yield an effective throughput of almost 1.5 Mbps.

With a T1 carrier, it is possible to dedicate channels to specific types of information by using multiplexing technology. For example, a company might dedicate two channels to an Internet connection, eight channels to voice communications, eight channels to video communications, and five channels to data (LAN) communications. That yields throughputs of 128 Kbps for Internet activity, 512 Kbps for voice traffic, 512 Kbps for video traffic, and 320 Kbps for LAN data traffic. The benefit of this division of channels is that a bottleneck in one area will not affect performance in the others. This process is often called *channel aggregation.*

ISDN has a few disadvantages. It is limited to a maximum throughput of about 1.5 Mbps, which makes it unsuitable as a network backbone. In addition, ISDN was not designed to provide 24-hour network access — although it is often used to do just that. Finally, ISDN does not provide bandwidth on demand as frame relay does.

Fiber Distributed Data Interface (FDDI)

Fiber Distributed Data Interface (FDDI) is a standard that uses fiber-optic cable and a token-passing media access control method to provide a transfer speed of 100 Mbps. FDDI was designed for high-end workstations and servers that need more bandwidth than a 10-Mbps Ethernet or 16-Mbps token ring can provide.

FDDI is often used to provide a high-speed connection between LANs in a metropolitan area network (MAN). The fiber-optic cable allows a maximum distance of 100 kilometers, but there are actually 200 kilometers of cabling due to its being an FDDI ring. FDDI also provides an optional dual counter-rotating ring that contains primary and secondary rings, which allow data to flow in opposite directions if the line breaks.

A token-passing method similar to the 802.5 standard is used to provide media access control. Note, however, the following difference. Unlike the 802.5 standard, which allows a computer to transmit only one data frame when it receives the token, a computer on an FDDI network can transmit as many frames as possible in a given time period when it receives the token. When time runs out, the computer releases the token and waits to receive it again. If a computer runs out of data to send before the time expires, the computer releases the token early.

One of the reasons FDDI provides higher throughput than 802.5 token ring is that multiple frames may be circulating on the network at the same time.

The topology of an FDDI network is a dual ring, as shown in Figure 6-3. FDDI uses a shared network technology, which allows multiple computers to transmit at the same time. Usually, however, only one ring is being transmitted on. This ring is referred to as the *primary ring*. The secondary ring is used as a backup in case the primary ring is broken. If a break occurs, the network is automatically reconfigured to transmit data on the secondary ring in the opposite direction.

Computers may connect to either or both rings. Computers that connect to both rings are referred to as *Class A stations*. Those that connect to only one ring are *Class B stations*. See Figure 6-4. Class A stations are responsible for helping reconfigure the network if the primary ring fails.

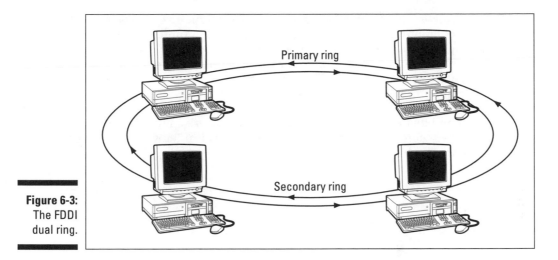

Figure 6-3:
The FDDI
dual ring.

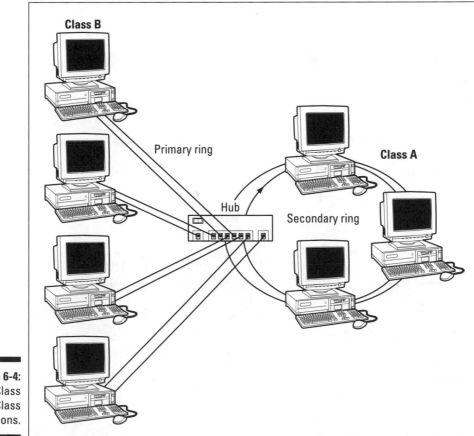

Figure 6-4:
FDDI Class
A and Class
B stations.

To detect faults, an FDDI network uses a technique called *beaconing*. When a computer detects a fault (see the beaconing Computer 3 at the top of Figure 6-5), it transmits a signal (called a *beacon*) until it receives a beacon from its upstream neighbor (see the beaconing Computer 2 at the bottom of Figure 6-5), as shown in Figure 6-5. This process continues until the only computer beaconing is the computer immediately downstream from the fault. This computer never receives a beacon because the fault lies between it and its upstream neighbor. When the network administrator determines which computer is beaconing, the administrator knows where to look for the cable break.

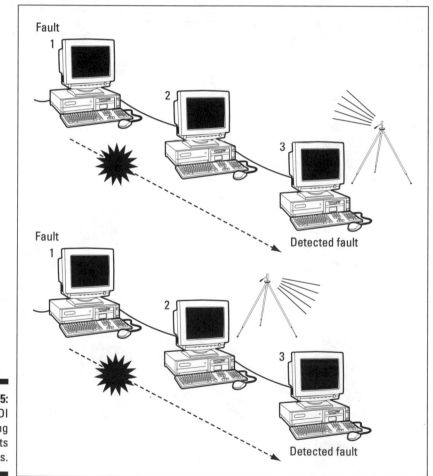

Figure 6-5:
FDDI
beaconing
detects
faults.

Following are the major advantages of FDDI that you should be aware of for the certification test:

- ✔ Immune to electromagnetic interference and noise
- ✔ Secure due to the extreme difficulty in tapping fiber-optic cable
- ✔ Provides long cable distances

The major disadvantage to FDDI is cost. Fiber-optic cable and FDDI adapters represent a significant cost, considering that fiber must be run to every desktop and every desktop must have an FDDI adapter.

Synchronous Optical Network (SONET)

Synchronous Optical Network (SONET) is a relatively new networking standard based on fiber-optic cable that delivers transfer speeds in excess of one gigabit per second. SONET is capable of delivering data, voice, and full-motion video. Some have compared working on a SONET network to drinking from a fire hose!

SONET uses a basic transmission rate of STS-1, which is equivalent to 51.8 Mbps. Higher speeds are achieved in integer multiples of the basic transmission rate. For example, STS-12 is equivalent to 622 Mbps (12×51.8 Mbps). As ATM gains popularity, look for SONET networks to provide the underlying Transport layer of ATM cells.

Prep Test

1 Which of the following networks uses a dual-ring configuration with fiber-optic cable?

A ○ ATM

B ○ FDDI

C ○ ISDN

D ○ Frame relay

2 Which of the following networks uses a fixed-length data cell to provide exceptionally fast switching?

A ○ ATM

B ○ FDDI

C ○ ISDN

D ○ Frame relay

3 Which of the following devices is found in an X.25 network?

A ○ DTE/DCE

B ○ CSU/DSU

C ○ Repeater

D ○ Terminator

4 Which of the following devices is used to convert digital LAN signals to bipolar digital signals?

A ○ DTE/DCE

B ○ CSU/DSU

C ○ Repeater

D ○ Terminator

5 Which of the following is considered a public network? (Choose all that apply.)

A ❑ ATM

B ❑ Frame relay

C ❑ PSTN

D ❑ Internet

6 If you need a digital line capable of transmitting between 6 Mbps and 45 Mbps, which type of line should you request from your provider?

A ○ T1

B ○ T2

C ○ T3

D ○ T4

7 Which type of switching is most appropriate for e-mail?

A ○ Basic switching

B ○ Circuit switching

C ○ Message switching

D ○ Packet switching

8 Which of the following network schemes incorporates the most overhead?

A ○ ATM

B ○ FDDI

C ○ X.25

D ○ Frame relay

9 Which of the following networks uses only fiber-optic cable? (Choose all that apply.)

A ❑ SONET

B ❑ FDDI

C ❑ ISDN

D ❑ Frame relay

10 Which of the following network schemes was designed to replace analog telephone lines?

A ○ ATM

B ○ FDDI

C ○ ISDN

D ○ Frame relay

Answers

1 B. FDDI uses a dual-ring fiber-optic network. Other characteristics you should associate with FDDI include token media access control and beaconing. Remember that FDDI is often implemented in MANs. *Review "Fiber Distributed Data Interface (FDDI)."*

2 A. ATM is so fast because all ATM equipment is tuned to process a 53-byte cell. *Review "Asynchronous Transfer Mode (ATM)."*

3 A. Don't confuse DTE/DCE with CSU/DSU. Remember that all terminals in an X.25 network are DTEs, and the access points into the X.25 network are called DCEs. *Review "X.25 Packet-Switching Protocol."*

4 B. The CSU/DSU is used to convert digital LAN signals into bipolar digital signals that can be transmitted over a digital line. The CSU/DSU also protects the provider's network from electrical surges on the subscriber's network. *Review "Digital lines."*

5 C, D. They're not free, but they are inexpensive compared to leased lines. You get what you pay for, however, so the quality of public networks is much lower. *Review "Public Network Services."*

6 C. Know the T-carriers for the test. T1 and T3 are the most popular. T3 is the big dog of leased lines. Remember, it's like drinking from a fire hose. *Review "T-carrier" in the "Digital lines" section.*

7 C. Message switching is the store-and-forward type of network. It's great for applications like e-mail, but inappropriate for any systems needing real-time network access. *Review "Message switching."*

8 C. Think old and slow. X.25 was developed at a time when phone switches could not provide high-quality connections, so the designers had to build in error detection and correction routines that are obsolete with today's high-quality switches. *Review "X.25 Packet-Switching Protocol."*

9 A, B. Need more fiber in your diet? Try one of these fiber-only standards. Both ATM and frame relay have the capability to make some use out of existing copper networks. *Review "Asynchronous Transfer Mode (ATM)."*

10 C. One day everyone will have an ISDN line run directly to his or her house. Telephone companies are rapidly replacing existing analog telephone lines with this new digital standard. *Review "Integrated Services Digital Network (ISDN)."*

Chapter 7

Expanding Networks

● ●

Exam Objectives

▶ Defining the communications devices that communicate at each level of the OSI model

▶ Selecting the appropriate connectivity devices for various token-ring and Ethernet networks (connectivity devices include repeaters, bridges, routers, brouters, and gateways)

▶ Resolving broadcast storms

● ●

*M*ost networks grow. More computers connect to the network. The network expands over a larger geographic area or becomes more concentrated in a smaller area. Networks tend to connect to other networks. All these things constitute network growth. As LANs outgrow their original design, some problems tend to arise, such as print jobs take longer; traffic-generating applications, like databases, require longer response times; broadcast storms arise; and from a general standpoint, everything just seems slower. Just as gardeners use tillers and fertilizer to make their gardens bigger, network engineers use hubs, repeaters, bridges, routers, and gateways to expand their LANs.

As network vendors attempt to differentiate their products by providing more functionality for less cost, the lines that determine the differences between these devices begin to blur. It's the network engineer's responsibility to identify the different capabilities of these devices and effectively use those capabilities to adjust to changes in the network's size.

The OSI model provides an excellent road map to follow when trying to differentiate between different networking devices. For the certification test, it is especially important that you be able to identify on which layers of the OSI model repeaters, bridges, routers, and gateways operate. Note that as you move from the lowest level of the OSI model to the highest (Physical layer to Application layer), devices offer more capabilities but also become more complex and more expensive.

For the test, it's a good idea to know the capabilities of the different connectivity devices. In real life, a network engineer also needs to know how to segment existing LANs into two separate LANs; join two dissimilar networks, such as Ethernet and token ring; and connect to other LANs to join into a large, corporate-sized network.

Quick Assessment

Defining the communications devices that communicate at each level of the OSI model

1 A(n) _____ is a device used to regenerate signals at the Physical layer of the OSI model.

2 A(n) _____ is a device used to forward packets from one segment to another at the Media Access Control sublayer of the Data Link layer in the OSI model.

3 A(n) _____ functions at the Network layer and forwards packets from one network to another.

4 A(n) _____ works at the four upper layers of the OSI model and translates data from one environment to another.

Selecting the appropriate connectivity devices for various token-ring and Ethernet networks

5 The central connection point for all computers in a star-wired network is called a(n) _____.

6 The device that combines signals from different data sources into a single stream of packets for transmission on a WAN is called a(n) _____.

7 A(n) _____ is a device that can bridge non-routable protocols and route routable protocols between two different networks at the same time.

8 Routers are _____ if their routing tables are created by administrators or _____ if they discover the network on their own.

9 Hubs are _____ if they have a power source and regenerate signals or _____ if they simply provide a physical connection.

Resolving broadcast storms

10 A(n) _____ can resolve a broadcast storm.

Answers

1   *Repeater.* See the "Repeaters" section.

2   *Bridge.* See the "Bridges" section.

3   *Router.* See the "Routers" section.

4   *Gateway.* Review the "Gateways" section.

5   *Hub.* See the "Hubs" section.

6   *Multiplexer.* Review the "Multiplexers" section.

7   *Brouter.* See the "Additional Network Expansion Devices" section.

8   *Static; dynamic.* Review the "Routers" section.

9   *Active; passive.* Review the "Hubs" section.

10   *Router.* See the "Routers" section.

Common Network Expansion Devices

Following is a quick reference for the devices described in this section and the OSI model layers to which they are related:

- ✓ **Repeater — Physical layer**
- ✓ **Bridge — Data Link layer (Media Access Control sublayer)**
- ✓ **Router — Network layer**
- ✓ **Gateway — Application layer**

Hubs are discussed also, but they don't fit into a single category as easily as the other devices do, partly because so many options are available.

Repeaters

Repeaters are the simplest of all network connectivity devices. They work at the Physical layer of the OSI model. Repeaters take a signal from one cable segment and regenerate it on another segment, as shown in Figure 7-1.

Repeaters have no intelligence: They don't recognize packets or data frames, or good data from garbled data. They simply regenerate a digital signal, bit for bit, from one segment onto another segment. The lack of intelligence in a repeater makes it a very fast device. It is well suited for the task of regenerating signals quickly and efficiently.

Using a repeater is the least expensive way to extend the length of a networking segment beyond the limit of a single piece of cable. Think of a repeater as the primary defense against signal attenuation. (*Attenuation* is the tendency for a signal to become weaker the farther it travels down a cable. Attenuation results from the natural resistance in copper wire.)

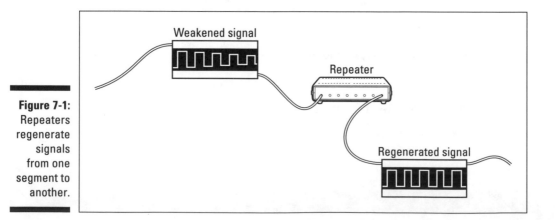

Figure 7-1:
Repeaters regenerate signals from one segment to another.

Repeaters do not enable any functionality on a network. For a repeater to work, protocols and the media access control method must be the same on all cable segments connected to the repeater.

It is possible to connect different physical media together with a repeater if the repeater has the appropriate connection ports. For example, a repeater could move Ethernet packets from a thinnet Ethernet cable to a fiber-optic cable as long as both segments shared the same media access control method and Ethernet packet format.

Hubs

A *hub* provides a common connection between devices in a star-wired network, as shown in Figure 7-2. Hubs are often referred to as multiport repeaters because they contain multiple ports and repeat a signal received on one port to all other ports.

Hubs are either active or passive. A *passive hub* is nothing more than a physical connection between wires. The passive hub doesn't regenerate or even monitor signals. An *active hub,* on the other hand, takes an active role in maintaining signals on the network. It monitors signals, regenerates the

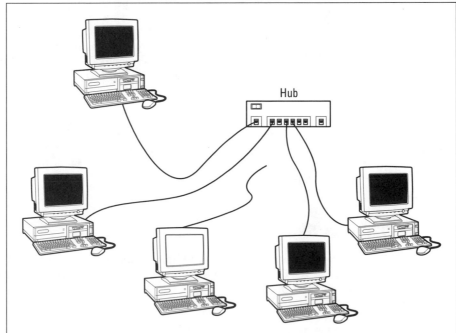

Figure 7-2:
Example of
connecting
a computer
with a hub.

signal, and may even deactivate malfunctioning ports. An active hub can detect collisions (two computers transmitting at the same time) and act as a traffic cop for the network.

The easiest way to determine whether a hub is active or passive is to check for a power cord. An active hub must have its own power source to regenerate signals and maintain network operations.

Hubs may also be referred to as smart, or intelligent, hubs. These are active hubs that have some form of administrative interface. They usually provide additional capabilities, such as Simple Network Management Protocol (SNMP) support or network segmentation, by grouping the ports on the hub into different logical networks. Most intelligent hubs have the capability to send administrative alerts when something out of the ordinary occurs on the network. Finally, smart hubs may maintain statistics on network performance, error rates, and uptime.

The administrative interface for an active hub can take a number of forms. It may be an SNMP-based application residing at an SNMP management station. The interface may be accessed by Telnetting to a port on the hub, in which case the port must have a valid IP address. The interface may even be activated by connecting a standard terminal to a serial port on the hub.

Multiple hubs are often linked together on a physical bus. Remember that this is called a star-bus topology. Adding additional hubs is one of the fastest ways to add additional computers to a network. In a configuration like this, the hubs are active, and often at least one is a smart hub with a management module capable of controlling all hubs on the bus. For this capability, usually all hubs must be the same make and model. Consequently, network engineers do not like to mix different brands of hubs in a single environment.

The basic purpose of a hub is to connect computers to a network. One of the fastest ways to add additional computers to the network is to add additional hubs. Hubs are available in configurations of 4, 8, 16, 24, and 48 ports. The more ports, the more expensive the hub. Most hubs that you work with will be 16- or 24-port hubs.

Bridges

Like a repeater, a *bridge* is used to connect segments or small LANs. A bridge, however, offers more capabilities because it operates at the Data Link layer of the OSI model.

Bridges can be used to do the following:

- ✔ Expand a segment beyond the normal distance
- ✔ Increase the number of computers that can operate on a LAN
- ✔ Reduce traffic bottlenecks resulting from too many computers on the LAN
- ✔ Link different physical media, such as thinnet and fiber-optic cable
- ✔ Link unlike network segments, such as Ethernet and token ring

Bridges do not recognize different protocols, but they do recognize different media access control methods. In fact, a bridge does most of its work at the Media Access Control sublayer of the Data Link layer. As a result, bridges are also referred to as a MAC layer bridge or device.

Throughout the rest of this section, I discuss something called a *routing table*. Unfortunately, the networking industry did not ask me before they started using this terminology. I would have told them that it was a bad choice of words. A routing table in reference to bridges is different than the routing table in reference to routers. If you find yourself getting the two confused, think of the routing table associated with bridges as a bridging table.

Each computer on a network has a unique identifier at the MAC level. This identifier is often referred to as the MAC, or hardware, address of the computer. The hardware address is the unique identifier burned into each network card at the factory. The bridge uses this identifier to do the following:

- ✔ Listen to network traffic
- ✔ Identify the source and destination address of each packet
- ✔ Build a routing table that identifies which computers are on which segments
- ✔ Forward packets to proper segments based on the routing table

Bridges forward packets based on the following algorithm:

1. If the source and destination addresses are on the same network segment, the packet is discarded because it will have already reached its destination before reaching the bridge.

2. If the destination address is listed in the routing table, the bridge forwards the packet to the segment containing the destination address.

3. If the destination is not listed in the routing table, the bridge forwards the packet to all segments except the segment the packet originated on.

The routing table of the bridge is built as the bridge listens to traffic on different segments. When a bridge hears a computer that it does not recognize transmit, it adds that computer's MAC address to the list of MAC addresses associated with that segment. The routing table is stored in the bridge's RAM and is dynamic. If the bridge is turned off, the routing table is destroyed and must be recreated when the bridge returns to service.

A common use of bridges is to segment networks to improve performance, as shown in Figure 7-3. If a bottleneck results when a group of computers sends each other a large amount of traffic (such as high-end graphics computers transferring large image files back and forth), a network administrator can use a bridge to put those computers on their own segment. After the high-traffic computers are segmented from the main network, their traffic will not interfere with the traffic on the rest of the network.

A large network is often created by bridging several smaller networks. Bridges have become popular networking devices for creating large networks for the following reasons:

- ✔ Bridges act like repeaters but have more intelligence. They regenerate data at the packet level instead of the raw signal level.

- ✔ Bridges have all the features of a repeater and accommodate more nodes.

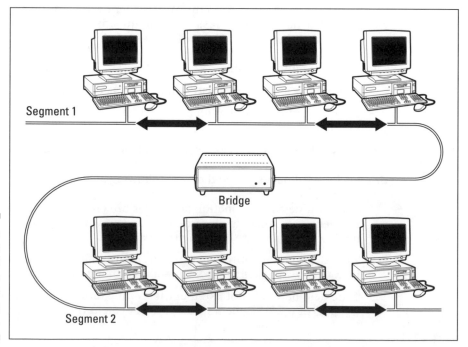

Figure 7-3:
Bridges are used to create multiple network segments.

> ✔ Bridges are better than repeaters at improving network performance because they have the capability to segment the network.
>
> ✔ Bridges are simple to install and transparent to users.
>
> ✔ Bridges are flexible and relatively inexpensive compared to routers.

Routers

Routers work at the Network layer of the OSI model. This means that they can direct, or route, packets across multiple networks. Unlike bridges, routers have enough intelligence to determine the best path through the network for a packet.

A router is a better choice than a bridge for large, complex networks that use multiple protocols and have multiple paths available between two points in the network. Routers also have the capability to share network information with other routers. So, collectively, routers can manage a network.

Another important feature of routers is their capability to confine broadcast traffic to a particular network. In a large network, too much broadcast traffic (traffic sent to the entire network instead of an individual computer) can bring a network to its knees. When this happens, it's called a *broadcast storm*. Routers prevent broadcast storms because, by default, they do not pass broadcast traffic from one network to another.

Routable protocols

Not all network protocols are routable. On the certification test, you have to distinguish between routable and non-routable protocols, so they are listed for you in Table 7-1.

Table 7-1	Routable and Non-Routable Protocols
Protocol	*Routable*
AppleTalk	Yes
DECnet	Yes
DLC	Yes
IP	Yes
IPX	Yes
NetBEUI	No
OSI	Yes
SNA	Yes

Most routers will accommodate multiple routable protocols if the protocols are enabled in the router configuration.

Routing packets

Routers talk only to other routers and computers on the same LAN as the router. Remember that routers connect multiple networks. Therefore, they are actually talking to a number of systems on a number of different LANs. It might be more appropriate to say that routers communicate with only computers on LANs that are directly attached to the router through one of the router's interfaces. They do not talk directly to remote computers.

If a router receives information for a remote computer, the router contacts the router that manages the remote network and hands off the information to that router for delivery to the computer. If a router can't contact the router for the remote network directly because there is more than one intermediate network, the router gives the information to whichever intermediate router can get the information to the remote network least expensively. This process continues until the information has been delivered to the remote computer.

A packet has a field for the source address and a field for the destination address. These fields can hold only one address at a time. Consequently, as routers pass information from one network to another, they strip the Data Link layer source and destination addresses and recreate them.

The routing table

A router uses a table of network addresses to determine how to handle incoming data packets. When the router receives a packet of information, it looks at the packet to determine the destination address. The router then looks in its routing table to find the appropriate network to send the packet to. When the router finds the network, it delivers the packet through its interface connected to that network.

Remember that the routing table mentioned here is different from the routing table used by a bridge.

The routing table contains the following information:

- ✔ Known network addresses
- ✔ Addresses of other routers
- ✔ Possible paths between routers
- ✔ Costs associated with using a particular path

Figure 7-4 illustrates the Windows 98 routing table. Notice the different parts of the table. Can you identify the routes?

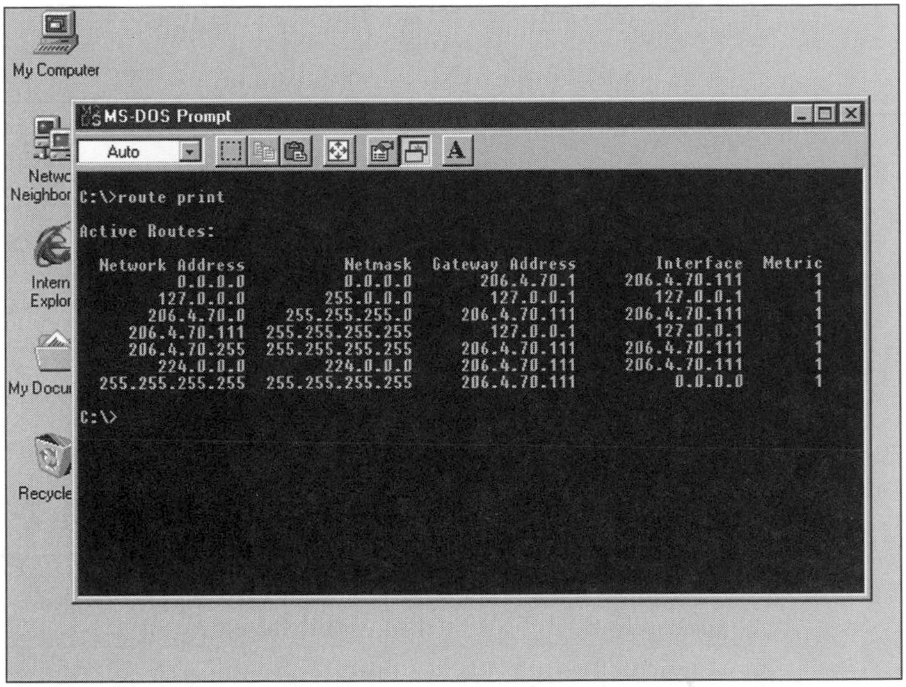

Figure 7-4:
The
Windows 98
routing
table.

Routing algorithms

Unlike bridges, routers must contend with multiple paths between two points in a network. Consequently, they need some method of choosing which path to use at a given time. This method, called a *routing algorithm,* selects the least expensive route through the network based on a number of criteria. Most algorithms use the hop count as the measure of cost.

A *hop,* in routing terminology, is a router. If a packet must travel through four routers to reach a destination through one route, the hop count for that route is four. If a route that requires only three routers is available, its hop count is three, and it would be the least expensive of the two routes. For the certification test, be familiar with the following algorithms. You won't need the details of their implementation, but you should be able to distinguish among them:

- **OSPF** (Open Shortest Path First) is a link-state algorithm that allows routers to respond quickly to changes in the network. Routes are calculated based on hop count, line speed, traffic volume, and cost. TCP/IP supports OSPF.

- **RIP** (Routing Information Protocol) is a distance-vector algorithm used by TCP/IP and IPX. It is not as efficient as OSPF.

✔ **NLSP** (NetWare Link Services Protocol) is an algorithm used by NetWare servers. It, too, is a link-state algorithm, but it supports only the IPX protocol.

Dynamic versus static routing

Routers receive their routing tables in one of two ways. Either an administrator builds the routing table by entering network numbers, routes, interfaces, and costs, or the router determines this information and builds its routing table through a discovery process. The discovery process automatically identifies possible routes in which to send packets and makes decisions dynamically on which route is the most efficient.

If the router must be configured manually, the router is using static routing. The router will not communicate its routing information to other routers in the network. If the router is allowed to discover the network configuration, usually by communicating with other routers, the router is a dynamic router. Table 7-2 summarizes the differences between static and dynamic routers.

Table 7-2	Static Routers versus Dynamic Routers
Static Router	*Dynamic Router*
Manual configuration of routes	Manual configuration of the first route and automatic discovery from then on
Always uses the same route, which is determined by a routing table entry	The route is chosen based on factors like cost and traffic
The route used is hard-coded and not always the shortest, most efficient route	Dynamically chooses alternate routes resulting in more efficient packet delivery
Static routes are more secure because all routes are known and are established by the administrator	Dynamic routes could possibly result in sending packets over an unsecure path

On the certification test, some questions will involve choosing among bridges, routers, and gateways. Other questions will involve strategically placing routers within the network to guard against broadcast storms. Remember the following benefits of routers:

✔ Segmenting large networks into smaller ones improves performance.

✔ Routers can act as a security barrier between segments by using filtering.

✔ Routers prohibit broadcast storms because broadcasts are not forwarded.

Finally, remember that routers are the nerve centers for the Internet. If an organization wants to connect its network to the Internet, it must properly implement routing. A gateway or a bridge will not enable an organization to connect to the Internet.

Gateways

Gateways operate at all layers above the network (Transport, Session, Presentation, and Application layers), enabling communications between different network architectures that use different network protocols. Gateways translate messages in one environment to a format acceptable for another environment. To do so, the gateway disassembles the packet of information by stripping the original protocol stack, and then reassembles the data in the packet with the new protocol stack required for the destination environment.

A good example of a gateway is an SMTP to X.400 e-mail gateway. The gateway converts SMTP messages to X.400 format for messages coming from the SMTP environment destined for the X.400 environment. Messages in the X.400 environment destined for the SMTP environment are converted in a similar way.

Gateways move data from one environment to another through a process of decapsulation and encapsulation using different protocol stacks, as shown in Figure 7-5. When any of the following characteristics are different between two environments, a gateway is required:

 ✓ Communications protocols, such as X.25 and Ethernet

 ✓ Data format structures, such as database record formats

 ✓ Languages, such as Windows Sockets (WinSock) and NetBIOS

 ✓ Architectures, such as SNA and client/server

One of the most common gateways (and one you should be familiar with) is the Microsoft SNA Gateway. The SNA Gateway converts traffic from LAN-based clients using a native LAN protocol (such as TCP/IP, IPX, or NetBEUI) to SNA traffic that can be routed and interpreted by host systems, such as IBM mainframes and AS/400s.

Gateways are task specific. Consequently, they are usually dedicated servers on the network. A gateway converting a large amount of traffic can require considerable resources on the server. Remember that conversions must occur in near real time to keep the gateway from becoming a bottleneck. Gateways also tend to be very expensive because of their complexity and resource requirements.

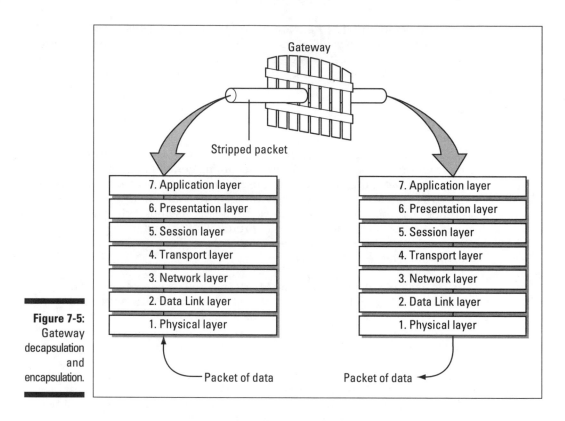

Figure 7-5:
Gateway
decapsulation
and
encapsulation.

Additional Network Expansion Devices

Many additional devices can be used on a network to increase functionality, improve throughput, or increase size. Most are simply hybrids of repeaters, hubs, bridges, routers, or gateways . Some are purely software, others are purely hardware, and still others are a mix of both. To make networking equipment less expensive, faster, and more functional, vendors have begun to blur the OSI boundaries that once identified where a device belonged.

Brouters

One device that blurs OSI boundaries is the *brouter,* which combines the advantages of a bridge and a router in a single networking device. A brouter can act like a router for routable protocols and like a bridge for non-routable protocols. An organization has to purchase only one device to accommodate all its connection needs. This results in a more cost-effective and manageable network.

CSUs and DSUs

CSU/DSU (channel service unit/data service unit) is used with digital leased lines and switched-56 digital dial-up lines. Because the lines are digital, a modem is not necessary. DDS sends data from a bridge or a router to the CSU/DSU. The CSU/DSU converts the LAN's digital signals into bipolar digital signals that are transmitted across the DDS line. The CSU/DSU also protects the service provider's network from electrical surges on subscribers' networks.

Multiplexers

Multiplexers are devices that combine multiple data sources, such as voice, video, and data, into a single data stream that can be transmitted over a WAN. At the receiving end, a demultiplexer separates incoming signals into signals that can be sent to the proper receivers (voice, video, or data).

Regardless of the data source, the information is brought together in the form of packets in a way that makes it transmittable. The packets are recombined at the receiving end. Some networking standards, such as frame relay, require a separate device to act as a multiplexer. Others, such as ATM, have a multiplexer built into the switch.

Prep Test

1 A repeater is a device used to regenerate signals and works at which layer of the OSI model?

A ○ Data Link

B ○ Application

C ○ Physical

D ○ Network

2 Which of the following devices works at the four upper layers of the OSI model?

A ○ Repeater

B ○ Bridge

C ○ Router

D ○ Gateway

3 Which of the following network devices can resolve a broadcast storm?

A ○ Repeater

B ○ Bridge

C ○ Router

D ○ Multiplexer

4 Which of the following network devices can connect dissimilar networks, such as Ethernet and token ring, and forward packets between them? (Choose all that apply.)

A ❑ Repeater

B ❑ Bridge

C ❑ Router

D ❑ Gateway

5 If multiple paths exist in which to send data, which device is capable of choosing the most efficient path?

A ○ Repeater

B ○ Hub

C ○ Router

D ○ Bridge

6 Which of the following are routing algorithms used to determine the most efficient path in which to route packets? (Choose all that apply.)

A ❑ XNS

B ❑ OSPF

C ❑ LAT

D ❑ RIP

7 If a network uses only the NetBEUI protocol, which of the following devices can be used to segment the network to reduce traffic?

A ○ Gateway

B ○ Multiplexer

C ○ Router

D ○ Brouter

8 Which of the following are advantages of using dynamic routers? (Choose all that apply.)

A ❑ Can choose a route based on factors like cost and amount of link traffic

B ❑ Can decide to send packets over alternate routes

C ❑ More secure because an administrator specifies each route

D ❑ Automatic discovery of additional networks and routes

9 Which of the following devices has the capability to translate packets from one protocol to another?

A ○ Repeater

B ○ Gateway

C ○ Bridge

D ○ Router

10 Which of the following devices works at the Network layer of the OSI model?

A ○ Repeater

B ○ Bridge

C ○ Router

D ○ Gateway

Answers

1 C. Repeaters work at the Physical layer. They are inexpensive and fast, but lack the intelligence to provide any additional capabilities. *Review the "Repeaters" section.*

2 D. Gateways work at the Application layer of the OSI model and require two complete protocol stacks for two different environments. Gateways work by a process of decapsulating and encapsulating application data. *See the "Gateways" section for more information.*

3 C. A router connects multiple networks at the Network layer of the OSI model and does not pass broadcast storms. *See the "Routers" section.*

4 B, C, D. Bridges, routers, and gateways can all connect dissimilar networks. Repeaters require that segments use the same access method (for example, CSMA/CD or token passing). *See the "Repeaters" section for more information.*

5 C. Unlike bridges, routers can accommodate multiple active paths between LAN segments and choose the most efficient path to route data. *See the "Routers" section for more information.*

6 B, D. OSPF (Open Shortest Path First) and RIP (Routing Information Protocol) are algorithms that determine the most efficient route to send packets. *See the "Routers" section for more information.*

7 D. A brouter is the best of both worlds in one box. It routes routable protocols and bridges non-routable protocols, such as NetBEUI, at the same time. *See the "Brouters" section.*

8 A, B, D. All are advantages of dynamic routers with the exception that dynamic routers aren't as secure as static routers. Static routers are more secure because an administrator eliminates the possibility of sending packets over an unsecure path by manually creating each route. *Review "Dynamic versus static routing."*

9 B. Only a gateway can translate one protocol and repackage the data into another protocol. *Review "Gateways."*

10 C. Routers work at the Network layer of the OSI model. *See "Routers."*

Part III
Selecting, Installing, and Troubleshooting Hardware and Media

The 5th Wave   By Rich Tennant

"If it works, it works. I've just never seen network cabling connected with Chinese handcuffs before."

In this part . . .

*I*f you're already a network engineer, this part will go by very quickly. But don't go through it so quickly that you miss a key point: You get credit for knowing only the Microsoft way of doing things.

This part is full of information about how to plan a network, from both the technical and the business side. Microsoft wants well-rounded MCSEs, people who can work effectively in both the technical and business worlds. The certification test reflects this desire, so don't be too quick to discount non-technical information.

In this part, you also find technical information about network adapters, cabling, and connections. Management aspects covered in this part include client system choices and troubleshooting procedures. For technical trouble-shooting information, check out Part IV.

Chapter 8
Network Adapters

• •

Exam Objectives

▶ Installing, configuring, and resolving hardware conflicts for multiple network adapters in a token-ring or Ethernet network

▶ Explaining the purpose of NDIS and Novell ODI networks

• •

*W*hen you connect computers together to form a network, you must install and configure network adapters so that the data traveling across the cable can get into the system. The exam tests you on installing and configuring a network adapter, including determining how to handle hardware conflicts and how to assign IRQs.

Hardware is the major focus of this chapter. Another exam objective that is touched on briefly involves two network standards — NDIS and ODI — that help ensure that adapter cards and protocol stacks from different vendors will work together. You can find more information about NDIS and ODI in Chapter 3.

This chapter describes the different types of network adapters. You find out about common computer bus architectures and how the bus architecture influences decisions about which adapter to use. You look at installing and configuring network adapters, including a review of the four settings that may need to be altered. You also find out about installing the necessary network adapter drivers.

This chapter gives you a basic understanding of the installation process. Each hardware manufacturer has a slightly different installation and configuration process. Therefore, for your first adapter installation, read the manufacturer's directions, and use this section for an overview of the process. Also remember that every computer system is a little different when it comes to available resources. The more devices you have installed in the system, the fewer resources are available to install additional devices. The chapter lists common settings for the most common devices found in most systems. You can use these lists to help answer some test questions, but remember to check the system by using a system utility to determine which resources are available when you install your first network adapter.

Quick Assessment

Installing, configuring, and resolving hardware conflicts for multiple network adapters in a token-ring or Ethernet network

1 NIC stands for _____ _____ _____.

2 The two major factors in selecting a NIC are _____ and _____.

3 Data in a computer travels across paths called _____.

4 When installing jumpers or switches, the four settings you may have to change are _____, _____, _____, and _____.

5 IRQ _____ is reserved for a video adapter.

6 IRQ 8 is reserved for the _____.

7 If you are using Microsoft DOS, Windows 3.1, or Windows 95, you can use the DOS command _____ to determine which IRQs are available.

8 _____ enables your network adapter to work directly with your computer's memory.

Explaining the purpose of NDIS and Novell ODI networks

9 The two versions of NDIS are Version 2, which is used by _____ and _____ systems, and Version 3, which is used by _____ and _____ systems.

10 The _____ standard is used primarily for adapters and drivers in Novell NetWare systems.

Answers

1 *Network interface card.* To review the use of adapter cards, turn to "It's All in the Cards: Network Adapters."

2 *Network cable; bus type.* Review the section on "Selecting an Adapter."

3 *Buses.* "Selecting an Adapter" discusses buses.

4 *Interrupt request; base input/output port; direct memory address; shared memory address.* Review the "Configuring an Adapter" section for more information on these settings.

5 *IRQ 2.* Table 8-1 is a complete review of all IRQs.

6 *Real-time clock.* Did you remember this IRQ number? Again, check out Table 8-1 for a complete list.

7 *MSD.EXE.* "Configuring an Adapter" has a complete review of IRQ issues.

8 *Direct memory address.* The "Configuring an Adapter" section discusses this.

9 *DOS and Windows 3.1; Windows 95 and Windows NT.* Review the "Installing an Adapter Driver" section for more information.

10 *ODI.* Review the " Installing an Adapter Driver" section.

It's All in the Cards: Network Adapters

The network interface card (NIC) makes the physical connection between a computer and the rest of the network. The NIC receives incoming data from the network through the network cable and turns it into bytes of information that the computer's CPU can understand. In turn, the NIC turns information from the computer into data that can be sent out over the network cable to other machines on the network.

Data in a computer travels across parallel data paths, called a *bus*. This side-by-side configuration allows the data to be transmitted in a group, a process called *parallel transmission*. Older computers, such as the original IBM personal computer, used an 8-bit bus. This allowed the bus to move 8 bits of information at a time. In 1984, this bus was expanded to 16 bits. Newer computers today have a 32-bit bus that moves 32 bits of information. You can compare this to a 16- or 32-lane highway with cars moving side-by-side, each carrying 1 bit of data. The wider the bus, the more data you can get from point A to point B in a given amount of time.

The data that goes out over a network cable, however, has to go single file, one bit at a time. This is called *serial transmission* and is similar to a single-lane road. The network adapter takes the parallel information it receives from the computer, converts the data into *packets,* and sends the packets out onto the network in serial form. The network adapter works also in the other direction. It takes the packets it receives from the network and converts them back into data that a computer can understand.

The NIC also has to tell the rest of the network its location. Every network adapter has a unique hardware address — for example, 00-85-39-A7-2B-99. The IEEE assigns blocks of addresses to companies that manufacture network adapters. These companies put a unique address from their block onto each chip in a process called *burning.* The chip is then placed on the adapter and that NIC has its address.

Selecting an Adapter

Questions on the exam about selecting an adapter focus on the type of adapter required. Two factors affect that decision.

The first factor is the type of network cable you have. The adapter must have the correct connector for the type of cable you are using. Chapter 10 reviews the types of network cables and connectors. Briefly, twisted-pair cable usually uses an adapter with an RJ-45 plug. Thinnet coaxial cable uses a BNC connector. Thicknet coaxial cable plugs into an AUI port. Fiber-optic cables are used mostly to connect networks together, so fiber-optic cable usually does not come to a computer.

When using thinnet coaxial cable, choose an adapter with a BNC connector.

The second factor affecting adapter selection is that the adapter you choose must match the type of bus in the computer. Following is a list of the most common computer bus architectures in use today: ISA, EISA, Micro Channel, VESA, PCI, and PCMCIA. In the accompanying figures, note the row of plugs along the edge, which match the slots inside the computer.

- ✔ **ISA** (Industry Standard Architecture), shown in Figure 8-1. This is the original type of bus used in the first IBM computers and its clones. Initially an 8-bit bus, it was expanded to 16 bits in 1984. ISA was the standard bus until 1988, when EISA was introduced.

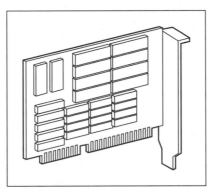

Figure 8-1:
ISA network
adapter.

- ✔ **EISA** (Extended Industry Standard Architecture), shown in Figure 8-2. In 1988, several computer manufacturers, led by Compaq, developed the EISA standard for computer buses and adapters. The EISA standard specifies a 32-bit bus. The EISA adapter can be used in a standard ISA slot on older computers, although this slows the adapter down to 16 bits.

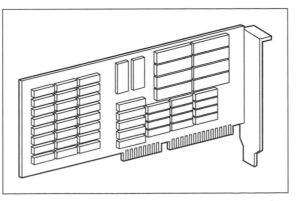

Figure 8-2:
EISA
network
adapter.

✔ **Micro Channel Architecture**, shown in Figure 8-3. Also in 1988, IBM developed Micro Channel to work with its new line of PS/2 computers. Micro Channel adapters can be a 16-bit or a 32-bit bus. Micro Channel is not compatible with ISA. Only IBM PS/2's have Micro Channel Architecture.

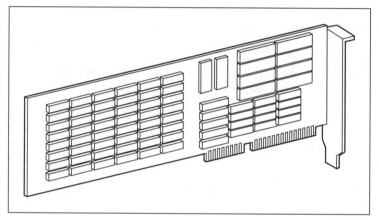

Figure 8-3:
Micro
Channel
adapter.

✔ **VESA** (Video Electronics Standards Association), shown in Figure 8-4. The introduction of Microsoft Windows 3.1 required a faster video processor to keep up with a faster graphical operating system. VLB, or VESA Local Bus, is a 32-bit bus that runs much faster than ISA and is less expensive than EISA. VESA was designed for video and later adapted to be used by network adapters and hard drive controllers.

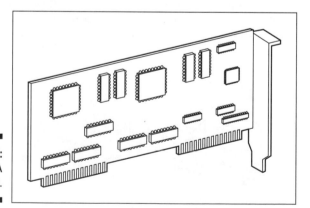

Figure 8-4:
VESA
adapter.

PCI (Peripheral Component Interconnect), shown in Figure 8-5. PCI is the newest 32-bit bus found in today's faster Pentium computers and Apple PowerPCs. PCI was designed to be not only fast but also compatible with Plug and Play. Microsoft Windows 95 is a Plug-and-Play operating system.

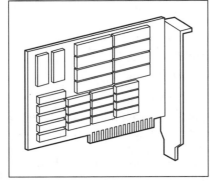

Figure 8-5:
PCI
adapter.

 PCMCIA (Personal Computer Memory Card International Association), shown in Figure 8-6. PCMCIA is the new type of bus used in today's laptop and notebook computers. The original PCMCIA standard, version 1.0, was designed for memory expansion in small computers. Version 2.0 was introduced to support other types of devices, such as network adapters and modems. A PCMCIA slot in a laptop computer looks similar to a thick credit card. One advantage to these types of cards is that they can be inserted or removed without having to reboot the computer.

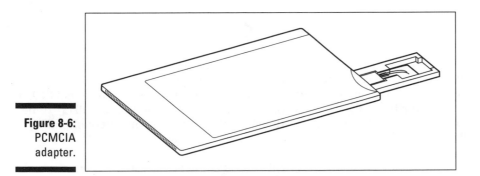

Figure 8-6:
PCMCIA
adapter.

If you have a choice of PCI and ISA, remember that PCI performs faster.

How do you determine which bus type is in a computer? The easiest way is to look inside the computer and match the expansion slot with the pins on the adapters in Figures 8-1 to 8-6. If that doesn't help, the documentation included with the computer should tell you the type of expansion slots.

If you still don't know, follow these guidelines:

- 386 or older computers probably have ISA, except if the computer was once a server, in which case it might have EISA.
- IBM PS/2 computers have Micro Channel.
- 486 computers have VESA and ISA slots.
- Newer Pentiums have both ISA and PCI; choose a PCI adapter because it will perform faster and better than an ISA adapter.

An IBM PS/2 uses a Micro Channel bus. A 486 has both VESA and ISA slots. A Pentium has both ISA and PCI slots.

Configuring an Adapter

After an adapter is installed, it must be configured — unless it's a PCI, Plug-and-Play adapter with Windows 95. With some older adapters, you must set jumpers or switches. With newer adapters, the included software looks at the other hardware in the computer and then selects settings not in use. The settings that might have to be changed are interrupt request, base input/output port, direct memory address, and shared memory address.

Interrupt request (IRQ)

Every computer has a number of built-in interrupt request lines that let devices tell the computer that they have something for it to do. Each device must have a unique IRQ to work properly. If two devices use the same IRQ, it is possible that neither will work. (These hardware conflicts are likely to be the focus of several exam questions!) Table 8-1 lists the most common IRQ settings.

For the exam, you must know which IRQs are available on a system, so Table 8-1 is a great candidate for memorization.

Table 8-1	Common IRQs
IRQ	**Typical Use**
0	System timer
1	Keyboard
2	Video adapter
3	Serial ports COM2 or COM4 if present; otherwise available
4	Serial ports COM1 or COM3 if present; otherwise available
5	Available unless used for second printer port LPT2 or sound card
6	Floppy disk controller
7	Printer port LPT1
8	Real-time clock
9	Available
10	Available unless used for primary SCSI controller
11	Available unless used for secondary SCSI controller
12	PS/2 mouse
13	Math coprocessor
14	Primary hard drive controller
15	Available unless used for secondary hard drive controller

If you are using Microsoft DOS, Windows 3.1, or Windows 95, you can use the DOS command MSD.EXE to determine which IRQs are available. If you are using Microsoft Windows NT, use the Resources tab under Diagnostic Tools in the Administrative Tools group.

Don't be confused by IRQs, especially the ones used by COM ports. Although COM1 and COM3 use the same IRQ, only one can be present in a computer. The same is true for COM2 and COM4. Also, the odd-numbered COM ports (1 and 3) use the even-numbered IRQ4; the even-numbered COM ports (2 and 4) use the odd-numbered IRQ3.

Base input/output (I/O) port

After the network adapter has the computer's attention, data is sent to the computer's processor. The computer uses the base I/O port to move data back and forth between the processor and the adapter. Like the IRQ, the base I/O port must be unique.

As with IRQs, if you are using Microsoft DOS, Windows 3.1, or Windows 95, you can use the DOS command MSD.EXE to determine which base I/O ports are available. If you are using Microsoft Windows NT, use Diagnostic Tools in the Administrative Tools group.

I/O addresses are given as hexadecimal numbers. The most common port used by network adapters is 300h, a hexadecimal number that refers to the beginning address of a block of memory. Other common addresses used as base I/O ports are 280h and 310h. Table 8-2 shows common I/O ports that you should know for the exam.

Table 8-2 may not be correct for all computers. It does, however, list the information you need to know for the exam.

Table 8-2	Common Uses of I/O Addresses
Port Number	*Device Using It*
200h	Game port
230h	Bus mouse
270h	LPT3
280h	Network adapter
2B0h	LPT1
2F8h	COM2
300h	Network adapter
310h	Network adapter
370h	LPT2
3F8h	COM1

Direct memory address (DMA)

Direct memory address, or DMA, enables a network adapter to work directly with the computer's memory rather than go through the computer's CPU.

Shared memory address

Because data can be sent to the adapter much faster than the data can be sent over the network, the computer requires a buffer area, called the *shared memory address,* to store the data until the network adapter is ready for it. This address, which must be unique to the network adapter, is usually set to D8000 or C8000 (sometimes written as D800 or C800). You shouldn't have to change it. In addition, any memory manager software must be instructed to exclude this address.

If an adapter does not come with software and you have to adjust these settings manually, you must change the jumpers or switches on the adapter. To change the setting of the jumpers, you place a small plastic cover over a pair of pins. The plastic cover, or jumper, has an internal metal connector. This completes the electrical circuit with the pair of pins. A pair that has a jumper cover over it is considered closed, and one without a cover is open. Figure 8-7 shows a set of jumpers.

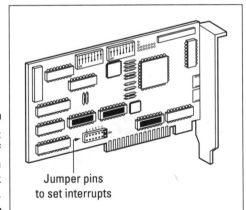

Figure 8-7: A block of jumpers on a network adapter.

Jumper pins to set interrupts

To change the setting of the switches, you simply flip the switch. Dual in-line package (DIP) switches are usually located on the side of the adapter at the metal plate that holds the adapter in the computer. These switches have two settings, labeled on and off, 0 and 1, or open and closed. Figure 8-8 shows a set of DIP switches.

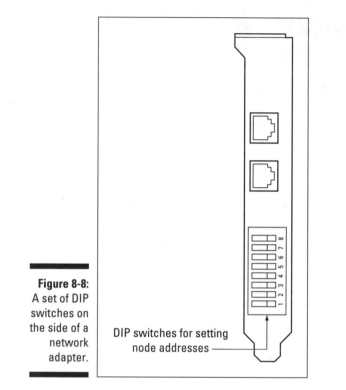

Figure 8-8:
A set of DIP
switches on
the side of a
network
adapter.

DIP switches for setting
node addresses

Installing an Adapter Driver

After installing and configuring a network adapter, the last thing to do is to install a device driver for it. The driver tells the operating system that a network adapter is installed and how to talk to the adapter. The two standards for drivers that you will see on the exam are

- ✔ Network Device Interface Specification (NDIS)
- ✔ Open Data-link Interface (ODI)

The main purpose for these standards is to allow network adapter manufacturers to write one driver that will work with many operating systems.

An important feature of these drivers is that more than one network protocol can be bound to the adapter. Thus, with only one adapter, you can use more than one type of network communications protocol. *Binding* is the process by which a protocol stack is joined with a network adapter driver to gain access to the adapter card for transmitting data.

NDIS was created by Microsoft and 3Com, a network adapter manufacturer. The two current versions of NDIS are version 2, which is a 16-bit driver used by DOS and Windows 3.1, and version 3, which is a 32-bit driver used by Windows 95 and Windows NT. These drivers are used to connect to another Microsoft system.

As with NDIS, ODI has both 16- and 32-bit versions. The 16-bit version is used by DOS and Windows 3.1 systems to connect to a Novell NetWare server. The 32-bit driver is used by Windows 95 and can be used instead of the NDIS driver to allow a Windows 95 system to connect to any type of server, not just a Novell server.

Prep Test

1 Assume that a computer has the following settings: a printer port at LPT1, a PS/2 mouse, a modem on COM1, and a video adapter. Which IRQ is available for the network card?

    A ○ IRQ7

    B ○ IRQ9

    C ○ IRQ4

    D ○ IRQ12

2 You need to buy a network adapter for an older IBM PS/2 computer. Which type of card should you buy?

    A ○ PCI

    B ○ ISA

    C ○ Micro Channel

    D ○ EISA

3 (True/False) PCI adapters are generally faster than ISA adapters.

4 IRQ12 is reserved for which of the following?

    A ○ PS/2 mouse

    B ○ Primary hard drive controller

    C ○ Floppy disk controller

    D ○ Keyboard

5 (True/False) NDIS drivers are used to connect to another Microsoft system.

6 (True/False) MSD.EXE can be used to determine an available port but not to determine what IRQs are available.

7 Port 270h is used for which device?

    A ○ COM2

    B ○ LPT3

    C ○ LPT2

    D ○ LPT1

8 (True/False) Although COM1 and COM3 use the same IRQ, only one can be present in a computer.

9 What process joins a network adapter driver with a protocol stack, allowing the stack to transmit data through the adapter?

A ○ Binding

B ○ Bonding

C ○ Installing

D ○ Booting

10 Which architecture is used for many laptop computers because it provides for adapter cards about the same size as credit cards? It provides Plug-and-Play capability as well.

A ○ EISA

B ○ ISA

C ○ PCMCIA

D ○ Micro Channel

Answers

1 *B.* IRQ 9 is available. IRQ7 is used by LPT1, IRQ4 is used by COM1, and the PS/2 mouse uses IRQ12. *Review "Interrupt request (IRQ)."*

2 *C.* IBM PS/2 computers use the Micro Channel Architecture for expansion cards, such as network adapters. *Review "Selecting an Adapter."*

3 *True.* PCI adapters are faster because they have a 32-bit bus as opposed to the 16-bit bus of an ISA or adapter. *Review "Selecting an Adapter."*

4 *A.* There's no easy way to know this other than memorizing the fixed IRQs. *Review Table 8-1 for a complete list of the reserved IRQs.*

5 *True.* NDIS drivers are used to connect to Microsoft systems. ODI drivers are for Novell systems. *Review "Installing an Adapter Driver" for a description of each of these standards.*

6 *False.* You can use MSD.EXE to determine open ports, as well as open IRQs. *Review Tables 8-1 and 8-2 for complete information on IRQs and ports.*

7 *B.* Check the manufacturer's documentation for a list of dedicated IRQs and base I/O ports. *Review Table 8-2 for the ports commonly used by certain devices.*

8 *True.* The same holds true for COM2 and COM4. *Table 8-1 has a complete list of reserved IRQs.*

9 *A.* The binding process joins the network adapter card driver and the protocol stack. *Review "Installing an Adapter Driver."*

10 *C.* The PCMCIA architecture is used in many laptop computers. *Review "Selecting an Adapter."*

Chapter 9

Troubleshooting Network Adapters

· ·

Exam Objectives

▶ Installing, configuring, and resolving hardware conflicts for multiple network adapters in a token-ring or Ethernet network

▶ Identifying common errors associated with components required for communications

▶ Diagnosing and resolving common connectivity problems with cards, cables, and related hardware

· ·

A system administrator must keep the system running, which is a tall order when you think about all the things that can go wrong in a networking environment. You must protect your system from environmental threats such as power outages, as well as the likes of Joe BackHoe, who might inadvertently cut your fiber-optic backbone segment. You also need to be able to diagnose network problems such as malfunctioning network adapter cards and cable interference, and computer problems such as hardware device conflicts and viruses.

Following are some preventive troubleshooting methods that will help reduce the number of problems you have with your network. No matter how hard you try, however, things *will* go wrong. Whether the problem is as minor as a user who has unplugged his or her network connection or as major as a crashed hard drive on the server, you will be faced with problems that need to be corrected immediately. System administrators have several diagnostic tools available to troubleshoot common Ethernet and token-ring networks, such as advanced cable testers, digital volt meters, time domain reflectors, and protocol analyzers.

This chapter describes what you should do to isolate problems, correct problems, and recover from data loss. The Networking Essentials exam will test your knowledge of specialized tools and require you to resolve the common networking problems mentioned in this chapter.

Quick Assessment

Diagnose and resolve common connectivity problems

1 To prevent losing data, you should _____ _____ your data often.

2 After you have corrected the problem, you should _____ what you did in case you have the same problem again.

3 A(n) _____ causes a copy of itself to be inserted into one or more other programs.

Identify common errors associated with components required for communications

4 You can divide a cable to see whether it has a break by using a(n) _____.

5 A tool that captures packets, decodes them, and determines which part of the network is causing problems is called a(n) _____ _____.

6 You can check the voltage in a network cable by using a(n) _____ _____ _____.

7 A device that tests a cable by emitting pulses of known amplitude on the cable is called a(n) _____ _____ _____.

8 Most network problems occur at the _____ layer of the OSI model.

Install, configure, and resolve hardware conflicts

9 _____ _____ can be used to discover and eliminate hardware conflicts on a Windows 95 system.

Answers

1 *Back up.* The "Isolating the problem" section covers backing up data.

2 *Document.* Read the section "Recovering from disaster" for more information about documenting solutions.

3 *Virus.* The "Viruses" section contains more information.

4 *Terminator.* The "Troubleshooting Ethernet" section talks more about terminators.

5 *Protocol analyzer.* This device is described in the "Protocol analyzer" section.

6 *Digital volt meter.* Digital volt meters are discussed in the "Digital volt meter (DVM)" section.

7 *Time domain reflectometer.* TDRs are discussed more in the "Time domain reflectometer (TDR)" section.

8 *Physical.* Most network problems occur and are solved at the Physical layer of the OSI model. This is mentioned in the "Common Errors with Communications Components" section.

9 *Device Manager.* Read the "Resolving Hardware Conflicts" section.

Troubleshooting the Network

To be able to determine the location of a network's problems, you must first know how the network performs under normal circumstances, which involves establishing a baseline of the network's performance. Then you will be able to predict — and avoid — some problems. And when a problem does occur, you will be able to identify what is causing it.

Isolating the problem

Before you can solve a problem, you must figure out what is causing it. The first thing to do is to make sure the user is not the problem (that is, that he or she isn't doing something incorrectly).

The second step is to make sure everything is plugged in and turned on. If a user can't print to the network printer, for example, make sure the cable to the printer is plugged in and that the printer has power.

The next step is to turn off everything that is part of the problem and then turn it back on again. If you think the problem may be associated with a disk drive and the drive hasn't crashed, make sure you have a good backup. Now would be a good time to make another backup on a clean tape to complement the most recent data backup.

Many times, these few steps will take care of the problems. When you encounter more serious problems, follow Microsoft's troubleshooting model, which is described next.

A troubleshooting model

Microsoft's troubleshooting model consists of five steps:

1. **Set the priority of the problem.**

   A server disk crash is much more important than Joe's not being able to surf the Web. You must assess the importance of the problem and decide how fast you must get it resolved in relation to the other issues you are working on.

2. **Collect the basic information you need to identify the problem.**

   Find out the last time the device worked properly and what has changed since then. Configuration changes, software upgrades, and the installation of new hardware are often responsible for problems.

3. **Make a list of possible causes.**

   Put these causes in order, with the most likely first.

4. Isolate the problem.

When you have a good idea of what is causing the problem, begin testing your ideas. Remember that you are performing controlled experiments at this point. Follow good scientific methods and make only *one* change to the environment at a time. Observe and document the results of each change for later review. Use network analysis tools such as advanced cable testers, time domain reflectometers, and digital volt meters to collect your data. Also, don't forget to review change logs, network documentation, and coworker knowledge when looking for answers.

5. Find a solution.

After you test your first idea, you will have solved the problem or have a better idea of what to do next. Reevaluate your proposed solution and try the next most likely one. When you finally correct the problem, document what you did in case the same problem occurs again.

Recovering from disaster

The only way to prevent data loss is by making frequent and dependable backups. Even fault-tolerant systems have the potential to lose data. If you have a system crash, the only thing standing between you and the unemployment line is a dependable backup.

An organization should implement a backup strategy that matches the level of importance of its data. If the loss of data would be damaging to the business, backups should occur more frequently than if the data is not critical. You should always back up critical data; this ensures that the system will be able to keep functioning if something does happen. Back up files that never change, such as program executables, occasionally.

You can use several types of backup strategies:

- **Full.** A full, or normal, backup makes a copy of every file. You may want to do a full backup every day if all your information is critical to running the company. This type of backup takes longer and uses more tapes. Because you have to use only one set of tapes, however, the restore process will be quicker and you can be back up and running sooner.

- **Normal with Incremental.** An incremental backup backs up all files that have changed since the last full or incremental backup. For example, you can do a full backup Friday, and then an incremental backup Monday through Thursday to back up only the files that change each day. This is a quicker way to back up data. If you have to restore data, however, you must restore the last full backup from Friday, and then restore the incremental backup from each day since then.

> ✔ **Normal with Differential.** A differential backup saves data that has changed since the last full backup. If you do a full backup Friday and then a differential backup Monday through Thursday, you will have to restore only the Friday backup and then the last day's incremental. This process takes a little longer to back up but is quicker to restore than an incremental backup.

You should periodically test your backups to make sure they will work when you restore. You can use a test server to restore the data to see whether all the information works correctly.

After you get the network running again, document what happened and what you did to correct the problem. This will make future problems easier and quicker to solve.

An incremental backup backs up data changed since the last incremental or full backup. A differential backup backs up all data changed since the last full backup.

Common Errors with Communications Components

The physical environment contains systems, cables, networking devices, and power supplies. A simple test can determine whether something is part of the physical environment. If someone threw it at you, would it hurt? If the answer is yes, it's probably in the physical environment.

Most network problems occur and are solved at the Physical layer of the OSI model.

Cabling and related hardware

Some of the most common causes of network failure are the physical media, the cable that connects a computer to the network, and malfunctioning network adapter cards. Problems with cabling and network adapter cards can include the following:

> ✔ **Cable break:** a cut or a break in the cable
>
> ✔ **Cable crimp:** a bend or a twist in the cable that prevents the flow of electrical or optical impulses
>
> ✔ **Cable interference:** running network cable too close to a source of high electromagnetic interference, such as cabling located too close to an electric motor or a fluorescent light ballast

An easy way to differentiate a cable problem from a computer problem is with the use of a laptop computer equipped with a network PC card. Unplug the computer experiencing the problem, and connect the laptop to the network cable. If the laptop can log on to the network, you can rule out the cable as the cause of the problem. If the laptop experiences the same network problems as the original computer, conduct further testing of the cable with a tool such as a time domain reflectometer or a network analyzer.

Electrical problems

A common problem organizations face is lack of clean power, that is, a constant voltage free of spikes and dips. Spikes occur when the power level exceeds a specified limit. A dip, sometimes called a brownout, occurs when the power level drops below the required amount necessary for a device to function.

A spike can occur at either the generating station or when someone shuts off a device that was drawing a lot of current. For just a moment, the voltage may increase significantly, blowing fuses or frying circuit boards. A brownout usually occurs in areas where the demand for power exceeds what the electrical company can provide. The result is low power levels that can destroy equipment such as electrical motors.

To combat the effects of dirty power, a company can install a power-conditioning unit or an environmental control system. The power-conditioning unit is like a big uninterruptible power supply (UPS) — so big that it can power an entire data center. The conditioner runs the incoming power stream through a series of electrical components and then delivers an even flow of electrical power. The environmental control system does the same thing but usually includes a high-capacity air conditioner to keep a data center at a constant temperature and humidity.

Viruses

A system administrator must also combat harmful programs written by hackers who want nothing more than to alter and destroy data. It seems that PCs have the same capability to contract viruses as humans do, usually with the same results! A *virus* is a sequence of code inserted in another program. When the program is run, the viral code is executed also. The viral code causes a copy of itself to be inserted into one or more other programs. Viruses are not distinct programs. They can't run on their own. However, a macro virus can attach itself to a macro within a document and, when the macro is executed, cause viral destruction.

A number of virus-protection solutions are on the market. All involve some form of periodic virus scanning. When a virus is detected, a variety of things may happen. The file may be automatically cleaned or it may be deleted, the user might be notified, and an event might be written to a log. If you are evaluating a virus protection package, remember to check whether the package will scan network drives and e-mail message stores; these are common locations for viruses to hide. Also check whether you can force a virus scan at a user's computer before allowing the user to access the network. These are just a few of the options you should look for in a good virus protection program.

Troubleshooting Ethernet

Ethernet, the most common network standard, is easy to install, but errors are still possible. Following are some errors that may develop in an Ethernet network:

- With 10BaseT, make sure you are using the right category of cable. Higher throughputs require higher quality cables. For example, you can achieve 10 Mbps on Category 3 cable, but you need Category 5 cable for 100 Mbps transmissions.

- Connectors must be pinned properly and crimped tightly. Too much unshielded or untwisted cable close to the connectors may cause loss of signal integrity.

- Coaxial cable must be terminated on each end. If there is a break in the cable, you can use a time domain reflectometer to locate the problem.

- Make sure specifications concerning cable distances and maximum number of nodes have not been violated.

- Malfunctioning hardware — NICs, hub ports, connectors, or other networking equipment — can cause partial or full loss of connectivity.

- Resource conflicts can result between base I/O ports, DMA shared memory, or interrupts.

Troubleshooting token ring

To troubleshoot a token-ring network, begin with the more obvious physical attributes of the network. Check for loose connectors. Check the manufacturer's design specifications to ensure that cable lengths or maximum node numbers haven't been exceeded. Also, make sure the correct type of cable has been used.

Following are other token-ring errors you might encounter:

- ✔ Base I/O, DMA shared memory, or interrupt conflicts
- ✔ Incorrect version of the adapter driver
- ✔ MAU ring-in and ring-out ports connected improperly
- ✔ Active MAUs unplugged or blowing a fuse
- ✔ Bad MAU ports
- ✔ Failed adapter card
- ✔ Adapter card set at the wrong ring speed (16 Mbps or 4 Mbps)
- ✔ Bent or broken pins on the adapter card
- ✔ Duplicate node addresses

A token-ring network can troubleshoot itself to some extent. It can even repair simple problems. If a token-ring network can't repair itself, it uses a process known as *beaconing* to help narrow down the source of the problem.

The token-ring beaconing process is different from the FDDI beaconing process, in that the token-ring version is always occurring at 7-second intervals. The first computer to power up on the network becomes the active monitor and announces to the network that it is the active monitor.

If a system doesn't receive an announcement from its upstream neighbor at the proper interval, that system transmits a packet to the entire ring containing the sending computer's network address and the network address of its upstream neighbor. The ring then tries to autoreconfigure to eliminate the malfunctioning system. This most often involves disabling a port on an MAU. If autoreconfiguration fails, manual intervention is required.

Common Connectivity Problems

Most network hardware problems come from one of three places:

- ✔ Network cable
- ✔ Cable connector
- ✔ Network adapter

Occasionally, a hard drive might crash in a server, or the power supply might go bad, or a router might quit working. Most everyday problems, however, are in the connections of computers to the network.

To help you diagnose problems with your network, you can purchase tools that range in price from a few dollars to several thousand dollars. Some of the more useful tools include the following:

- Advanced cable tester
- Digital volt meter (DVM)
- Time domain reflectometer (TDR)
- Optical time domain reflectometer (OTDR)
- Protocol analyzer

Advanced cable tester

An advanced cable tester tests the integrity of a piece of cable. Generally, one end of the cable is plugged into the tester and the other end is plugged into the tester's receiver. The cable tester then sends a signal down the cable. The receiver receives the signal and sends it back to the tester. This type of tester determines the cable's attenuation, resistance, and other electrical and physical properties. Some testers also show you how each wire in the cable is pinned.

If you are planning on using an old piece of cable, it is a good idea to test it with a cable tester to see whether it works properly.

Digital volt meter (DVM)

One of the most common devices used for testing copper cable is a digital volt meter (DVM). The DVM measures continuity in the cable and can determine whether the cable is continuous and can carry network traffic, or broken and will bring the network down. A continuity check can also reveal a short, where two pieces of conductor touch each other.

Time domain reflectometer (TDR)

A time domain reflectometer (TDR) sends sonar-like pulses along a cable to detect breaks, shorts, or cable imperfections. If a fault is detected, the TDR analyzes it and displays the results. A TDR can usually locate the fault within a few feet of the actual problem. TDRs are used heavily during the installation of new cables in a network. They are probably the most common type of cable testing device.

Optical time domain reflectometer (OTDR)

An optical time domain reflectometer (OTDR) performs the same function on optical cable as a TDR does for copper cable. The sonar-like pulses are generated from a light source. Full breaks in a fiber-optic cable can be detected by simply placing a flashlight at one end of the cable and looking at the other end. Partial breaks or imperfections are much more difficult to detect because light will still pass through the cable. An OTDR is required to detect anything other than a full break in the cable.

Protocol analyzer

A protocol analyzer disassembles a packet of information to identify the cause of a problem. It also can generate statistics of network traffic. Most hardware protocol analyzers have built-in TDRs.

The following is a list of some of the common problems that a protocol analyzer can detect:

- Faulty network components
- Configuration and connection errors
- LAN bottlenecks
- Traffic fluctuations
- Protocol problems
- Unusual traffic patterns

Protocol analyzers can also be used to characterize or baseline a network by performing the following functions:

- Identify the most active computers
- Capture packets for generating trend analysis
- Determine which protocols are most heavily used
- Determine which protocols are using the most bandwidth
- Capture and analyze packets to determine whether routing is efficient

Popular network analyzers include the following:

- ✔ Hewlett-Packard Network Advisor
- ✔ Network General Sniffer
- ✔ Novell LANalyzer
- ✔ Microsoft Network Monitor (SMS version)

Resolving Hardware Conflicts

You need to be familiar with a few common errors associated with the use of network adapters. Most modern networking architectures are not tolerant of multiple adapters in the same computer on the same physical cable. Problems arise because the same computer appears to have multiple addresses. Adding multiple network adapters running the same protocols to the same physical cable rarely improves the performance of a system. Instead, it can decrease system performance dramatically or cause the system to stop functioning completely.

Installing multiple network adapters in a system connected to different network segments is common. If routing is enabled, the system will act as a router and move information from one network to another. Routing can represent significant overhead on a system. System performance levels may drop as a result of enabling routing.

Another common error to watch out for is connecting the wrong network segment to the wrong adapter. In this case, the system does not function on either network because its interface to each network does not have an appropriate address for that network. In addition, incorrect routing tables will cause a system to have difficulty sending or receiving data.

Hardware conflicts can be difficult to troubleshoot. The first place to check for a hardware conflict in Windows 95 is the Device Manager tab in the System Control Panel applet. Figure 9-1 shows a Device Manager free of any hardware conflicts. If a conflict existed, Device Manager would highlight the device with either a yellow question mark or a red exclamation point. The yellow question mark indicates that the operating system could not identify the device. The exclamation point indicates that the device was identified, but it is trying to use the same resources as another device. Double-click on the device to see the details of the conflict.

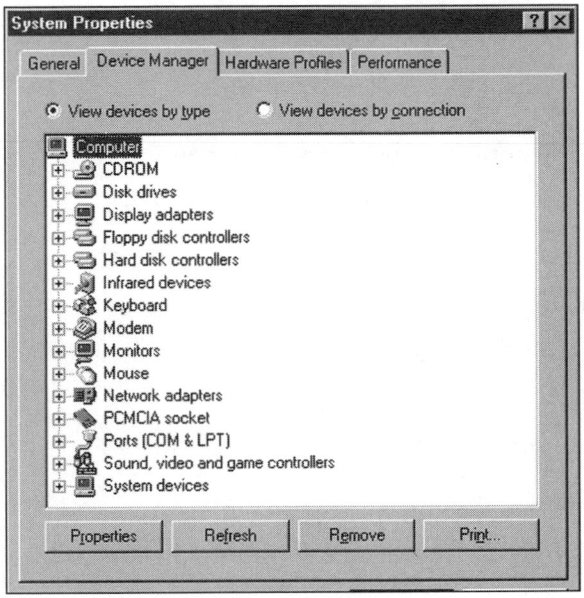

Figure 9-1:
Device
Manager.

If you find a device conflict, you can select the device with the problem and use the tabs in Device Manager to view information about the device driver and the system resources being used by the device.

If the system can detect which devices conflict with the one in question, it will list those devices. Device Manager also enables you to change the resources being used by the device to remove the conflict.

When devices are designed to use the same resources and only those resources, a device conflict can develop that can't be resolved. In such a situation, you must either remove one of the devices or define a different hardware profile for each conflicting device. Hardware profiles are created through the Hardware Profiles tab on the System Control Panel applet.

Prep Test

1 What is the first thing you should do when trying to correct a problem?

A ○ Make all the changes you think are necessary

B ○ Eliminate user error

C ○ Reboot

D ○ Back up critical data

2 Which diagnostic tool operates on a packet level?

A ○ Time domain reflectometer

B ○ Digital volt meter

C ○ Protocol analyzer

D ○ Performance monitor

3 Which of the following are common causes of network failure? (Choose all that apply.)

A ❑ Cable break

B ❑ Cable splice

C ❑ Cable interference

D ❑ Faulty network adapter card

4 Which utility can be used to detect hardware components that are not functioning properly?

A ○ Hardware Manager

B ○ Device Manager

C ○ Conflict Manager

D ○ System Manager

5 What type of backup makes a copy of all files that have been changed since your last full backup?

A ○ Full

B ○ Incremental

C ○ Differential

D ○ Retro

6 What is the first step in the Microsoft troubleshooting model?

A ○ List the possible causes

B ○ Set the priority of the problem

C ○ Isolate the problem

D ○ Reboot

7 What tool can check for breaks in cables?

A ○ Digital volt meter

B ○ TDR

C ○ Advanced cable tester

D ○ All of the above

8 At what layer of the OSI model do most network problems occur?

A ○ Physical layer

B ○ Data Link layer

C ○ Network layer

D ○ Transport layer

Answers

1 *B.* Make sure there actually is a problem with the system and that you're not fighting a training issue. *See the section on "Isolating the problem."*

2 *C.* The protocol analyzer captures, counts, and disassembles packets. *The section "Common Connectivity Problems" covers the different types of instruments for testing your network.*

3 *A; C; D.* Network failures are commonly caused by cable breaks, cuts, crimps, interference, and faulty network adapter cards. *Review "Cabling and related hardware" for more information.*

4 *B.* Hardware conflicts can be difficult to detect and troubleshoot. The first place to check for a hardware conflict is the Device Manager tab in the System Control Panel applet. Keep in mind that Device Manager is available only on computers running Windows 95 or Windows 98. *See "Resolving Hardware Conflicts" for more information.*

5 *C.* A differential backup backs up all files that are "different" from the last time a full backup was run. *See the "Recovering from disaster" section for more information about types of backups.*

6 *B.* The first thing you should do is prioritize your issues, and take care of the most immediate needs first. *See "A troubleshooting model" for more information.*

7 *D.* All these can test for cable breaks. *The "Common Connectivity Problems" section talks more about these.*

8 *A.* Most problems occur and are resolved at the Physical layer of the OSI model. *Review "Common Errors with Communications Components" for more information.*

Chapter 10

Cabling and Connections

· ·

Exam Objective

▶ Selecting the appropriate media for various situations

· ·

*T*his chapter describes how to connect computers to form a network. In particular, you find out about the types of connections, cable, and wireless systems you would choose given specific exam scenarios. This exam objective receives a chapter all to itself primarily because of the technical nature of the material. This is one of the most technical chapters in the book. Many technologies discussed in this chapter are special-purpose technologies that you may not have had any experience with, such as wireless and analog signaling.

A large portion of the chapter consists of descriptions of the different physical media. You need to know the differences in characteristics of each type of physical media. A few examples of these characteristics are the transmission speed and signaling scheme for a particular media, or its relative cost and ease of installation. Pay particular attention to the differences between wireless connections and cable connections and the differences between copper-based media and fiber-optic media.

The chapter also describes some potential problems with the different types of media available. For example, copper-based media suffers from the effects of attenuation and interference. Fiber-optic cable does not. Fiber-optic cable, however, is very expensive and very fragile. This is just one example of the trade-off decisions that a network designer must make when designing a network.

In the discussion of signaling, pay close attention to the way analog signaling is accomplished. Most people have a good grasp of digital signaling because it is so common. Analog signaling is a little different.

When you complete this chapter, you'll be well equipped to answer cable-related questions, and you'll know the appropriate signaling strategy for different scenarios.

Quick Assessment

1 _____ is effective for about 100 feet and is very susceptible to light sources such as sunlight or bright office lights.

2 The two types of signaling are _____ and _____.

3 Digital signaling is also known as _____.

4 The two types of bit synchronization are _____ and _____.

5 The two types of multiplexers are _____ and _____.

6 Twisted-pair cable comes in two types: _____ and _____.

7 The two types of coaxial cable are _____ and _____.

8 The six factors in deciding the type of cable to use are _____, _____, _____, _____, _____, and _____.

9 The loss of signal strength is called _____.

10 The electrical energy released from a cable that can foul other transmissions is called _____.

Answers

1   *Infrared.* Check out the "Infrared" section for more information.

2   *Digital, analog.* Review "Signal Transmission" for an overview of the two types of signaling.

3   *Baseband transmission.* Again, review "Signal Transmission" if you are confused.

4   *Asynchronous, synchronous.* If you named them, can you decide when one method over the other is used? If not, review "Analog signaling."

5   *Frequency-division multiplexer, time-division multiplexer.* Review the "Multiplexing" section for more information.

6   *Unshielded, shielded.* Review the "Twisted-sister cable" section on unshielded and shielded twisted pair.

7   *Thinnet, thicknet.* See "Coaxial cable" and Figure 10-2 for more information.

8   *Cost, installation, security, shielding, distance, speed.* Review Table 10-1 for an explanation of each of these.

9   *Attenuation.* Review "Attenuation."

10   *Interference.* Review "Interference."

Signal Transmission

After you understand the ways in which you can transmit data and the vehicle by which you do it, you'll be better equipped to mix and match solutions to come up with the right answers to exam questions. To review, signaling is a way of sending data. The two types of signaling are digital and analog. This section describes each method. The next section describes the medium used for each type.

Digital signaling

When using digital signaling, a computer can transmit and receive at the same time. Digital signaling is also known as *baseband transmission*. Baseband systems use a single frequency to send signals in the form of electrical charges or light pulses. Electrical charges have one of two voltage levels, either on or off. Devices connected to baseband systems can both transmit and receive a signal at the same time.

Don't be confused by the use of *digital signaling* instead of *baseband transmission.* They're the same!

As the baseband signal travels down the cable to its destination, the signal becomes weaker. If the cable length is too long, the signal becomes distorted and can't be read by the receiving computer. For this reason, repeaters are used to receive the signal and rebroadcast it in its original strength. (For more about repeaters, see Chapter 7.) This process can be used to increase the effective length of the cable.

Analog signaling

Analog transmission can go in only one direction. If you need to send both voice and data, analog is probably the correct choice. Analog, also known as *broadband,* uses analog signals to transmit data. Broadband divides the cable into multiple channels, and each channel has its own frequency. Any device tuned to this frequency can read the data that is transmitted. A cable TV system uses broadband transmission to send TV signals into houses. This type of cable could be used to transmit data and voice signals on the same cable.

Broadband transmission is in only one direction, so a device can either send or receive. You can compensate for this in two ways to allow data to flow in both directions:

✔ **Mid-split broadband** divides the cable into two channels, each using a different frequency or different range of frequencies. One channel transmits data, and the other channel receives data.

✔ **Dual-cable broadband** uses two cables, both attached to each device. One cable transmits and the other receives.

During analog or digital signaling, both the transmitting device and the receiving device must cooperate with each other. They must know when the signal begins and ends and how to tell which signal is the one it wants to see. This process is called *bit synchronization*. The two types of bit synchronization are asynchronous and synchronous.

Asynchronous bit synchronization requires a start bit at the beginning of the message and a stop bit at the end. When you're ready to send data, the start bit is sent to both the transmitting machine and the receiving machine to synchronize the signal clock in each system. When the transmission is complete, the stop bit is sent to tell both machines that the transmission has ended.

Asynchronous transmissions use parity to determine whether the transmission was received correctly. The three parity options are even, odd, and none:

✔ In **even parity,** the sum of the bits sent is even.

✔ In **odd parity,** the sum of the bits is odd.

✔ In the **none** option, no parity checking is used.

Asynchronous transmissions use a lot of computer resources and are very inefficient for high-speed transmissions.

In *synchronous bit synchronization,* the sending and receiving systems agree on a clock management method and continuously synchronize their clocks. The receiver is always waiting for data, and the sender transmits the data as it becomes ready.

Multiplexing

Multiplexing is another consideration in data transmission. In *multiplexing,* a single high-bandwidth (high-capacity) channel is used to transmit many lower-bandwidth channels. Likewise, many low-bandwidth channels can be combined to form one high-bandwidth channel. A multiplexer/demultiplexer (MUX) is the hardware device that combines these channels and then separates them at the receiving end.

Both broadband and baseband transmissions can use multiplexing. Each has its own type of multiplexer:

- ✔ **Frequency-division multiplexing (FDM)** is the broadband type of multiplexer. The channels are on different frequencies, with an area of unused frequencies separating them. These unused ranges act as buffers to keep the signals from overlapping and becoming distorted. Cable TV uses this type of multiplexing.

- ✔ **Time-division multiplexing (TDM)** uses time slices to separate channels and is the only way to provide baseband transmissions with multiple channels. A system is given a certain amount of time to broadcast information on all available bandwidth, and then the next system in line is given the chance to transmit.

Battle of the bands: Baseband versus broadband

Both types of signaling have good and bad points. Broadband (analog) is more versatile because it can be divided into channels, but it is generally more expensive and requires two cables or two channels to receive and transmit at the same time. Baseband (digital) can both send and receive at the same time. Most networks today use digital signaling.

Remember that baseband uses digital signals and is used by most networks today. Broadband uses analog signals and can allow multiple uses of a single cable.

It's the Media's Fault

Cost and speed are two factors you should consider when selecting a physical media. You must consider also the difficulty associated with cable installation and maintenance, the amount of information that will be transmitted, the number of computers attached to the network, and the distance between these computers. No set formula exists: You must weigh all the factors and come up with an answer that balances performance and price.

Bandwidth

In a network environment, *bandwidth* is how many data bits can be sent across the network at a given time. Bandwidth is measured in megabits per second (Mbps), where 1 Mpbs means 1 million bits would be transmitted in 1 second. Most networks transmit at about 10 Mbps. Many of the newer technologies can transmit up to 100 Mbps, and some fiber-optic networks can transmit at almost 2 gigabits per second (2 Gbps), or 2 billion bits per second.

Attenuation

Have you ever been driving down the road listening to the radio and the station you're listening to starts to fade out? Well, this happens to network signals too, and is called *attenuation*. As the signal travels farther down the cable, it gets weaker as part of the signal is absorbed into the media. Different media can transmit signals different distances, and this affects the length of the cable. Copper cable, such as twisted pair and coaxial, can carry signals for only a short distance; fiber-optic cable can be used over a much longer distance.

Interference

As an electrical signal travels down a wire, some of the signal leaks out of the wire. If this energy, called *noise*, is strong enough, it can interfere with other signals in a process called *electromagnetic interference*, or *EMI*. (If you've driven under high-voltage power lines and your radio signal has faded out, interference is the culprit.) With enough interference, the signal is unreadable by the computer receiving and trying to understand it.

Plenum

In most newer office buildings, a space exists between the false ceiling and the floor above where telephone, electric, and network cabling is run. This area is called the *plenum*, and is used also to circulate air throughout the building. If a fire occurred, the burning cable would be in the air circulating in the building. Most cable's outer layer is PVC (polyvinyl chloride), which is cheap and easy to work with, but also gives off toxic fumes when it burns. For this reason, most fire codes require plenum-grade cabling in this area. This cable is resistant to fire and does not give off as many fumes. As you've probably guessed, this type of cable is more expensive to buy and install.

Cable Types

The most common way to connect computers on a network is with cables. The many different types of cable can be divided into three categories: twisted pair, coaxial, and fiber-optic.

Twisted-sister cable

The cable that runs from your telephone into the wall is probably a twisted-pair cable. Most computer networks are connected with cable similar to telephone cable. Inside a twisted-pair cable are pairs of copper wire wrapped in color-coded insulation. Each pair is wrapped and then twisted around its partner, thus the name twisted pair. This twisting prevents *crosstalk,* which occurs when the signal from one cable is mixed with the signal from another cable. Twisted-pair cable comes in two types: unshielded and shielded, as shown in Figure 10-1.

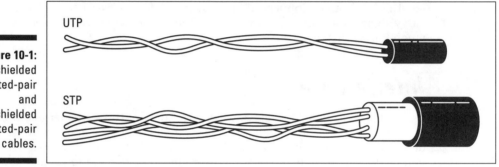

Figure 10-1:
Unshielded
twisted-pair
and
shielded
twisted-pair
cables.

Unshielded twisted pair

Probably the most commonly used cable in computer networks is unshielded twisted pair, also known as UTP. The major difference between UTP for networks and telephone cable is the number of pairs inside the cable: Telephone cable uses four wires in two pairs, and UTP for networks uses eight wires in four pairs. The connector that each type of cable uses is different as well. Telephone cable uses RJ-11 connectors, and UTP network cable uses RJ-45 connectors, which are larger to allow for the extra pairs of cable. The network server uses a cable that connects to a hub, which splits the signal and sends it out over other UTP cables to each computer.

The Electronic Industries Association and the Telecommunications Industries Association (EIA/TIA) have broken down UTP cables into categories. Older telephone cable is usually referred to as Category 1. For a data network, the minimum required cable is Category 3 with a data transmission speed of 10 Mbps. (Cat 3 wiring is a voice and data grade wire that meets the IEEE 802.3 specs for 10BaseT.) Most computer networks today are Category 5, which is capable of transmission speeds of 100 Mbps.

Although unshielded twisted-pair cable is an inexpensive, easy-to-install network cable, it also has its bad side. UTP is very susceptible to interference, and too much interference can cause the signal in the cable to become unusable. Another problem with UTP is attenuation, which affects the length of the cable that can be used. For UTP, the maximum length of a single segment is 100 meters (328 feet).

Shielded twisted pair

The other type of twisted-pair cable is shielded twisted pair (STP). The main difference between UPT and STP is that in STP the pairs of cable are wrapped in a copper or foil wrapping that keeps out interference. This wrapping is grounded electrically, which reduces interference even more. The maximum cable length is the same as UTP, but STP is stiffer, which makes it harder to install. STP also requires special connectors for electrical grounding. This, along with the shielding, makes STP more expensive as well.

Coaxial cable

Coaxial cable, also known as coax, is like the cable used for cable TV. Coax cable consists of a central core conductor, which is either a solid copper cable or several strands of copper wire twisted together, surrounded by a layer of plastic foam insulation. Next is a second conductor, which is usually a woven mesh of metal, and then a plastic casing around the entire cable. Figure 10-2 shows a cross-section of coaxial cable.

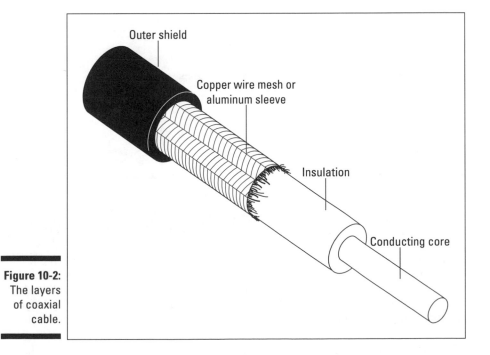

Figure 10-2:
The layers of coaxial cable.

The inner conductor carries the data; the outer conductor provides protection from interference and crosstalk. The inner conductor wire is thicker than that of twisted pair, which prevents the loss of signal strength (attenuation) and allows the signal to travel farther than the 100-meter limit of twisted pair. The two types of coax cable are thinnet and thicknet.

Thinnet

Thinnet cable is lightweight and flexible and is probably the second most common cable used in networks after UTP. Thinnet cable is run from computer to computer without the need of a hub. On a single network, cable is usually run from a starting point, through every computer on the network, to an ending point. Thinnet cable normally has a BNC connector on each end, as shown in Figure 10-3. This connector plugs into the BNC T connector, and the bottom end of the T connector plugs into the network adapter. At each end of the cable, a terminator tells the signal that it has reached the end of the road.

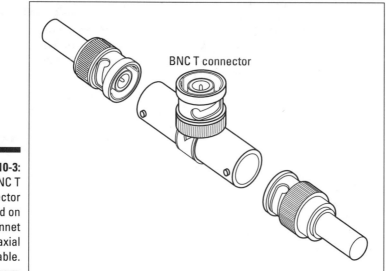

BNC T connector

Figure 10-3:
BNC T
connector
used on
thinnet
coaxial
cable.

Cable companies rate coax cable based on its thickness and resistance to current. Thinnet cable is rated as RG-58, and cable TV cable is RG-59.

Thinnet cable has a maximum segment length, the distance between each computer, of 185 meters (607 feet). This is almost twice as long as UTP, and thinnet is also more resistant to interference. It is also easy to install and very flexible. The maximum transmission speed, however, is only 10 Mbps. In addition, thinnet coax is slightly more expensive than twisted-pair cable.

Thicknet

Thicknet is a thicker form of coax than thinnet. Thicknet is classified as either RG-11 or RG-8. Thicknet uses one cable run throughout an area rather than run from computer to computer like thinnet. A transceiver is placed wherever a connection is needed along the cable. The transceiver is attached to the cable with a vampire tap that pierces the cable and makes a direct connection with the central core of the cable. A drop cable is run from the transceiver to the computer, connecting to an attachment unit interface (AUI) port on the computer's network card. The AUI port that the drop cable attaches to is a 15-pin connector referred to as a DB-15 connector.

Like thinnet, thicknet has a maximum transmission speed of 10 Mbps. Because of its thickness, thicknet cable is very resistant to interference and allows a long maximum cable length of 500 meters (1640 feet). It is, however, very expensive, very stiff, and very hard to work with during installation. For these reasons, thicknet is now used mostly for a backbone cable that runs throughout a building and connects networks to each other. Figure 10-4 shows the connection of a computer to a thicknet backbone.

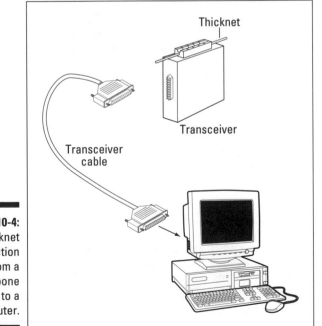

Figure 10-4:
A thicknet
connection
from a
backbone
to a
computer.

Fiber-optic cable

Fiber-optic cable does not carry data on an electric signal but instead uses light. For this reason, fiber-optic cable is not susceptible to interference like copper wires and does not produce a signal that can be tapped into and stolen. This makes fiber-optic cable very fast and secure.

Fiber-optic cable consists of a central glass-core fiber surrounded by a layer of glass casing with a plastic cover around the entire cable. Figure 10-5 shows a section of fiber-optic cable. The glass casing reflects the light signal back onto the central fiber and keeps it moving down the cable. The signal travels in one direction; because of this, fiber-optic cable normally consists of two fibers together, one for each direction.

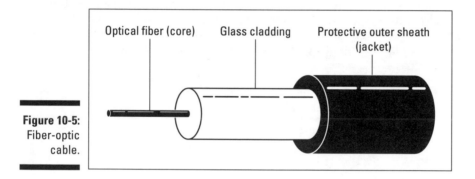

Figure 10-5: Fiber-optic cable.

Fiber-optic cable can carry signals a long distance — 2 kilometers (6,562 feet). It is very fast, 100 Mbps or more, and is not bothered by interference. It is, however, very difficult to install and is the most expensive cable type. In addition, only someone trained to install fiber-optic cable should install it.

Choosing the correct cable

When choosing the correct cabling setup, given a set of scenarios on the exam, you have to consider many things. For example, you might be asked to determine the correct cabling based on a company's budget or security concerns. Memorizing Table 10-1 will prepare you to answer these questions.

Table 10-1	Factors in Determining Cable Choice
Factor	*Explanation*
Cost	How much can be spent? The more you can buy, the faster and more secure the network will be.
Distance	How long do the cables need to be? If the distances between computers are long, you must use cables capable of carrying data those distances.
Speed	How fast does the network need to be? Generally, the faster you need your network to run, the more the cable will cost. This cable is also usually more difficult to install and maintain.
Security	Does the network need to be secure? If your network needs to be very secure, you may want to consider using fiber-optic cable, which is very hard to tap into to steal data. If a company wants the most security it can buy and money is no object, fiber-optic is your answer.
Installation	How easy is the cable to install and work with? Fiber-optic cable is very difficult to install and therefore should be installed only by a professional.
Shielding	Will the cable be used in an area where it will require more shielding, such as in a factory? The more shielding needed in the cable, the more expensive it is.

In the real world, you wouldn't buy cable until you knew for sure which type of cable you would need for the network! You would ask various questions about the company's needs before making a major purchase. These same questions will help you answer exam questions. Table 10-2 lists the major characteristics used to compare different types of media.

Table 10-2	Comparison of Cable Types				
Cable Type	Maximum Cable Length	Transmission Speed	Ease of Installation	Interference	Cost
UTP	100 meters	10 to 100 Mbps	Very easy	High	Least expensive
STP	100 meters	16 to 500 Mbps	Fairly easy	Low	Expensive
Thinnet	185 meters	10 Mbps	Easy	Low	Inexpensive
Thicknet	500 meters	10 Mbps	Difficult	Low	Very expensive
Fiber optic	2 kilometers	100 Mbps to 2 Gbps	Very Difficult	None	Most expensive

Wireless Media

Wireless media is a viable solution for companies that need to connect sites that would be too expensive to connect with physical cables. This is sometimes referred to as a *wireless bridge*. Another popular use of wireless technology is mobile computing. Laptop or palmtop users who must constantly move about with their devices can't be inhibited by dangling wires.

Wireless networks are becoming more and more popular. More manufacturers are offering wireless equipment and prices are coming down. A few wireless offerings, such as scatter-infrared technology designed for laptop users, can be used with traditional wired networks as well. Faced with these scenarios, you need to be comfortable with the types of wireless media, so this section is a review. Pay attention to speed — one of the items you need to factor in when you're looking at an exam question.

Radio wave

Radio wave broadcasts are similar to the signal broadcast from a radio station. Two types of radio wave broadcasts are in use:

- Narrow band
- Spread spectrum

Narrow band, also referred to as single frequency, uses a transmitter and a receiver tuned to the same frequency. Because this is a radio signal broadcast, it does not require line of sight to work. The signal is high frequency, however, so it cannot pass through steel or load-bearing walls. Narrow-band transmission is also fairly slow, transmitting at about 4.8 Mbps.

Spread-spectrum radio broadcasts signals over a range of frequencies. The frequencies that spread spectrum uses are divided into channels. The network adapters tune in to a specific channel for a specific length of time, and then switch to the next channel. All computers on the network are synchronized to a particular sequence that controls how long each channel is used before the adapters switch to the next channel. Because this switching sequence is known only to the computers on the network, other computers can't listen in. Spread spectrum is very slow, transmitting only about 250 Kbps (1000 Kbps equals 1 Mbps).

Microwave on high for four minutes

Microwave systems use satellite antennas to transmit information between sites. Microwaves are good for connecting buildings in small, short-distance areas such as an office park or a college campus. These systems must have line-of-sight points to function, and are useful across large bodies of water or flat land areas such as deserts.

To use a microwave system, you must have two radio receivers, one to generate the signal and the other to receive the broadcast. The two directional antennas must be pointed at each other, and are often put on top of buildings or towers to get them above surrounding objects such as trees.

Infrared

Infrared (particularly scatter infrared) is a good choice for warehouse environments. This is because infrared is effective for only about 100 feet and is very susceptible to other light sources such as sunlight or bright office lights. Infrared has a transmission speed of about 10 Mbps. Following are the three basic types of infrared networks:

- **Line of sight.** This version works only when the receiver and transmitter have a clear line of sight.

- **Scatter.** In a scatter-infrared network, the transmitter bounces the signal off walls and ceilings until it eventually hits the receiver.

- **Reflective.** A reflective network uses optical transmitters that send the signal to a common point that then reflects the signal to the receiver, similar to the way a mirror reflects your image.

Prep Test

1 What do you call the weakening of a signal the farther it travels?

A ○ Interference

B ○ Attenuation

C ○ Crosstalk

D ○ Bandwidth

2 Which type of cable meets fire code specifications for false-ceiling installation?

A ○ PVC

B ○ Plenum

C ○ Fire-safe cable

D ○ Fiber optic

3 What do you call the amount of data a network can transmit at one time?

A ○ Interference

B ○ Signaling

C ○ Crosstalk

D ○ Bandwidth

4 Which of the following types of cable can be used in a 100 Mbps network? Choose all that apply.

A ❑ Category 3 unshielded twisted pair

B ❑ Category 5 unshielded twisted pair

C ❑ Thinnet coaxial

D ❑ Thicknet coaxial

E ❑ Fiber optic

5 Suppose that four computers are on a network and you want to run thinnet coaxial cable to connect them. Which computer will be too far away for this to work?

A ○ Computer 1: 310 feet

B ○ Computer 2: 345 feet

C ○ Computer 3: 275 feet

D ○ Computer 4: 335 feet

E ○ None

6 What type of connector does thinnet coaxial cable use?

A ○ BNC

B ○ AUI

C ○ RJ-45

D ○ RJ-11

7 What is the minimum grade of cable that can be used for data transmission?

A ○ Category 1

B ○ Category 3

C ○ Category 4

D ○ Category 5

8 Which type of wireless system bounces signals off walls and ceilings until it reaches the receiver?

A ○ Spread-spectrum radio

B ○ Reflective infrared

C ○ Microwave

D ○ Scatter infrared

9 (True/False) Lasers need a clear line of sight to work properly.

10 Which system uses a single frequency to transmit?

A ○ Narrow-band radio

B ○ Spread spectrum

C ○ Reflective infrared

D ○ Modulated laser

Answers

1 *B.* Attenuation is the weakening of a signal as it travels. *Review "Attenuation" and "Signal Transmission" for more information on attenuation and signaling.*

2 *B.* Plenum-grade cable meets fire codes. *Review the "Plenum" section.*

3 *D.* Bandwidth is the measure of a network's speed when transmitting data. *Review the "Bandwidth" section as well as Table 10-1.*

4 *B; E.* Category 5 unshielded twisted pair and fiber optic are the only two types of cable certified to carry data at 100 Mbps. *Table 10-2 lists the types of cables and their specifications.*

5 *E. None.* The maximum cable length of thinnet coaxial cable is 185 meters, or 607 feet. *Table 10-2 lists cable lengths.*

6 *A.* Thinnet cable uses BNC connectors, unshielded twisted-pair cable uses RJ-45 connectors, and thicknet cable uses AUI connectors. *Review "Thinnet" and "Thicknet" to cover this material.*

7 *B.* Category 3 is the minimum classification used to carry data. *Review the "Unshielded twisted pair" section.*

8 *D.* Scatter infrared bounces signals off walls and ceilings to reach the receiver. *See the "Infrared" section to review how infrared works.*

9 *True.* If there is not a clear line of sight, the laser beam will not reach its intended receiver. *Review the "Infrared" section.*

10 *A.* Narrow-band radio uses a single radio frequency to transmit data. *Review the "Radio wave" section.*

Chapter 11

Client Systems

Exam Objectives

▶ Identifying common errors associated with components required for communications

▶ Diagnosing and resolving common connectivity problems with cards, cable, and related hardware

*T*his chapter familiarizes you with a number of network operating system clients. Remember, though, that you are studying for a Microsoft certification exam. Consequently, don't expect to be quizzed too much on OS/2, UNIX, and Macintosh networking clients. Instead, become familiar with Windows 95 and Windows NT Workstation. Older versions of Microsoft operating systems such as Windows, Windows for Workgroups, and MS-DOS are also fair game, but not heavily emphasized. The Networking Essentials exam won't question you on the specifics of various network operating system clients, but it does reference these clients in different scenarios. As such, a working understanding of each client system as well as the Microsoft workhorse operating systems (Windows 95 and Windows NT) will enable you to sail right through the client questions on the test.

In the old days of networking, a network operating system was an add-on component to the client operating system. As early as the first release of Windows for Workgroups, Microsoft products provided networking support as part of the client operating system. The marrying of the two systems increased networking speed, reliability, and efficiency. Although modern client operating systems come with networking support built in, a network adapter card must be installed in the machine before it can connect to the network. In this chapter, you examine the different types of card architectures. You also find out about installing network adapter cards and their various settings, such as IRQs, base I/O ports, and base memory address. Finally, you look at troubleshooting tips for resolving conflicts with the previously mentioned network adapter card settings. For additional troubleshooting tips on cables and related hardware, refer to Chapter 9.

Quick Assessment

1 _____ is a Microsoft desktop operating system that supports multiple processors to provide true multitasking.

2 _____ is an operating system used primarily for servers running the TCP/IP protocol for network communication needs.

3 _____ supports advanced power management and Plug-and-Play hardware, so it is the preferred operating system for laptop computers.

4 _____ is IBM's operating system for PCs.

5 A(n) _____ is a hardware line to the CPU that a device can use to request service.

6 The _____ provides a channel through which data flows from the CPU to the system hardware.

7 The _____ identifies a location in system RAM where a network adapter card stores data to be transferred to or from the CPU.

8 A(n) _____ _____ refers to all protocol layers that must work together for a system to communicate on a network.

9 The _____ bus is used in most Pentium computers and supports the Plug-and-Play standard.

10 _____ _____ _____ is the bus designed by IBM that allows the CPU to be freed from handling device I/O on cards that support bus mastering.

Answers

1 *Windows NT Workstation.* For more details, look through the "Windows NT Workstation" section.

2 *UNIX.* A good overview of UNIX is in the "UNIX" section.

3 *Windows 95.* Read the "Windows 95" section.

4 *OS/2.* Check out the "OS/2" section for more information.

5 *IRQ.* Read the "Troubleshooting network adapters" section.

6 *Base I/O port.* Read the "Troubleshooting network adapters" section.

7 *Base memory address.* Read the "Troubleshooting network adapters" section.

8 *Protocol stack.* Look over the "Protocol stacks" section to find out more.

9 *PCI.* Review the "Card installation" section.

10 *Micro Channel Architecture.* The "Card installation" section provides a good overview of PC architecture.

Client Operating Systems

Concentrate on the Microsoft operating systems. Windows NT Workstation and Windows 95 are the most popular operating systems in use today and are emphasized on the certification test.

Windows 95

Windows 95 is the successor of Windows 3.11, Windows for Workgroups, and MS-DOS. Windows 95 offers the following enhancements over these older versions of Microsoft operating systems:

- **More intuitive user interface.** The interface is easy to learn and use. Because of desktop design features such as icons, the interface is easy to administer and manage for novices and experts alike.

- **32-bit operating system architecture.** The architecture offers superior resource handling, which results in a more stable operating environment. The crash-resistant 32-bit subsystems included with Windows 95 also improve stability.

- **Preemptive multitasking.** In a preemptive multitasking environment, the operating system takes responsibility for allocating resources. Previous versions of Microsoft operating systems used cooperative multitasking, which depended on the applications to voluntarily release resources.

- **Plug-and-Play technology.** Hardware written to the Plug-and-Play standard can identify itself and its settings to the operating systems. If a device is reconfigured or a new device is added, the operating system recognizes the change and reacts accordingly.

- **Integrated networking support.** Windows 95 includes 32-bit networking components that allow the operating system to function in all major networking environments such as Microsoft Networks, NetWare, UNIX, and Banyan. The operating system also includes network services such as file and print sharing.

- **Centralized security and system policies.** Windows 95 uses pass-through security to allow user accounts to be located on a network server. User accounts may be based on Microsoft, Banyan, or Novell directory services. This allows a network administrator to develop centralized security and account management.

- **Built-in support for mail, fax, and other telecommunications functions.** A universal in-box is provided for all applications written to the Messaging Applications Programming Interface (MAPI). The Telephony Applications Programming Interface (TAPI) is provided also to ensure consistent modem operations across applications.

- ✓ **Support for mobile services.** Windows 95 supports the PCMCIA standard and hot docking and undocking of devices. This allows a computer running Windows 95 to change from a network computing device to a mobile computing device without reconfiguration.

- ✓ **Multimedia capability.** Two new 32-bit components have been added to Windows 95: the CD-ROM file system (CDFS) and the video playback engine. Both greatly improve the performance of multimedia applications for business and entertainment.

- ✓ **Long filename support.** Windows 95 uses a virtual file allocation table (VFAT) to provide support for filenames up to 255 characters long. Filenames can be mixed case and can include spaces. An 8.3 format filename is also created to maintain compatibility with older operating systems.

Windows NT Workstation

Windows NT Workstation can function alone as a desktop operating system, or it can be a part of a network in either a workgroup or a Windows NT domain. Windows NT Workstation supports multiple processors as well as preemptive multitasking for true multitasking performance.

NT Workstation also provides local security for files, folders, printers, and other resources. Users must be authenticated by either the local computer or a directory services provider. NT Workstation can use an NT domain or directory services from Banyan or Novell to authenticate users.

Another benefit of NT that improves system stability is the way that NT supports applications. Each application is run in its own memory space. If an application fails, it will not affect the operations of other applications.

You need to be able to differentiate between Windows 95 and Windows NT for the certification test. **Windows 95** has

- ✓ Less demanding hardware requirements
- ✓ Broader application and device compatibility
- ✓ Better mobile support through advanced power management and Plug and Play

Windows NT Workstation provides

- ✓ Higher performance
- ✓ Greater reliability through stability
- ✓ Better security features

OS/2

If you know that OS/2 is IBM's PC operating system, you know everything you need to know about this client for the test. OS/2 was developed before Microsoft Windows but failed in the marketing wars. (Bill Gates may have dropped out of Harvard, but he aced Marketing 101.) The newest version of OS/2 is a 32-bit operating system and provides 32-bit networking support. This makes networking operations fast.

Unfortunately, most of the functionality you are accustomed to having with Microsoft operating systems is not present. OS/2 Versions 2.1 and older do not support Windows Internet Name Service (WINS) or Dynamic Host Configuration Protocol (DHCP). This makes implementing OS/2 in large networks problematic at best. To enable OS/2 in a Microsoft networking environment, you would use the LAN Manager 2.2c client.

MS-DOS

MS-DOS is a 16-bit operating system, so it is somewhat challenged when it comes to high speed or heavy loads. Microsoft, however, has developed a fully functional MS-DOS networking client. The client, which is often referred to as LAN Manager for MS-DOS, includes a full redirector. The redirector is the software that allows a client to browse network resources and map drives to share folders.

MS-DOS clients do not participate in the process that maintains the browse list of network resources. Consequently, a network that contains only MS-DOS machines will not have a browse list, and connecting network resources may be difficult. The solution to this problem is to place a machine with any other Microsoft operating system on the network. The machine will become the browse master, and a browse list will become available to all clients on the network.

Macintosh

Macintosh clients are provided by Apple Computer as part of the Macintosh operating system. Macintoshes use AppleTalk as their communications protocol. Remember that if AppleTalk is used on either a token-ring or an Ethernet network, it is referred to as TokenTalk or EtherTalk, respectively.

Windows NT Server supports the AppleTalk protocol with its File and Print Services for Macintosh (FPS for Mac) product, which is included with Windows NT Server. FPS for Mac allows an NT Server to emulate an AppleShare file-and-print server.

On the Macintosh side, Mac TCP is another common protocol. Mac TCP, which is TCP/IP for the Macintosh, can be used with TokenTalk and EtherTalk cards as well as with dial-up connections. If a dial-up connection is used, Mac PPP is most often the dial-up protocol. MAC PPP is an implementation of the Point-to-Point Protocol designed to be used on Macintoshes.

UNIX

It may seem odd to talk about UNIX as a networking client because UNIX is so often used to provide network services. Almost all network operating systems, however, have both server and client capabilities.

When you think UNIX, think TCP/IP. TCP/IP is by far the most common protocol used with the UNIX platform. TCP/IP allows UNIX-based systems to interact with Microsoft Windows NT Servers. You could probably think of a number of ways that a UNIX system could act as a client to an NT Server. Following are two common methods.

Most often, when a UNIX system acts as a client to an NT Server, it is for network printing support. If the NT Server is using the TCP/IP protocol and has TCP/IP printing support loaded, the NT Server can accept incoming print jobs from a UNIX machine and direct them to a Windows NT printer.

Another occasion when a UNIX computer may act as a client to an NT Server is when the UNIX client uses FTP to move a file from the NT Server to the local system. The NT Server must be running an FTP service.

Although Windows NT and Windows 95 include support for many common UNIX utilities such as TELNET, RCP, RLOGIN, and REXEC, support consists of only the client side of the application. Windows NT and Windows 95 do not include the server components of these utilities.

Installing and Troubleshooting Network Adapters

Network adapter cards are often referred to as NICs, or network interface cards. NICs are produced by many hardware vendors, including Intel, 3COM, and IBM.

Card installation

One of the keys to NIC installation and configuration is to get the right card for the type of bus used in the system. Common buses include ISA, EISA, PCI, and Micro Channel Architecture (see Table 11-1).

Table 11-1	PC Bus Architectures
Bus Type	**Description**
ISA	Industry Standard Architecture is found in IBM PC, AT, and XT computers. The card originally supported an 8-bit data path, but was upgraded to support a 16-bit bus path.
EISA	Extended Industry Standard Architecture was introduced by a consortium of computer manufacturers called the "Gang of Nine." The EISA bus supports a 32-bit data path and provides compatibility for ISA.
Micro Channel	Micro Channel Architecture was introduced as part of IBM's PS/2 program. Micro Channel can function as either a 16-bit or a 32-bit bus, but is architecturally and electrically incompatible with ISA and EISA. It allows the CPU to be freed from handling device I/O by supporting bus mastering.
PCI	Peripheral Component Interconnect is used with most Pentium-based computers and Power Macintoshes. The PCI bus includes a very fast 32-bit architecture, but the PCI bus is probably more famous for providing Plug-and-Play support.

Depending on the system you are using and the NIC you are installing, setup procedures vary. The amount of work depends on the sophistication of the hardware. With Plug-and-Play hardware, you may need to only insert the new hardware, turn the system on, and start using the new hardware.

With older systems and older network architectures, you might have to locate available IRQs, base memory addresses, and base I/O ports as well as make determinations about access speeds and media connectors. These settings might then be applied to the NIC through jumpers or DIP switches.

Troubleshooting network adapters

If Plug and Play (sometimes affectionately known as Plug and Pray) is unsuccessful, or if the hardware doesn't support it, you must manually configure several options. You can use the MSD and WINMSD utilities to determine which interrupts, base I/O ports, and base memory addresses are free.

An *interrupt request line (IRQ)* is a hardware line over which devices can send requests to the CPU for service. IRQs are built into the computer's hardware and are assigned different levels of priority so that the CPU can make a determination about which request to service if multiple requests are received at the same time. Each device in the computer must use a different IRQ. IRQ 3 and IRQ 5 are the most common interrupts used for NICs; if available, IRQ 5 is the recommended interrupt.

The *base I/O port* provides a channel through which information flows from the CPU to the system hardware. The port appears to the CPU as a memory address. Each device in a system must have a different base I/O port. The most common base I/O ports for NICs are 300 to 30F and 310 to 31F.

The *base memory address* identifies a location in the computer's RAM. This location is used by the network adapter card as a buffer area to store data frames. Each device in a system must have its own base memory address. The most common base memory address for NICs is D8000. Be aware that some NICs do not have a base memory address because they do not use any system RAM.

Usually, installation falls somewhere between automatic configuration and manually setting options on a card. Most modern NICs include a setup or configuration utility that enables you to set various options and run diagnostics through a software interface. With such a utility, a NIC can be reconfigured without taking the case off the computer. You may still have to locate available resources, but automatic configuration will be quicker and less prone to error than manually configuring all the options.

OS configuration

The operating system configuration process for installing and configuring a NIC is sometimes referred to as the *binding process*. After all device drivers and protocols have been installed, an administrator may need to specify a number of configuration options, such as which protocols are bound to which adapters, specific protocol settings such as the data frame size and timeout values, and the priority of different protocol stacks. In Microsoft operating systems, the priority of the protocols is defined by choosing the default protocol, which is the protocol the operating system tries to use first to fulfill any requests for network resources.

Setting the most-used protocol at the top of the binding order under Windows NT improves network performance because that protocol will be tried first. This should minimize the number of timeouts that occur before a request is fulfilled. Unbinding unused protocols improves system performance, too.

Protocol stacks

Network protocols are often developed in modules, which are referred to also as layers. These modules, or layers, are collectively referred to as either a protocol suite or a protocol stack. (The network designers apparently couldn't decide on a good name for the design so they developed several synonyms for the same thing.) Each layer is responsible for a particular task or set of tasks. This makes design a little easier because each designer can focus on one small piece of the puzzle at a time.

You've seen one approach to defining a protocol stack. It's the OSI seven-layer model. Although protocols have been designed with strict conformance to the OSI model, rarely are protocol stacks implemented with all seven layers. Usually, some of the layers are combined. The OSI model remains an excellent reference model, but it is not a practical implementation.

Translating a protocol specification into hardware and software can be a difficult task. Many designers interpret ambiguous specifications in different ways. The result is hardware and software — written to the same specification — that is incompatible. Designers and administrators have faced these problems enough times over the years that support for open systems is growing.

Open systems are sets of hardware and software standards that can be generally applied throughout an industry. The OSI reference model has been used as one basis for developing open systems. Unfortunately, the TCP/IP community (by far the largest in the industry) has not embraced open systems. They argue that their protocol is already highly functional and open because it is available to everyone. Consequently, the impact of the OSI model and open systems has been relatively small.

Many protocol stacks are available, but for the certification test you need to be familiar with only the ones that affect local area networking the most. These protocol stacks are the following, all of which are covered in Chapter 3:

- Internet protocols (TCP/IP)
- NetWare (IPX/SPX)
- AppleTalk
- IEEE 802 family

Prep Test

1 To enable OS/2 in a Microsoft networking environment, which networking client would you need to install?

   A ○ DOS client

   B ○ OS/2 client

   C ○ LAN Manager 2.2c

   D ○ Enabling OS/2 in a Microsoft networking environment isn't possible

2 Which of the following are common uses of a UNIX client in a Microsoft NT networking environment? (Choose all that apply.)

   A ❑ Printing from a UNIX machine via TCP/IP printing support to an NT print server

   B ❑ Browsing an HTML file from a UNIX machine on an NT Web server

   C ❑ Moving a file via FTP from an NT file server to a UNIX machine

   D ❑ Sending an e-mail message via SMTP from a UNIX machine to an NT exchange server

3 Which of the following network client operating systems supports advanced power management and Plug-and-Play hardware, making it the preferred operating system for laptop computers?

   A ○ UNIX

   B ○ OS/2

   C ○ Windows NT Workstation

   D ○ Windows 95

4 Which of the following network client operating systems, developed by IBM, was a forerunner of Microsoft Windows?

   A ○ UNIX

   B ○ OS/2

   C ○ Novell NetWare

   D ○ DECnet

5 Which of the following are the most common base I/O ports for network adapter cards? (Choose all that apply.)

   A ❑ 200 to 20F

   B ❑ 300 to 30F

   C ❑ 210 to 20F

   D ❑ 310 to 31F

6 Which of the following is the most recommended IRQ for a network adapter card, if the port is available?

A ○ IRQ 1

B ○ IRQ 3

C ○ IRQ 5

D ○ IRQ 7

7 Which of the following is the most common base memory address for a network adapter card?

A ○ D1000

B ○ D8000

C ○ D9000

D ○ E9000

8 Which of the following are valid protocol stacks? (Choose all that apply.)

A ❑ Internet Protocol (TCP/IP)

B ❑ NetBEUI stack

C ❑ NetWare (IPX/SPX)

D ❑ AppleTalk

9 The PCI bus architecture that provides support for the Plug-and-Play standard has a(n) _____ -bit local data bus.

A ○ 8

B ○ 16

C ○ 16 or 32

D ○ 32

10 Which of the following bus architectures, developed by IBM, allows the CPU to be freed from handling device I/O by supporting bus mastering?

A ○ EISA

B ○ ISA

C ○ Micro Channel

D ○ PCI

Answers

1 *C.* To enable OS/2 in a Microsoft networking environment, you would use the LAN Manager 2.2c client. *Review "OS/2."*

2 *A, C.* Two common occasions when a UNIX machine acts as a client on a Windows NT network are TCP/IP printing support and retrieving files via FTP. *Review "UNIX."*

3 *D.* Windows 95 supports Advanced Power Management (APM) and Plug and Play on PCI buses with PCMCIA adapters. Windows 95 also has lower resource requirements. These features make Windows 95 your best choice for laptops. *Review "Windows 95" and "Windows NT Workstation."*

4 *B.* Remember that even though Microsoft wrote the majority of the operating system way back when Bill Gates was only sort of rich, IBM owns the rights. That explains a few things. *Review "OS/2."*

5 *B, D.* Base I/O ports provide a channel through which data can move between the device and the CPU. The most common base I/O ports for NICs are 300 to 30F and 310 to 31F. *Review "Troubleshooting network adapters."*

6 *C.* The recommended interrupt, if it is available, for a network adapter card is IRQ 5. *Review "Card installation."*

7 *B.* The most common base memory address for network adapter cards is D8000. *Review "Troubleshooting network adapters."*

8 *A, C, D.* The group of protocols that come together to provide a communications path for a system are referred to as a protocol stack or sometimes as a protocol suite. Common stacks are IPX/SPX, TCP/IP, AppleTalk, OSI, and SNA. *Review "Protocol stacks."*

9 *D.* Don't miss the bus! (Sorry, I couldn't resist.) The PCI is the most modern of all bus architectures. It uses a 32-bit local bus found in almost all Pentium computers and provides advanced computing features such as Plug and Play. *Review "Card installation."*

10 *C.* Micro Channel had a lot of potential in the early days. It was fast, configuration was almost automatic, and it supported bus mastering, which greatly reduced the load on the CPU. Unfortunately, IBM Micro Channel never caught on as an industry standard. *Review "Card installation."*

Part IV

Installing and Troubleshooting Network Clients and Servers

In this part . . .

This is where the rubber hits the road. Now that you have a plan, it's time to put the plan into action. So far in this book, I have discussed a number of different technologies from a somewhat theoretical perspective. Now it's time to see how some of those standards are implemented. It's time also to match the correct technologies to different networks.

On the certification test, implementation is tested heavily, almost as heavily as standards and terminology. After all, most MCSEs work as technology experts. Part of that job requirement is the ability to make things happen. By the time you finish this part, you should feel comfortable tackling almost any network implementation assignment.

One of the key troubleshooting skills that many IS professionals are lacking is problem determination. You use problem determination to break a problem into smaller pieces, and then you eliminate the pieces one by one until the problem is obvious. In addition to understanding the technical information in this part, you need to understand basic problem determination procedures. If you develop a set of questions to ask to locate a problem with a particular technology, you can quickly answer the troubleshooting questions on the test. If you don't develop a systematic procedure, you are left with a trial-and-error approach and will find the troubleshooting questions frustrating. Troubleshooting is the topic you should concentrate on in this part, because the test contains lots of troubleshooting questions.

Chapter 12
Clients and Servers

● ●

Exam Objectives

▶ Implementing a NetBIOS naming scheme for all computers on a given network

▶ Comparing a client/server network with a peer-to-peer network

▶ Comparing a file-and-print server with an application server

▶ Comparing user-level security with access permission assigned to a shared directory on a server

● ●

*C*lient systems represent the majority of systems on a network. When configuring client systems in an organization, you must consider a number of factors. The certification test stresses the NetBIOS naming scheme, type of networking model, and type of security model.

Understanding NetBIOS is essential to planning a naming scheme for network clients, for groups, and for accessing resources. After you define a scheme, you then must decide which network model is best suited to the organization. The decision between client/server and peer-to-peer networking generally isn't difficult because Microsoft has a magic number of users that defines when each should be used. You may need to take off your shoes and socks to do some quick calculation as to whether you have more than the recommended users for a peer-to-peer network, but that is allowed when taking the certification test. In fact, they even supply you with a calculator!

In larger networks, specialized servers such as file-and-print servers, application servers, communications servers, and Web servers handle the workload generated by the clients on the network. For the certification exam, be aware of the specific task accomplished by each type of server.

After the naming scheme, network model, and servers are in place, it's time to implement security. System administrators can set password policies that require a minimum number of characters in a password and that cause passwords to expire on a regular basis. Two security models, password-protected shares and access permissions, are presented in this chapter, and you examine them to see which is the more secure.

Quick Assessment

Implementing a NetBIOS naming scheme

1 Another name for the client component of a Microsoft operating system is a(n) _____. Each network operating system supplies this component to allow a computer to access resources from a server.

2 Shared _____ and shared _____ are the most common examples of shared resources on a network.

3 The _____ _____ _____ uses the format \\ServerName\ShareName.

Comparing client/server and peer-to-peer networks

4 A(n) _____ is a group of computers that do not share a common set of user accounts.

5 A(n) _____ is a group of computers that do share a common set of user accounts as well as a common security context.

6 Servers in a Microsoft Windows NT domain environment are usually _____ _____ servers.

7 In a(n) _____, all members are treated equally, and all members act as both a client and a server in equal proportions.

Comparing file-and-print and application servers

8 A(n) _____ server is used to process data flow and e-mail messages between networks.

9 A(n) _____ server is primarily responsible for storing data and files.

10 A(n) _____ server stores and runs large databases.

Comparing user-level security to a shared directory

11 (True/False) When using user-level security on a Windows 95 computer, the person sharing the information must give the person accessing the information a password in order to connect to the share.

Answers

1 *Redirector.* In the "Resource names" section, look for information about the Universal Naming Convention to find out more about redirectors.

2 *Directories; printers.* Check out the "Resource names" section.

3 *Universal naming convention.* More on this in the "Resource names" section.

4 *Workgroup.* Check out the "Workgroup model" section on connecting network clients to workgroups or domains.

5 *Domain.* Check out the "Workgroup model" section.

6 *Windows NT.* You'll want to pay close attention to the section on workgroups and domains. Refer to the "Client/Server Network versus Peer-to-Peer Network" section for more information.

7 *Workgroup.* You'll want to pay close attention to the section on workgroups and domains. Refer to the "Client/Server Network versus Peer-to-Peer Network" section for more information.

8 *Communications.* Read the " Different Types of Servers " section.

9 *File-and-print.* Read the "Different Types of Servers" section.

10 *Application.* Read the "Different Types of Servers" section.

11 *False.* When using user-level security, a user's ability to access a share is determined by the account he used to log on. Read more about security in *"Share-Level versus User-Level Security."*

Implementing a NetBIOS Naming Scheme

For computers on a network to communicate, they need a way to identify themselves to one another. This can be accomplished by using various naming schemes. In this section, you examine the NetBIOS naming scheme and how it works with network names for accounts, computers, and resources.

Account names

An *account* is a collection of all the information that relates to an individual user or group of users on a network. This information includes user name, password, and permissions. Individual users are grouped in one of two possible models: domain or workgroup. Unique account names are used to identify different workgroups and domains just as they are used to identify individual user accounts.

Computer names

You've heard the saying, "You can call me Dan or you can call me Stan, just as long as you don't forget to call me for dinner!" It's not important to that person what name he goes by, just as long as he gets something to eat. Well, much in the same way, a computer may have many titles that it can answer to depending on which protocol, process, or device it is communicating with at the moment. Because all computing processes aren't able to use the same naming scheme to communicate, we need a process for translation (or name resolution) from one method to another.

For example, suppose that a data frame addressed to a computer is sent along the network. The receiving computer contains a MAC address of 00-60-98-06-32-01, which identifies the computer. The address consists of hexadecimal code; at the Physical level a computer is known by this code. Numbering systems like this are easy for computers to understand, but are difficult for mere mortals to use and remember. A name such as Sales Printer would be easier for people to use.

All Microsoft networking is based on NetBIOS (Network Basic Input/Output System). NetBIOS is an application programming interface that you implement as a service under Windows NT. A NetBIOS name, also known as a NetBIOS computer name or a *friendly name,* offers a way to identify each computer in a Microsoft network. The name must be 15 characters or less and unique to the network. Networks that use the TCP/IP protocol must convert the NetBIOS computer name to an IP address before communications can occur. This can be accomplished by using the Windows Internet Name Service (WINS), or the Domain Name Service (DNS), or both.

All computers in a Microsoft network must have a NetBIOS computer name. Implementing a NetBIOS naming scheme is fairly straightforward. As mentioned, names must be 15 characters or less and they must be unique. The following illustrates an example in which the computer name is derived from department and associate names. The corresponding MAC address and IP address are listed to illustrate two additional ways to identify the same computer:

Computer Name	MAC Address	IP Address
ENG_SUSAN	00-60-98-06-32-01	131.107.2.200
ENG_ROB	00-58-23-05-12-09	131.107.2.201
SALES_JIM	00-34-38-67-32-91	131.107.2.150
SALES_LISA	01-66-21-78-99-07	131.107.2.151
ADMIN_KYLE	01-45-77-78-21-56	131.107.2.65
ADMIN_AMY	00-21-37-56-87-09	131.107.2.66

Resource names

Every resource on the network, whether it is a printer or a shared folder, must have a NetBIOS name. Regardless of whether a computer is a member of a domain or a workgroup, that computer has the capability to make resources available to other computers through file shares and print shares. When you *share* a file or a printer on your computer, other users can access the files in the shared directory or send print jobs to the shared printer.

Access rights are the types of access a remote user has to a shared file or printer. These access rights vary depending on whether the computer sharing the resource is a member of a domain or a workgroup. Figure 12-1 shows the dialog box for sharing a directory as well as how to set a password for the shared directory. (This is covered in more detail in the "Share-level security" section later in this chapter.) Figure 12-2 shows the dialog box for sharing a printer. Notice the different options and remember which ones relate to printers and which relate to directories.

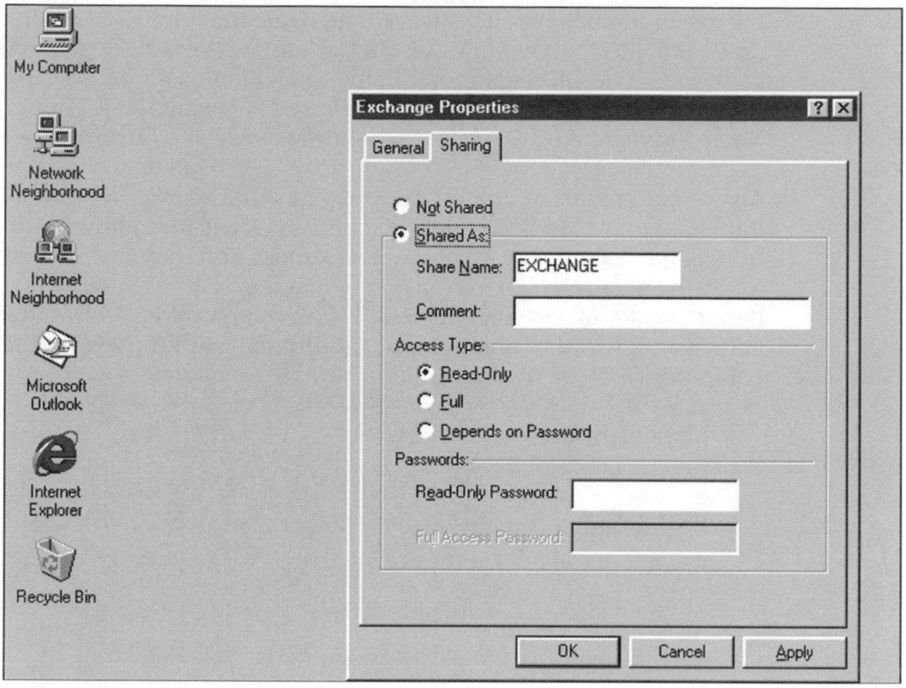

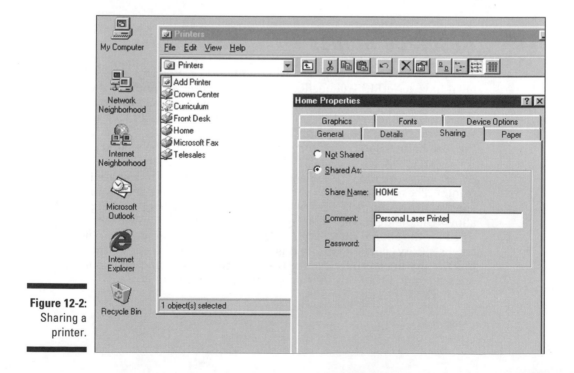

Figure 12-1:
Sharing a
directory.

Figure 12-2:
Sharing a
printer.

To access a shared resource, the client component, which is a software driver on the local machine, provides the capability to attach to the resource. The client component on a Microsoft operating system is sometimes referred to as a *redirector* because the client component (at least for directory access) is implemented as a file system driver. File system drivers handle requests such as a COPY or MOVE command on a local machine. Because the redirector is implemented as a file system driver, it can request a remote file and execute a command such as COPY just as if the file were on the local machine.

Implementing network client components (remember, they are known also as *redirectors*) as file system drivers makes interacting with shared resources easy. Redirectors for Microsoft operating systems exist for all major network operating systems, including Microsoft Windows NT, Novell NetWare, Banyan Vines, and VAX systems. When a user generates a file request, the operating system first determines whether the file is local or remote. If the file is remote, operating system components determine which network contains the resource by looking at the NetBIOS computer name for the remote server, and then forward the request to the appropriate redirector on the client machine. The appropriate redirector then establishes a connection with the remote server to complete the file request.

Client computers using Microsoft 32-bit operating systems such as Windows 95 and Windows NT can use a universal naming convention (UNC) name to access file and printers directly from other systems. A UNC name has the following format:

```
\\Computer_Name\Share_Name
```

For example, if I were to go to my Start menu, select Run, and then type \\Rhino\Memos, a new window would appear on the screen showing me the contents of my shared folder Memos that resides on my laptop identified with the NetBIOS name Rhino.

DOS and Windows applications do not support the universal naming convention. Therefore, on older versions of Microsoft operating systems, such as Windows and DOS, a drive letter must be mapped to a share name and an LPT port must be mapped to a printer share for the system to be able to use the resource. To map a share, I would use a command such as the following:

```
net use H: \\Computer_Name\Share_Name
```

I could then access the information in *Share_Name* by using the H drive on the local system. Mapping an LPT port to a shared printer works in a similar fashion. The command syntax is

```
net use LPT2: \\Computer_Name\Share_Name
```

You might not use command syntax at all. In Windows 95 and Windows NT, connecting to shared resources is very easy. The most common way to access a resource is to browse through the Network Neighborhood until you find the resource, and then double-click it. Navigation is the same as if you were accessing your local hard drive. Okay, maybe it's a little slower, but it looks the same. This method is a temporary way to gain access to a shared resource.

If you will be accessing a shared resource frequently, you may want to map the resource to a drive letter. After you find the resource through Network Neighborhood, the procedure of mapping a drive is simple. Right-click on the shared resource, and then select Map Network Drive. You are presented with a dialog box that asks what drive letter you want to use and whether you want this mapping re-created every time you log on, as shown in Figure 12-3. This method of mapping a drive letter to a shared resource has the advantage of establishing a more permanent link, but the amount of drives you can map is limited. You have only 26 available drive letters to work with and at least two or more are already in use on your computer. (Drive A is your floppy disk drive and drive C is your hard drive.) The decision between mapping a drive letter or simply accessing the resource depends on how often the resource will be used.

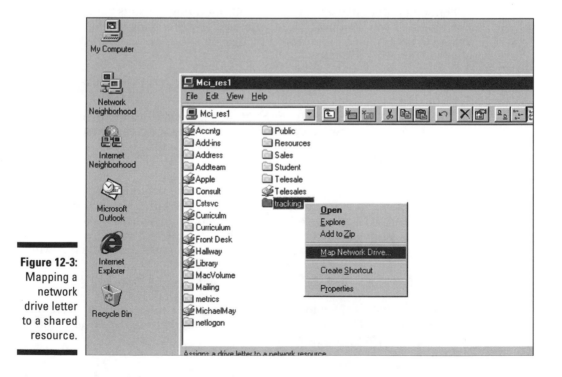

Figure 12-3:
Mapping a
network
drive letter
to a shared
resource.

Client/Server Network versus Peer-to-Peer Network

The two basic models of networking are client/server networks and peer-to-peer networks. This section points out the key differences between the two models, and illustrates how network communications are established for a Windows 95 client in both a client/server and a peer-to-peer network.

On the certification test, Microsoft uses synonyms for the two networking models. Be sure to remember that another name for a client/server network is a *domain,* and another name for a peer-to-peer network is a *workgroup.*

Adding a Windows 95 computer to a domain or a workgroup is accomplished in the same way for each environment. Figure 12-4 shows the Identification tab from the Network Configuration dialog box. Notice the Computer Name and Workgroup fields. The computer name is the NetBIOS name used to identify the computer on the network. The workgroup name is the NetBIOS name of the workgroup or domain to which the computer belongs.

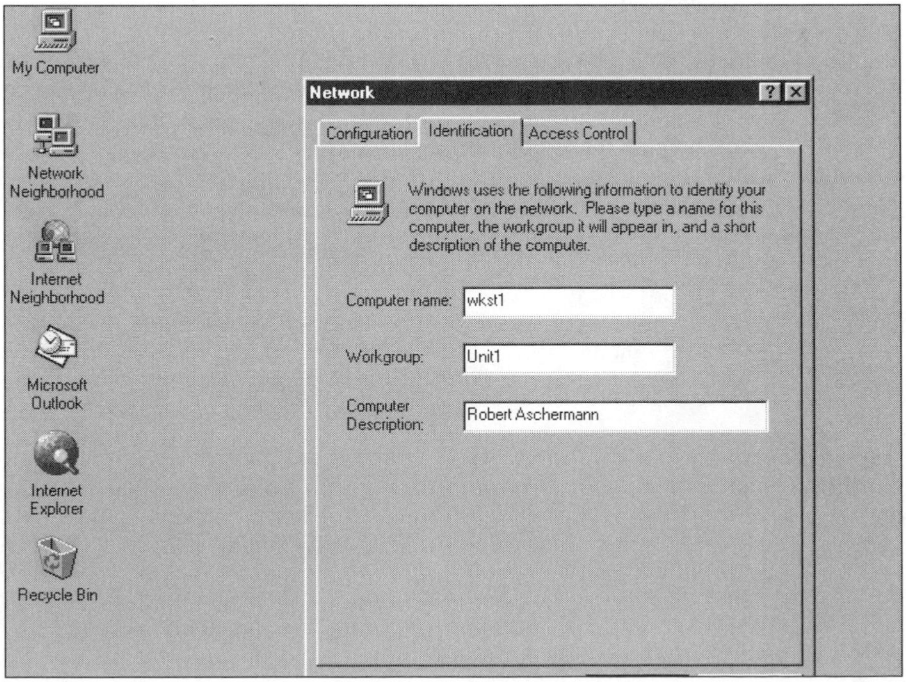

Figure 12-4:
Workgroup and domain configuration.

Microsoft often reuses terminology in a way that can be confusing. A Microsoft domain maintained by Windows NT Servers is not the same as a DNS domain. A *DNS domain* is simply a hierarchical name space used to map friendly names to IP addresses. An example of a friendly name would be `www.microsoft.com`. *Microsoft domains* are logical groupings of computers that share the same security information through the use of domain controllers.

Workgroup model

A *workgroup* treats all members equally. Each computer can be both a client and a server. Because a workgroup has no centralized administration or security, large workgroups are difficult to maintain.

For complete access to network resources, every user in the workgroup must have a user account on every machine. For example, if a workgroup has five users and five machines, and all users need access to all machines, twenty-five user accounts must be maintained.

User accounts and passwords associated with a particular user may have the same name on each computer or different names. The latter method increases the administrative efforts required to maintain a workgroup.

A workgroup environment has no single administrative authority. Consequently, each user must act as the administrator for his or her computer.

Workgroups have some advantages. They

- ✔ Are easy to set up.
- ✔ Work well for small departmental LANs that do not require centralized security.
- ✔ Do not require dedicated servers, so they are less expensive to implement.
- ✔ Do not require a dedicated full-time administrator.

For the certification test, workgroups are considered to be a valid network configuration for a network that contains fewer than ten computers, has no centralized security requirements, has no need for centralized administration, and must minimize cost. If all these requirements are *not* met, a domain should be used.

Domain model

A *domain* is a logical grouping of computers that share the same security provider. In other words, a domain is a central database of user accounts and passwords. Each user in the domain has one account and one password that provide the user access to every resource on the network that the user is allowed to access.

A Windows 95 computer joins a domain by specifying the name of the domain in the Workgroup field of the Identification tab of the Network Configuration dialog box. (Refer to Figure 12-4.) When you specify the domain name, the computer becomes part of the browse list for that domain. The computer does not *appear* in the browse list, however, unless file-and-print sharing is turned on for that computer, thus enabling its server component.

For a computer to be able to log on to a domain, you need to set the appropriate configuration options. Figure 12-5 shows the logon configuration dialog box on a Windows 95 computer.

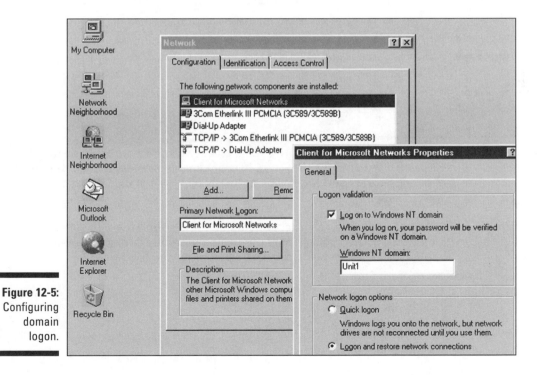

Figure 12-5:
Configuring
domain
logon.

To be able to participate in a domain, the Microsoft redirector, otherwise known as the Client for Microsoft Networks must be installed. One of the configuration options for the client is the capability to specify a Windows NT domain that provides security user accounts. This will provide user account authentication when a user logs on to the computer.

After installing the client, you will notice that on the Configuration tab of the Network control panel application, you have the ability to specify the Client for Microsoft Networks in the Primary Network Logon field. If this option is chosen, the user will be presented with the three-field logon dialog box shown in Figure 12-6. If Windows is specified in the Primary Network Logon field, the user will be presented with the standard two-field logon box, which does not include the Domain field.

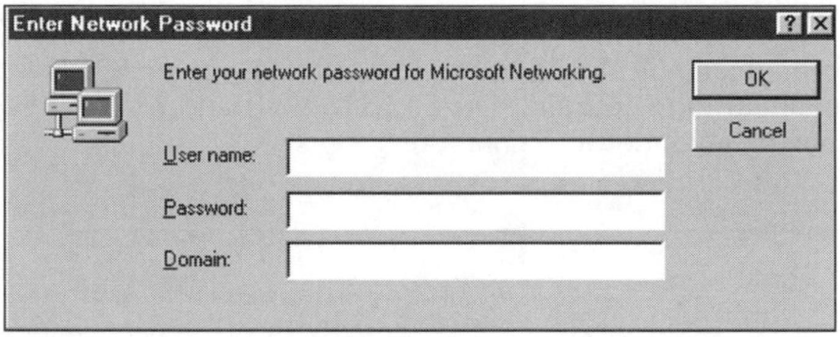

Figure 12-6:
Windows
NT Domain
logon
dialog box.

Different Types of Servers

In an environment with more than ten users, a peer-to-peer network in which computers act as both clients and servers will probably be insufficient. As a result, most networks have dedicated servers to meet the needs of multiple users and to provide services such as e-mail, database access, and printing.

Servers can perform a variety of complex tasks, but are often specialized in larger networks to handle only a specific task. For example, in a Windows NT network, different types of servers can include the following:

- ✔ File-and-print servers
- ✔ Application servers
- ✔ Communications servers
- ✔ Web servers

File-and-print servers

File-and-print servers are responsible for managing access to network resources such as shared directories and printers. A common use of this type of server is to create home directories for all network users. Each user would have a shared directory for storing his or her personal files, which would typically be mapped to the MS-DOS drive letter designation of H:\. When users open a file from their home directory, it is downloaded from the remote network location into the computer's memory for use. Basically, file-and-print servers are for data and file storage.

Application servers

Application servers provide the server-side functionality for client/server applications. A common use is for large databases that store vast amounts of data that's available to clients. Although application servers and file servers both contain data, the difference between the two is evident when you look at how the servers handle a request. When you request a file from a file server, the file is downloaded to your computer. When you query a database on an application server, the database stays on the server and only the results of the query are downloaded to your computer.

Communications servers

Communications servers process e-mail messages and data flow between the server's own network and remote networks. Using the Remote Access Service (RAS) under Windows NT, communications servers also can communicate with remote users dialing in with a modem or over the Internet. Due to the risk of outside intrusion on these types of servers, extra precaution is taken to secure access as much as possible.

Web servers

Web servers are used to host Internet or intranet sites. Users can browse HTML files, send e-mail, communicate in discussion groups, and download files from a Web browser such as Microsoft's Internet Explorer or Netscape Communicator. Web servers often serve as a connection device to databases residing on application servers and files stored on file-and-print servers.

Share-Level versus User-Level Security

After security is in place for the physical components of a network, a system administrator needs to ensure that network resources will be secure from hackers, unauthorized users, and uninformed users. Two security models have emerged to keep hardware and data safe:

- ✓ Password-protected shares, also known as share-level security
- ✓ Access permissions, also known as user-level security

 Once again, Microsoft likes to refer to these two security models by their synonyms. Be sure and remember that another name for password-protected shares is *share-level security* and another name for access permissions is *user-level security*.

Share-level security

Access control is used to determine the level of security on a system. If *share-level security* on a Windows 95 computer (remember, it's also known as password-protected shares) is chosen, a user at a computer can use only passwords to secure resources. This is the level of resource security used in workgroups. A user could share a directory from his or her computer with one of the following permission levels:

- ✓ Read-only (the ability to read files, but not to delete or add files to the directory)
- ✓ Full-control (the ability to read files as well as add and delete files in the directory)

Each permission level can be protected with a password.

Before remotely accessing a shared directory that has been protected with share-level security, users wanting access must receive the appropriate password from whomever established the shared directory. Upon attempting to open the shared directory, users are asked to provide a password. If they provide the read-only password, they have read-only permission. If they provide the full-control password, they have full-control permission. If they do not provide either password, they have no access to the shared directory.

User-level security

User-level security (also known as access permissions) is based on user accounts. In this security scheme, a user sharing a resource may grant different levels of permissions to individual user accounts. For example, I might share a directory and grant Johnny's user account read-only permission and Suzie's user account full-control permission.

When Johnny accesses the shared directory with his user account, he can only read the directory and the files within it. Suzie can do anything she wants. Neither was challenged for a password when they accessed the resource because their user accounts were already authenticated in the domain when they logged on. Their access permissions are based on their user accounts. Because access is granted at logon for individual user accounts, user-level security (access permissions) is a more secure security model than share-level security (password-protected shares).

Implementing a security model

Now that you have an understanding of the two types of security models, you may be wondering how they are implemented. On a Windows 95 computer, you implement a security model through the Access Control tab in the Network Control Panel application, as shown in Figure 12-7. Choose Share-level access control or User-level access control. If you select User-level, you must also provide the name of either a Windows NT Server or a Windows NT domain; this name is used to locate the central database of user accounts.

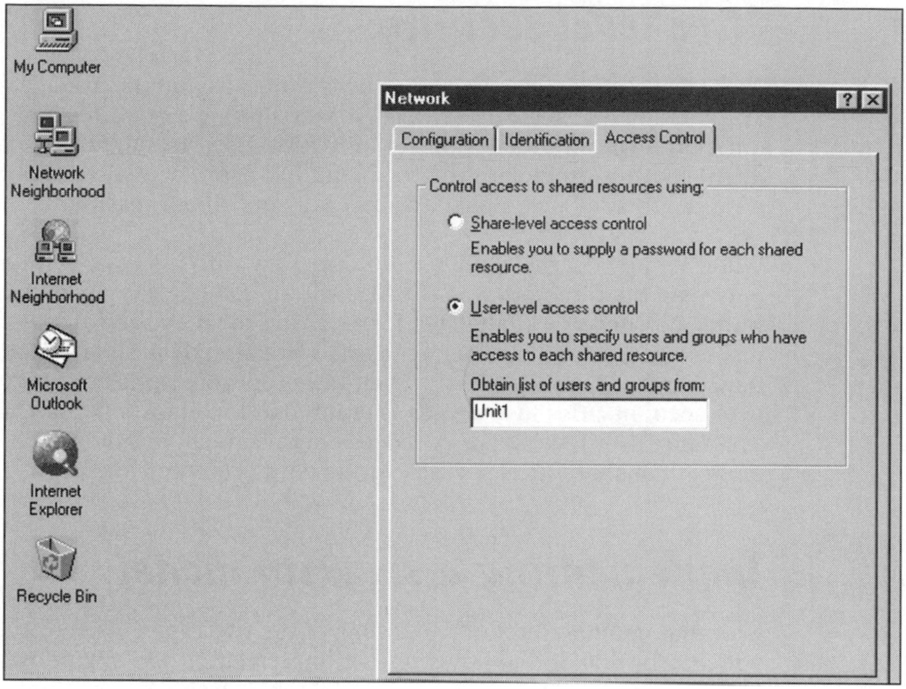

Figure 12-7:
Setting
access
control.

Prep Test

1 Which of the following is another name for a peer-to-peer network?

A ○ Domain
B ○ Servergroup
C ○ Workgroup
D ○ Companion networking

2 Which of the following is another name for a client/server network?

A ○ Domain
B ○ Servergroup
C ○ Workgroup
D ○ Realm

3 Which of the following is a valid example of the universal naming convention (UNC)?

A ○ \rhino\memos
B ○ rhino\memos
C ○ \\rhino\memos
D ○ //rhino/memos

4 In Windows NT, the server is responsible for processing connection requests made by what device that resides on the network client?

A ○ Director
B ○ Redirector
C ○ Client
D ○ Provider

5 Which security model provides access to resources as a result of a user logging onto the network?

A ○ Password-protected shares
B ○ Share-level security
C ○ NTFS security
D ○ User-level security

6 Which of the following servers is primarily responsible for storing large databases and processing queries for data?

A ○ File-and-print server
B ○ Application server
C ○ Web server
D ○ Data server

7 What is the maximum number of characters that a NetBIOS name can contain?

A ○ 15

B ○ 12

C ○ 256

D ○ 32

8 NetBIOS names can be created for which of the following network components? (Choose all that apply.)

A ❑ Individual user accounts

B ❑ Domains

C ❑ Workgroups

D ❑ Shared printers

9 Which of the following are true for a peer-to-peer network? (Choose all that apply.)

A ❑ Works well for small departmental LANs that do not require security

B ❑ Requires at least one dedicated server

C ❑ Is difficult to set up

D ❑ Does not require a dedicated full-time administrator

10 Which networking security model is the most secure?

A ○ Password-protected shares

B ○ Access permissions

C ○ Share-level security

D ○ NTFS security

Answers

1 *C.* On the certification test, Microsoft uses synonyms for the two networking models. Remember that another name for a client/server network is a domain, and another name for a peer-to-peer network is a workgroup. *Review "Client/Server Network versus Peer-to-Peer Network."*

2 *A.* On the certification test, Microsoft has a habit of using synonyms for the two networking models. Be sure and remember that another name for a client/server network is a domain, and another name for a peer-to-peer network is a workgroup. *Review "Client/Server Network versus Peer-to-Peer Network."*

3 *C.* The UNC name allows 32-bit Microsoft operating systems to access shared resources without first mapping drives or LPT ports. To connect to a remote resource, it must be specified by using the following syntax: *Computer_Name**Share_Name*. *Review the "Resource names" section.*

4 *B.* Redirector is the generic name given to a client component in a Microsoft operating system. Redirectors are implemented as file system drivers for accessing network resources, which is similar to the process for accessing local resources. Each network operating system must provide its own redirector for the client. *Review the "Resource names" section.*

5 *D.* User-level security assigns security permissions when a user logs onto the network. *Review "Share-Level versus User-Level Security."*

6 *B.* Application servers are used to store and run large databases. *Review "Different Types of Servers."*

7 *A.* NetBIOS names are limited to 15 characters or less. Review *"Implementing a NetBIOS Naming Scheme."*

8 *A, B, C, D.* For computers on a network to communicate, they need to identify themselves to one another. The NetBIOS naming scheme can be used to create network names for accounts, groups of accounts, computers, and resources. *Review "Implementing a NetBIOS Naming Scheme."*

9 *A, C, D.* Peer-to-peer networks are easy to set up and work well for small departmental LANs that do not require security. Additionally, peer-to-peer networks do not require a dedicated full-time administrator and do not require dedicated servers, so they are less expensive to implement. *Review "Client/Server Network versus Peer-to-Peer Network."*

10 *B.* Access permissions are more secure because users are more likely to give away a password to a resource than their network logon password. *Review "Share-Level versus User-Level Security."*

Chapter 13

Administration

● ●

Exam Objectives

▶ Choosing an administrative plan to meet specified needs, including performance management, account management, and security

▶ Choosing a disaster recovery plan for various situations

▶ Selecting the appropriate hardware and software tools to monitor trends in the network

▶ Identifying and resolving network performance problems

● ●

*T*his chapter is an overview of network administration. I describe a number of decisions that network administrators must make to create and maintain their networks, including how to organize user accounts, how to protect data, what level of documentation is appropriate, and which network operating system to choose. Some choices are dictated by what already exists in the environment or by political concerns. Other choices, however, can be based solely on the merits of competing technologies.

Choosing the right technology can be a difficult task requiring research and testing. This chapter describes a number of technologies that you may be faced with and the criteria you should consider when making a decision. One of the most important sections in this chapter is the fault tolerance section. *Fault tolerance* refers to methods for protecting data on your disks.

The proper use of user accounts and groups is another important objective that you should focus on for the test. Finally, performance tuning is touched on briefly. The test does not stress detailed knowledge of performance tuning. It does stress your understanding of the basic concepts, such as creating a baseline and identifying which resources may be bottlenecks in certain situations.

If you are already a network or system administrator, you may disagree with some of the points made in this chapter. That's fine. Just remember that the reason you bought this book is to pass a Microsoft certification exam. Microsoft, like others, has its opinions concerning system administration. Because it's their test you're taking, you get credit for knowing only their answer.

Quick Assessment

Choosing an administrative plan to meet specified needs

1 _____ is a fault-tolerant method that results in an exact duplicate of the data.

2 _____ is a fault-tolerant method that requires a minimum of three disks and can regenerate data on-the-fly if a disk is lost.

3 Rights and permissions should be assigned to _____ .

4 User accounts should be _____ within a user account database.

Choosing a disaster recovery plan

5 A good _____ procedure is the only way to ensure that data is protected.

6 _____ are small self-replicating programs that can alter or destroy data on a system.

7 A(n) _____ protects systems in case of a power failure.

Selecting the appropriate tools

8 _____ is the utility provided with Windows NT for performance analysis.

Identifying and resolving network performance problems

9 A(n) _____ should be created to track changes in network performance over time.

10 Performance monitors track the usage of _____, such as processor, memory, disk, and network.

Answers

1   *RAID level 1 — disk mirroring.* Check out the "Fault-tolerant systems" section.

2   *RAID level 5 — disk striping with parity.* Check out the "Fault-tolerant systems" section.

3   *Groups.* More on user and group administration in "Creating a Network Environment."

4   *Unique.* Check out the "User accounts" section.

5   *Backup.* Read the "Protecting the Environment" section.

6   *Viruses.* Review the section on "Virus protection" to find out what to do about these.

7   *UPS.* Check out the "UPS" section.

8   *Performance Monitor.* Review "Monitoring network performance."

9   *Baseline.* Review "Monitoring network performance."

10   *Resources.* See "Monitoring network performance."

Creating a Network Environment

Creating a network environment involves a lot of planning. The environment may consist of multiple network operating systems as well as different topologies and standards. User accounts should be organized to provide central administration. Application requirements must be considered to ensure that users have access to resources they need. A method for documenting changes should also be defined.

Network software

By *network software,* I mean the primary network operating system (NOS) used in an environment, such as Novell NetWare, Banyan Vines, or Microsoft Windows NT. At a minimum, the NOS should provide directory services (centralized account and password management) and the capability to secure resources based on those accounts and passwords.

The choice of which NOS to implement must take into account cost, performance, features, and politics. The choice is best made based on the merits of the technology, but political concerns often corrupt the decision-making process.

One school of thought says that standardizing on one NOS reduces support costs, thereby making a single NOS the most effective way to create a network environment. Another school of thought says there is no one best NOS for all jobs, so the choice of NOS should be based on the individual job. This increases support costs, but gives the company the flexibility to do more than its competitors.

User accounts

Each user in a network should have one private user account. Furthermore, user accounts should be unique to the network.

By having a single user account, the user has only one password to remember and can access all resources that he or she has permission to access without having to log off and back on each time a different resource must be accessed. It also reduces the administrative load associated with maintaining user accounts.

Groups

Groups are collections of user accounts that can be treated as a logical entity. Groups are implemented in different ways depending on the operating system, but they all have the same purpose. When rights and permissions are assigned to groups instead of to individual user accounts, administration is much easier.

With Windows NT, the process of creating users and groups and assigning rights and permissions is summarized with the acronym AGLP:

- ✔ Accounts
- ✔ Global groups
- ✔ Local groups
- ✔ Permissions

The process begins by creating user accounts in a Windows NT domain. Then global groups are created in the domain, and the user accounts are placed into the appropriate global groups. Local accounts are then created in the resource domains, and appropriate permissions for various resources are assigned to the local groups.

The final phase involves placing the appropriate global groups from the account domain into the correct local groups in the resource domains. This completes the process of granting rights and permissions to user accounts.

All rights and permissions should be based on group membership, not individual user accounts. Consequently, all administration can be accomplished from the accounts domain by simply moving users into and out of the global groups in the accounts domain. An administrator can quickly see what permissions a user has for a resource by looking at the groups to which the user belongs.

Protecting the Environment

Protection can mean many things. For some, it means to prevent unauthorized access of resources. For others, it means protecting valuable data from disk crashes or power outages. This section describes some of the ways you can protect the networking environment from both data loss and unauthorized access.

Security

Security is primarily based on user accounts, passwords, and access rights. Other levels of security, however, are available. One level that is often overlooked is physical security. File servers and printers used to print sensitive material should be kept in a locked room.

When you begin to work with user accounts and passwords, you should first develop an effective account policy. An *account policy* refers to the use of passwords. Passwords should be unique, should be at least six characters long, should contain numbers as well as uppercase and lowercase letters, and should not be reused within a reasonable time period. In addition, a user account should be locked out after a specified number of failed logon attempts, with only the administrator able to unlock the account.

After you have secure user accounts and passwords, the next step is to determine which user accounts will be able to access which resources and how much access those accounts should have. Assign the most restrictive permissions that will still allow the user to perform his or her job. For example, if a user needs to only read a file, do not put the user in a group with change permission; put the user in a group that has only read permission.

Virus protection

With the proliferation of viruses, some type of virus protection software is strongly recommended for every system exposed to a public network. Most viruses are just nuisances, but it takes only one destructive one to ruin your day.

Virus detection software, such as McAfee or InocuLAN, is loaded on each computer on the network and then scans the local hard drive and floppy drive for viruses. These scans can be scheduled periodically or can be forced to occur every time a file is accessed. You usually have the choice to scan all files or just executables. Some virus scanners even integrate with a screen saver and use that idle time to scan entire volumes.

If a virus is detected, you can instruct the system to notify you and log the detection. Some systems automatically repair the affected file. Repairs usually involve removing the virus code from the file; if that is impossible, the only repair option is to delete the file.

Several server-based virus detection programs are available. When loaded on the server, they protect all server volumes. Some will scan incoming and outgoing information for traces of viruses. If a trace is detected, the affected file must be repaired before it can be transmitted to the client or stored on the server. The most advanced server-based virus detection programs integrate with the Microsoft BackOffice suite to scan information stored in the Exchange Server message store, SQL Server databases, and SMS repositories. WWW servers store all their information as files in directories, so they can be protected with basic server-based virus detection.

UPS

The uninterruptible power supply (UPS) is a key component in a data protection plan. The UPS provides a constant power supply to critical systems in case of a power failure in the main power supply.

A UPS provides power in one of two ways. The most common source is a battery that is constantly charged by the main power supply. When the main power supply fails, the battery begins to discharge. The battery continues to power the systems connected to it until the systems shut down or the battery dies. If power is restored through the main system before the battery dies, the UPS switches the servers back to main power and begins recharging its battery.

More expensive UPS devices get their power from a rotary system, such as a diesel generator. These systems take a little longer to come online after a failure in the main power system, but they can generate more power and sustain it over a longer period.

A good (or smart) UPS will do the following:

- Prevent additional users from logging on to a server after a power failure
- Send an alert message to the administrator when a power failure occurs
- Gracefully shut down systems before the power source is depleted

The UPS is located between the server and the wall plug-in that the server would use if the UPS weren't present. The server is connected to the UPS in one of two ways: with a power cord or with a serial cable that connects to RS-232 ports on both the UPS and the server. The serial connection provides the real communications channel between the UPS and the server.

A UPS agent performs the process of reconfiguring the operating system of the server to prevent users from logging on, to send messages, and to shut down the server. The agent is software loaded on the server that interprets signals coming from the UPS and makes requests of the operating system based on those signals.

Following are some considerations when implementing a UPS:

- ✔ The UPS must support the basic power requirements for the systems that will be attached to the UPS.
- ✔ A good UPS needs to be able to communicate with the server about the power state. This usually requires a UPS agent that is compatible with the operating system running on the server.
- ✔ The UPS should guard against surge protection. Repairing a power outage in the main system often results in power spikes and unpredictable power. The UPS should condition the incoming power to eliminate these spikes, or should not switch back to main power until the main power system is stable.
- ✔ The life span of the battery is an important factor. Batteries degrade over time, and if not replaced could result in a failure in the backup system.
- ✔ A method must be available for warning an administrator when a power failure occurs.

Fault-tolerant systems

Fault-tolerant systems protect data by duplicating it to different disks or by splitting data across multiple physical disks. Fault-tolerant systems offer data redundancy. In a redundant system, data is still available even if part of the data system fails.

Fault-tolerant systems are not a replacement for good data backups! Backups are the only way to ensure that data is protected. It is possible to lose all data in a redundant system.

Fault tolerance has been standardized into a series of levels to allow hardware and software manufacturers to work together. These levels are referred to as redundant arrays of inexpensive disks (RAID) and range from 0 through 10. Microsoft Windows NT offers the following RAID levels of fault tolerance:

- ✔ RAID 0 (disk striping)
- ✔ RAID 1 (disk mirroring)
- ✔ RAID 5 (disk striping with parity)

Microsoft chose to implement level 5 instead of levels 2, 3, and 4 because level 5 evolved from the previous levels. Level 10 is not supported by Microsoft because its implementation of RAID is software-based, and level 10 (mirrored drive arrays) is highly dependent on the hardware being used.

Software RAID is effective, but given the choice between software and hardware implementations, you should choose hardware. Hardware implementations offer speed and flexibility that can't be matched by software implementations. Software RAID is often referred to as "poor man's RAID."

Disk striping (RAID level 0) divides data into 64K blocks and spreads it across multiple physical disks. The result is referred to as a *stripe set.* A stripe set combines multiple areas of unformatted free space into one large logical drive, which is what the user interacts with. A stripe set must contain at least 2 but no more than 32 physical drives. Stripe sets can contain areas from different types of drives, such as SCSI, ESDI, and IDE. Figure 13-1 is a diagram of a system using disk striping.

Disk striping offers a few advantages. First, combining free space from multiple disks makes better use of disk space. Second, spreading data over multiple disks and adding multiple disk controllers improves disk performance.

Be aware that disk striping does not provide any fault tolerance because losing a single disk in the array will result in losing all the data.

Disk mirroring (RAID level 1) duplicates a partition from one physical drive to another. A *mirror* is an exact binary copy of a partition. Any partition on a disk can be mirrored, including the system and boot partitions on a Windows NT server, and a copy of the data is always available. It's almost like having a continuous backup. When data is written to one disk, it is written also to the other. Figure 13-2 is a diagram of a system using disk mirroring.

Figure 13-1:
Disk
striping
(RAID
level 0).

	Data		
	= Data		

	Disk 0	Disk 1	Disk 2	Disk 3
Stripe 1	0	1	2	3
Stripe 2	4	5	6	7
Stripe 3	8	9	10	11
Stripe 4	12	13	14	15
Stripe 5	16	14	18	19
Stripe 6	20	21	22	23

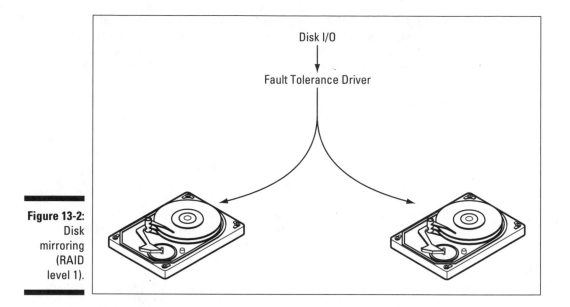

Disk I/O

Fault Tolerance Driver

Figure 13-2:
Disk
mirroring
(RAID
level 1).

Disk mirroring is the only way to protect boot and system partitions on a Windows NT server. If a drive containing the boot and system partitions fails, a fault-tolerant boot disk can be created that will allow you to boot the system from the mirrored copy of the boot and system partitions.

One disadvantage to disk mirroring is that it requires at least two disks, and one of the disks is pure overhead. In a mirrored system with two 2GB drives, only 2GB worth of data space (not 4GB) is available, which is 50 percent overhead. Hard disks are relatively inexpensive, so that may not be much of an issue. For large storage devices, however, disk mirroring represents a significant investment.

Another disadvantage to disk mirroring is write performance. Remember that each piece of data must be written to both disks. This takes extra time. Read performance, however, is improved because the operating system reads from both disks simultaneously if the hardware supports it.

A minor variation of disk mirroring that requires an additional hard drive controller is called *disk duplexing*. In a mirrored system with only one hard drive controller, having a mirrored copy of the disk may not be enough protection because you can't access either copy of the data if you lose your hard drive controller. With two hard drive controllers, as shown in Figure 13-3, you can implement disk duplexing. Duplexing results in higher performance and a higher level of fault tolerance because you can lose a drive and a hard drive controller and still have access to your data.

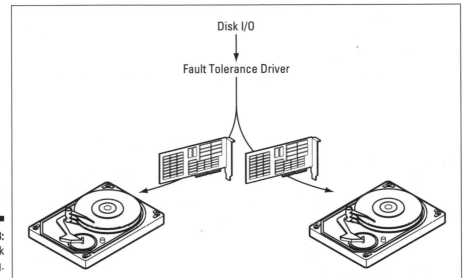

Disk I/O

Fault Tolerance Driver

Figure 13-3:
Disk
duplexing.

Disk striping with parity (RAID level 5) is the most popular approach to fault tolerance. It requires a minimum of three disks and will accommodate a maximum of 32 disks.

Data is striped across all drives in a fashion similar to RAID 0 (disk striping) with the addition of a parity block. The parity block contains a mathematical result generated by running an algorithm against all data blocks. Think of the data as a set of rows striping across all disks. Each row has a parity block, but the parity block for each row is alternated across each of the disks, as shown in Figure 13-4. Notice the location of the parity blocks.

The parity block for each stripe (row) is used to reconstruct the data in the event of a disk failure. The reconstruction process uses the same mathematical algorithm used to create the parity block to reconstruct the missing data from the remaining data and parity blocks. It's like an algebraic equation. If you know the values of all the variables (data blocks), you calculate the answer (parity block). If you know the answer (parity block) and the values of all but one of the variables (data blocks), you can calculate the value of the missing variable.

RAID level 5 can handle losing a single disk without any serious consequences. System performance will suffer as missing data is rebuilt in RAM, but the data can be recovered. If you lose a second disk before recovering the first, however, you lose the entire data set. Why? Refer to the example of the algebraic equation in the preceding paragraph. When two or more variables in the equation are unknown, it is impossible to solve the equation.

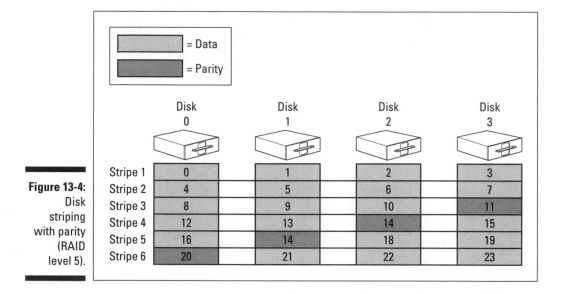

Figure 13-4:
Disk
striping
with parity
(RAID
level 5).

Disk striping with parity usually speeds up disk performance, but it may also reduce processor performance due to the number of mathematical calculations. Striping with parity also decreases overhead as more disks are added to the array. Overhead is calculated as 1 divided by the number of disks in the array. With three disks, overhead is equivalent to $1/3$ total disk space. With 32 disks, overhead is calculated as $1/32$ total disk space.

I can't stress enough the importance of good backups. Fault-tolerant arrays can be lost. In that situation, your only action is to recreate the disk array and reload your data from a backup. Don't be surprised if you see this situation in a test question.

Managing the Network Environment

One of the jobs of a network administrator is to ensure reliable network performance. If you were to look at a utilization graph for a network over a sufficiently long period of time, such as a day or a week, you would see a series of peaks and valleys that represent periods of high and low utilization.

The administrator must ensure that the network has enough resources available to handle the worst peaks. This is accomplished by analyzing the peaks and then deploying resources strategically throughout the network. A schedule might also be developed that diverts underutilized resources to areas that experience significant peaks.

The administrator should attempt to smooth out the peaks and valleys by permanently reassigning resources from underutilized areas to areas that are experiencing heavy loads. This is more of a preemptive procedure because the effects of peak periods will become less pronounced.

Monitoring network performance

Four basic resources are involved in any type of computer performance monitoring:

- ✔ Processor
- ✔ Memory
- ✔ Disk
- ✔ Network

Depending on the performance problem you are trying to focus on, you will emphasize one or more of these basic resources. For example, if you want to monitor the effects of running a mathematically intensive application, you would monitor the processor. Remember, though, that performance is a characteristic of all these resources working together. Don't forget to look at the entire system when evaluating a performance problem or establishing a baseline.

Most advanced operating systems include a built-in network monitoring utility. Such a utility can be used to establish a baseline for performance monitoring and preemptive troubleshooting.

A *baseline* is a realistic picture of resource usage for a system. Baselines use a representative sample of performance data taken from a system at different times over a period of time. A good baseline allows a network administrator to characterize system resource usage during various periods. If the administrator suspects a performance anomaly, the administrator can compare current statistics with baseline statistics to determine whether an anomaly exists.

Information used in performance tuning and troubleshooting comes from a number of sources. The most common include the following:

- ✔ Event logs that record errors and other significant events on a system
- ✔ Usage statistics that track who is using resources and how the resources are being used — often referred to as *auditing*
- ✔ Performance statistics that indicate resource usage in terms of processor utilization, memory usage, network adapter throughput, and so on

Microsoft Windows NT includes a tool called Performance Monitor that is used to track performance and establish baselines. Performance Monitor can display data in a graphical format that plots usage of a resource as a continuous line over time. Performance Monitor can also be used to generate reports and to log data for trend analysis. Logging data and storing that data in an archive is part of the process of establishing a baseline.

Segmentation

If you discover through your performance analysis that a network is overutilized, a common method for improving network performance is segmentation. Occasionally, a bottleneck can result from a group of computers sending each other a large amount of traffic (such as high-end graphics computers transferring large image files back and forth). A network administrator can use a bridge to put a group of computers on their own segment so that their traffic will not interfere with the traffic on the rest of the network.

Segmentation is most often accomplished by installing bridges or routers in strategic locations throughout the network. Segmentation with routers is performed to provide network security. One of the best ways to prevent unauthorized access to data over a network is to use a router to filter packets from network addresses that do not have permission to send data to the secure network. Segmentation with routers is often a part of setting up a network firewall.

Hardware upgrade policy

Every organization should have a hardware upgrade policy based on performance requirements. After a certain level of performance for a resource has been agreed on, it becomes the network administrator's responsibility to monitor that resource and notify management before performance is affected.

It is management's responsibility to provide adequate resources for the growth of the company. That includes proper budgeting and cost-benefit analysis. As an organization grows, its information systems need to grow along with it.

Correctly sizing resources can be tricky business. With so many unknowns, forecasting growth and planning for resources can be reliably accomplished in only the short run. If you overestimate your needs, you end up spending money on resources you don't need. If you underestimate your needs, performance suffers. Most administrators try to estimate what they need and then plan for a little growth.

Prep Test

1 Which disk fault-tolerance method makes a duplicate of a partition from one drive to another?

A ○ RAID 0
B ○ RAID 1
C ○ RAID 5
D ○ RAID 10

2 Which disk fault-tolerance level actually offers no fault tolerance?

A ○ RAID 0
B ○ RAID 1
C ○ RAID 5
D ○ RAID 10

3 Which fault-tolerant method is used most often and involves calculating a parity block?

A ○ RAID 0
B ○ RAID 1
C ○ RAID 5
D ○ RAID 10

4 What is the only fault-tolerant method that can be used to protect a system or boot partition on a Windows NT server?

A ○ RAID 0
B ○ RAID 1
C ○ RAID 5
D ○ RAID 10

5 Which procedure is the only way to ensure data protection?

A ○ Fault tolerance
B ○ Backup
C ○ Mirroring
D ○ Striping

6 What can you use to provide power to devices during a power failure?

A ○ UPS
B ○ Monitor
C ○ Generator
D ○ Battery

7 What do you call the small self-replicating programs that can alter or destroy data on a system?

A ○ Worms

B ○ Trojan horses

C ○ Viruses

D ○ @$!#%

8 You should assign rights and permissions to _____ rather than _____ to make administration easier.

A ○ Accounts, groups

B ○ Users, resources

C ○ Groups, user accounts

D ○ Resources, users

9 Which of the following should characterize user accounts in a networking environment?

A ○ Replicated

B ○ Duplicated

C ○ Unique

D ○ Reused

10 Which of the following is a realistic picture of how a system performs over a representative time sample?

A ○ Snapshot

B ○ Baseline

C ○ System log

D ○ Performance chart

Answers

1 *B.* Disk mirroring is the process of duplicating an entire partition from one physical drive to another. There are no data stripes. The entire partition is mirrored. *Review "Fault-tolerant systems."*

2 *A.* Data is spread across multiple physical disks, but without parity, data can't be recovered if one of the disks fails. Level 0 improves performance, but it offers no fault tolerance. *Review "Fault-tolerant systems."*

3 *C.* Level 5 is the same as level 0 except that a parity block is included for each stripe. This allows regeneration of data as long as a second drive does not fail before the first one is recovered. *Review "Fault-tolerant systems."*

4 *B.* Here's a little tidbit from the NT operating system. You may or may not see a question like this on the test. Occasionally the test reaches beyond what you might think you need to be prepared for. *Review "Fault-tolerant systems."*

5 *B.* Don't rely on fault tolerance to save your data. It is possible to lose fault-tolerant arrays. If that happens, the only thing that will save you is a good backup of your data. *Review "Protecting the Environment."*

6 *A.* Uninterruptible power supplies are used to protect servers and networking components. Most are based on a battery system and will alert an operating system as to the state of power so that the operating system can take action to protect data. *Review "UPS."*

7 *C.* Nasty little things. Most are just annoying, but some are downright vicious. Implement a virus detection and correction plan and don't forget to periodically update your virus definition files. *Review "Virus protection."*

8 *C.* Always remember AGLP when working with Microsoft operating systems. Accounts go into global groups, which go into local groups, which are assigned permissions. *Review "Groups."*

9 *C.* Keeping user accounts unique improves security, enhances the ability to audit resource usage, and makes administration simpler for the administrator as well as the user. *Review "User accounts."*

10 *B.* A performance baseline helps you determine whether something is out of the ordinary on a system or whether the company has outgrown the system. Think of this as trend analysis. *Review "Monitoring network performance."*

Part V
The Part of Tens

The 5th Wave   By Rich Tennant

"I can never remember — are the bubble
lights VESA or PCI?"

In this part . . .

Here, all the various troubleshooting sections are brought together. You find out about preventative maintenance tasks, such as making backups, and a number of troubleshooting tools to use in problem determination procedures. In addition, a quick review is presented to make sure you're ready for the test.

I hope you've scheduled your test by now. If not, what's the problem? It's time to get ready to go. Once the clock is ticking, it's show time. If you spend too much time thinking about questions, you'll either run out of time or talk yourself into a bunch of incorrect answers. The best way I know to keep you from second-guessing yourself is to pump you full of information. Use this part as your final review before going into action. After you start the test, be alert and trust in yourself. You'll pull through.

Chapter 14
Ten Test Day Tips

Review Your Best Notes before the Exam

I always have my best notes in the car with me to review just before the exam. Some people say that if you don't know it by test time, you probably won't know it. I disagree. Just minutes before the exam, it's nice to quickly review material that's guaranteed to be on the exam. This is a great time to look at those standards charts. Find a quiet room, take a minute to clear your mind, focus on the task ahead, and cram. It's amazing how much information can be stored in short-term memory and then dumped. This won't get you through the test successfully if you didn't also do your homework, but it might get you over the top if you are borderline ready.

Make Sure You Have Enough Paper

Most Sylvan testing centers are no longer using scratch paper. Instead, they give you a dry-erase board and a marker. For me, this is more difficult and messy than using scratch paper. You also don't have as much room to work with because you can't write as small. You can ask for additional boards, or you can request real scratch paper. Just remember that either way, you have to turn in your scribbling before you get your test results.

Relax!

I understand how difficult these exams can be, especially if you have never taken a Microsoft exam before. Your mind can play tricks on you if you are nervous. Just remember everything you discovered in this book, and you should do fine! As a Sylvan test administrator, I have seen the coolest people lose it on the test. (Those scenario questions are murder.) Needless to say, those folks didn't successfully complete the test. Remember that the timer doesn't actually start until the first test question is displayed. You have all the time you need to create tables and other notes on your scratch paper before you start the test.

Write Your Standards Tables

Memorize your cabling standards tables for Ethernet, token ring, and FDDI before going into the test. Then before you start the test, write all the information you can remember on your scratch paper or dry-erase board. This will help you keep 10Base2, 10Base5, 10BaseT, 10BaseFL, 100BaseT, and so on straight. Focus on cable lengths, transmission speeds, cost, and flexibility for ease of installation.

Don't Rush but Don't Take Your Time

It's better to have a few minutes left to review your answers than to have to answer a bunch of questions in two minutes. Even if you feel you have enough time to complete the exam, you may be presented with a few gigantic scenario questions near the end. Find the scenario questions and at least read them before answering all the other questions. This will give you a little extra time to think about them. Also, another question on the test might provide some insight into a scenario question.

Did you know that even though the timer expires, you can continue working on the question you are on? Keep this in mind if you are on a mind-boggling question for which you need plenty of time. Sylvan, however, is always making subtle changes to their testing software. Use this tip at your own risk, because the situation could change at any time.

Diagram Complex Questions on Paper

For questions with text-based scenarios, draw the physical layout on scratch paper. By drawing the layout while you are interpreting the answer, you may be able to discover and eliminate one or more multiple-choice answers. This process may help you eliminate wrong answers you might not have been able to figure out otherwise. This tip is especially helpful if you are a visual learner. Drawing diagrams is especially helpful when answering questions about hubs, bridges, repeaters, and routers. When faced with a scenario question, diagram the solution to make sure it's reasonable.

Don't Go Back and Change Your Answers

Studies have shown that your first instinct when answering a question is usually correct. I tend to fool myself into thinking that I answered the question incorrectly, and I change my answer. One test taker in the newsgroup said he went back and changed two answers that he now feels were originally correct. Before you change an answer, make sure you have overwhelming evidence that another answer is the correct one. Then again, a question you receive later in the exam may give away the correct answer in a previous question.

Mark Questions You're Unsure Of

I like to use the scratch paper to write down the number of the question and the two possible answers to which I have narrowed down my response. When I return to this question later, I can immediately pick up my thought process where I left off. Here is an example of what my scratch paper looks like after I'm finished:

6. **A** or C?

22. B or C?

41. Is this a trick? I think it's B, maybe C. . . .

The answer I think is most likely the correct answer is written darker or underlined.

Some Questions Use the Same Problem

Some complex scenario questions use the same problem but present a different proposal to solve the problem. You will know these questions because they are preceded by a blue screen. (No, this is not the blue screen of death, but it may as well be. I hate these scenario questions!) If you read the problem carefully the first time, you won't have to read it for every subsequent question that uses the same problem. Do, however, glance at the scenario to make sure nothing significant has changed.

Save Time on Scenario Questions

On the scenario questions that use required and optional results, you can save a minute or so if the proposed solution does not meet the required results. You do not need to determine whether the proposed solution also meets the optional results; just select the answer that says, "The proposed solution does not meet the required result or any of the optional results," and move on.

Chapter 15

Ten Online Resources

In This Chapter

▶ MCSE resources on the Internet

▶ Other MCSE resources

*M*CSE exam resources are like arrows. The more arrows you have, the better your odds of hitting a bull's-eye and passing the Networking Essentials exam. Here is a collection of resources available to help on your journey to MCSE enlightenment.

Some of the best information available for passing these MCSE exams is on the Internet. You can share information with hundreds of other MCSE hopefuls like yourself. Many outstanding resources are available with the most up-to-date information.

Microsoft Certified Professional Magazine Online

One of the best sites I've found on the Internet for corresponding with others who have taken these certification tests is at the following address:

```
www.mcpmag.com
```

Go to the Forum section of this Web site. You will find not only people who are studying for the test just like yourself, but also those who share their test-taking experiences with the rest of the group. I visited this site nearly every day while I was studying, and it kept me on the right track.

Figure 15-1 shows the opening page for the *MCP Magazine* Web site. Notice the link for back issues of *Microsoft Certified Professional Magazine*. The back issues contain test-taking hints, suggestions, and articles relating to the exams. These are professional articles by certified trainers and engineers who have completed the process you are engaged in.

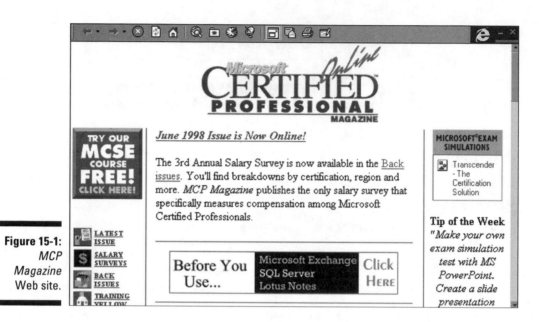

Figure 15-1:
MCP
Magazine
Web site.

Try this Web site. Then after you have passed the Networking Essentials exam, you can post your experiences for those still studying.

Cramsession.com

Cramsession.com is one of the many sites I've seen on the Internet for exam-related information. For a last-minute cram session:

```
www.cramsession.com
```

has everything you need. Use this site when you are just days away from your exam or as a guideline for exam objectives as you first begin studying.

Learnquick.com

One of the few sites that I visit often for MCSE information is the Accelerated MCSE Training page:

```
www.learnquick.com
```

This site is an invaluable source of information for MCSE hopefuls. The information is clear and accurate. A link for "Study Help" (see Figure 15-2) not only has information about different topics related to MCSE exams but also offers software, study guides, and white papers. I definitely recommend this site as one of the best MCSE resources on the Internet.

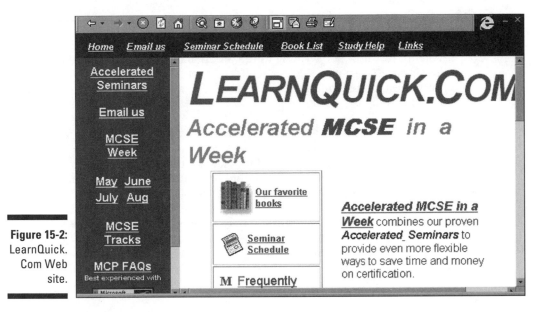

Figure 15-2:
LearnQuick.
Com Web
site.

MCSE Mailing List

A very helpful resource for determining what the exam covers is the MCSE mailing list. You can subscribe to this list and receive e-mail much like a forum. The information, however, is compiled and sent to you every day. While you read the various posts and brain dumps on exams, you can compile your own text file for each exam you are preparing to take. Copy important test hints and paste them into your exam-specific document. After a few weeks, you can create quite a large document. If you know you are going to take an exam a few months down the road, begin by compiling your document now, and you'll have an invaluable resource later!

To subscribe to the MCSE mailing list, send an e-mail message to majordomo@saluki.com with the following in the message:

```
SUBSCRIBE mcse your email address
```

For example:

```
SUBSCRIBE mcse cbran@capstonetechnology.com
```

If you are having trouble subscribing to the MCSE mailing list, contact Scott Armstrong (mailing list administrator) at `saluki@saluki.com`.

MCSE Mailing List Archives

If you are just now subscribing to the MCSE mailing list, you could be missing some very valuable exam information. Visit the gigantic vault of information in the mailing list archives. You can find the archives at the following address:

```
www.saluki.com/mcse_archive/index.html
```

See hundreds, if not thousands, of messages from users. If you had been a member of the mailing list, these would have arrived in your e-mail box as an easy-to-read digest containing about 20 to 30 messages.

After the page finishes loading, you may have to use your browser's find feature to search the subject line for relevant topics, such as TCP/IP. When you get some hits, display the message and read the post. I encourage you to keep a text file for each exam so you can cut and paste important information for studying.

Microsoft Training and Certification Page

Head directly to the source at the following address:

```
www.microsoft.com/train_cert
```

Here you'll find information on new exams, beta exams, and certification requirements. Figure 15-3 shows the opening page for the Microsoft Training and Certification Web site. A link on the site that you'll definitely want to visit is "Find an Exam," where Microsoft outlines the sections and topics covered on each certification exam.

In addition to exam objectives, the site offers other Microsoft resources such as course information, white papers, and case studies. Training and Certification is an important place to monitor if you are interested in taking a beta exam or if you need to check whether any of your exams are being retired. After you complete your MCSE, it is valid until an exam is retired; then you have a grace period to study for a replacement exam. For example, if you pass the Windows 95 client exam, you will eventually have to update when Windows 95 is no longer a valid client.

Figure 15-3:
Microsoft
Training
and
Certification
Web site.

Microsoft Training and Certification Download Page

Another site for a number of different downloads, such as exam/course grids, self-test software, and case studies is at the following:

```
www.microsoft.com/Train_Cert/download/downld.htm
```

The Microsoft self-test software looks exactly like the real test. These tests contain questions from the beta exams that were not included in the final exam. Use this resource a few days before your exam to determine your weak areas, or use it earlier as an indication of the material being tested.

Transcender Self-Test Software

The best self-test software I have seen for preparing for the real exams is Transcender exam simulation software. Transcender software can be purchased at the following:

```
www.transcender.com
```

These exams are challenging — and are probably more difficult than the real Microsoft tests! Each question includes an in-depth explanation as to why the answer is correct. As with most self-test software, you can use it to determine your weak areas a few days before the exam or as a guideline to prepare your studying.

Although the software is helpful for becoming certified, it is much more expensive than the competition. If money is no object, get some Transcender self-test software and get certified! Figure 15-4 illustrates Transcender's guarantee that you'll become Microsoft certified. Transcender will return your money if you fail an exam twice using its product.

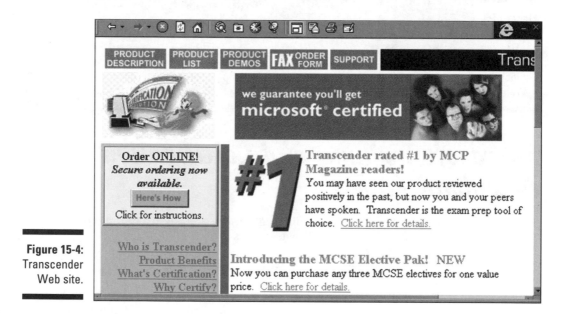

Figure 15-4: Transcender Web site.

TechNet

If you have not been using Microsoft's *Technical Information Network (TechNet),* get your hands on a copy. This monthly subscription CD is packed with information on Microsoft products and technologies. As shown in Figure 15-5, *TechNet* also includes resource kits that you would otherwise have to go and buy. The ability to search for relevant information is the most important feature of this product. I have used it for nearly every test I've taken.

You receive one copy of *TechNet* when you become a certified professional on an operating system. You get a year's subscription when you become a certified engineer. If you've been using *TechNet,* here are a few tips to improve your search results:

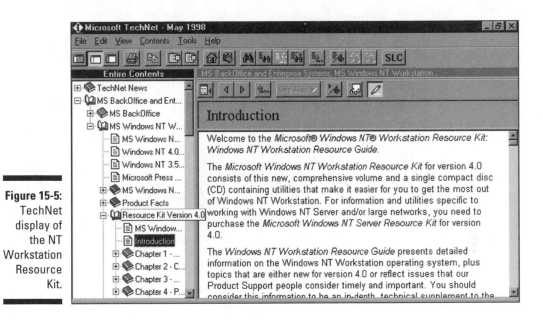

Figure 15-5:
TechNet
display of
the NT
Workstation
Resource
Kit.

✔ Define a subset. I usually create a subset called NT that contains only information related to NT.

✔ Adjust NEAR when searching to less than eight. I like to use three to four. This means that in a phrase such as *NT near NetBIOS*, the words can't be more than three to four words apart.

✔ Check the option to jump to the first highlight in a topic. If you don't check this, you will have to search the article for the hit, which wastes time.

You can use this tool along with all the others to get the most out of studying for your exam.

Part VI

Appendixes

"We're looking for applications that work well on a particularly open and distributed network."

In this part . . .

Turn here when it's time to check out how well you've studied. Included are two sample exams similar to the one you'll see at test time. You have more than 30 pages of questions to test your Networking Essentials knowledge. You'll also find an appendix of requirements for Microsoft Certified Professional status and an appendix about the contents of the companion CD — which includes demo tests and a collection of test tips from the book.

Appendix A
Practice Exam 1

● ●

▶ 90 minutes

▶ 42 correct answers to pass

▶ 53 questions

▶ No peeking!

● ●

1 Suppose that you own a small accounting firm with eight employees. You currently do not have any requirement to share data between accountants. You also want each employee to manage the security of his or her computer. Which network model is best for your company?

A ○ Client/server

B ○ Server-based

C ○ Peer-to-peer

D ○ User-level

2 Which statement best describes share-level security?

A ○ User accounts are maintained centrally, and permissions are granted based on those accounts.

B ○ Permissions to shares are controlled on each machine by using a single password.

C ○ An administrator defines who can access which network folders.

D ○ There is no security; all shared data is available to everyone on the network.

3 Suppose that you work for an advertising firm that has 15 computers. Over the next few months, you anticipate that your company will grow significantly. Each person on staff needs access to a graphics library and an article database to do his or her job. Which network model is best for your company?

A ○ Multimaster domain model

B ○ Server-based

C ○ Workgroup

D ○ Peer-to-peer

4 Which statement best describes a star topology?

A ○ All computers are connected to a single hub.
B ○ All computers are connected linearly on a single cable.
C ○ All computers are connected in a ring fashion with a single cable.
D ○ All computers are connected directly to the router.

5 Which method is used to control traffic on an Ethernet network?

A ○ CSMA/CD
B ○ Bus arbitration
C ○ Token passing
D ○ CSMA/CA

6 What is the common name for a 10BaseT network?

A ○ Ethernet
B ○ Fast Ethernet
C ○ FDDI
D ○ Token ring

7 Which of the following is a network layer protocol? (Choose all that apply.)

A ❑ AppleTalk
B ❑ Telnet
C ❑ ARP
D ❑ IPX

8 At which layer of the OSI model does a router function?

A ○ Physical layer
B ○ Network layer
C ○ Transport layer
D ○ Data Link layer

9 At which layer of the OSI model does a bridge function?

A ○ Physical layer
B ○ Network layer
C ○ Transport layer
D ○ Data Link layer

10 Suppose that you have two separate networks, one running TCP/IP and the other running IPX/SPX. Which device could you use to connect these two networks?

A ○ Gateway
B ○ Bridge
C ○ Hub
D ○ Brouter

11 ISDN is sometimes used to connect remote offices. Which of the following best describes an ISDN line?

A ○ It has a maximum throughput of 45 Mbps.

B ○ It has two B channels and one D channel.

C ○ It has a maximum throughput of 1.544 Mbps.

D ○ It is an analog connection technology.

12 Suppose that you have remote offices in New York, Chicago, and Albany. You need to connect these three offices with a WAN. You must have a transfer rate of at least 1 Mbps between sites. Which technology would be best suited for your requirements?

A ○ ISDN

B ○ Fast Ethernet

C ○ T1

D ○ 56K modems

13 Suppose that your company wants to consolidate all voice, video, and data communications on a single WAN connection. Which technology allows you to multiplex all three together?

A ○ ISDN

B ○ Ethernet

C ○ ATM

D ○ Switched-56K

14 What is the maximum length of a 10BaseT Ethernet cable?

A ○ 100 meters

B ○ 300 meters

C ○ 500 meters

D ○ 1000 meters

15 Suppose that your computer is 600 feet from the nearest hub. Which device would allow you to overcome this distance problem on your 10BaseT Ethernet network?

A ○ Router

B ○ Brouter

C ○ Repeater

D ○ Category 5 UTP cabling

16 What is the minimum cable requirement to run 10BaseT Ethernet network?

A ○ Category 5 UTP

B ○ Category 5 STP

C ○ Fiber optic

D ○ Category 3 UTP

17 Which of the following is a measure of the amount of signal loss in a cable?

A ○ Crosstalk

B ○ Attenuation

C ○ Signal-to-noise ratio

D ○ Interference

18 Suppose that Joe is unable to communicate on the network, but all other computers you check work fine. What is a probable cause for Joe's problem?

A ○ The network software was not installed.

B ○ Joe has forgotten his password.

C ○ The NIC in Joe's machine is defective.

D ○ The router Joe is connected to is down.

19 You have the following ports defined on your machine: COM1, COM2, LPT1, LPT2. Which IRQ is available for use with a network card?

A ○ IRQ 2

B ○ IRQ 5

C ○ IRQ 7

D ○ IRQ 10

20 What can you use to look at the packets being sent out on the network by your new Windows NT server?

A ○ Performance monitor

B ○ SNMP

C ○ Traffic analyzer

D ○ Protocol analyzer

21 After investigating a connectivity problem, you are certain the problem is the length of the cable connecting the machine with the hub. What can you use to test the cable to see whether it meets specifications?

A ○ Network analyzer

B ○ Protocol analyzer

C ○ Time domain reflectometer (TDR)

D ○ Tape measure

22 You want to ensure that your server is protected against power loss and power surges. What can you install to protect your server?

A ○ RAID disks

B ○ UPS

C ○ AutoBoot software

D ○ SNMP

23 Which tool is used to create and manage user accounts?

A ○ Account Manager
B ○ Server Manager
C ○ User Manager for Domains
D ○ Network Manager

24 Which RAID level would protect your data from a drive failure on the server?

A ○ RAID 9
B ○ RAID 3
C ○ RAID 5
D ○ RAID 7

25 Which method could you use to protect against both a drive failure and a controller failure?

A ○ Disk mirroring
B ○ RAID 1
C ○ Disk duplexing
D ○ RAID 5

26 By what name is 10Base2 cabling also known?

A ○ Thinnet
B ○ Thicknet
C ○ UTP cabling
D ○ Fast Ethernet

27 Which of the following statements best describes broadband transmissions?

A ○ Digital signaling over a single frequency
B ○ Digital signaling over a range of frequencies
C ○ Analog signaling over a single frequency
D ○ Analog signaling over a range of frequencies

28 Suppose that you're concerned that corporate data — especially the data on laptops — might be accessed by another company. Which method would best protect the data on your company's computers?

A ○ Compression
B ○ RAID 5
C ○ Encryption
D ○ Data mirroring

29 Which of the following protocols is routable? (Choose all that apply.)

A ❑ NetBEUI

B ❑ AppleTalk

C ❑ TCP/IP

D ❑ IPX/SPX

30 Which statement best describes the characteristics of NetBEUI?

A ○ Small, fast, efficient, non-routable

B ○ Routable, small, fast

C ○ Industry standard, cross platform, routable

D ○ Slow, non-routable

31 Suppose that your company has two divisions that need to communicate. Division 1 is running NetBEUI and using share-level security to share data between machines. Division 2 is using TCP/IP and user-level security to share data between machines in a server-based environment.

Required result: Both divisions must be able to share data.

Optional results: You want to standardize your company on a single routable network protocol, and you want to isolate broadcast traffic between the two divisions.

Proposed solution: Install a router connecting the two divisions. Install TCP/IP on Division 1 computers and configure them to support user-level security.

The proposed solution produces which of the following results?

A ○ The required result and both optional results

B ○ The required result and one of the optional results

C ○ The required result and none of the optional results

D ○ None of the results

32 Suppose that your company has two divisions that need to communicate. Division 1 is running NetBEUI and using share-level security to share data between machines. Division 2 is using TCP/IP and user-level security to share data between machines in a server-based environment.

Required result: Both divisions must be able to share data.

Optional results: Communications between the divisions must be fast; and you want to isolate broadcast traffic between the two divisions.

Proposed solution: Install a bridge between the two divisions. Install TCP/IP on all Division 1 computers and configure them for user-level security.

The proposed solution produces which of the following results?

A ○ The required result and both optional results

B ○ The required result and one of the optional results

C ○ The required result and none of the optional results

D ○ None of the results

33 Suppose that your network is experiencing a lot of broadcast storms. Which device could help isolate the broadcast traffic?

A ○ Bridge

B ○ Repeater

C ○ Hub

D ○ Router

34 Suppose that you are configuring your network with two segments. You want to route TCP/IP across both segments, but also allow NetBEUI broadcasts to be transmitted between the two subnets. Which device can you install to best facilitate this?

A ○ Router

B ○ Brouter

C ○ Bridge

D ○ Repeater

35 Suppose that you have remote offices in New York, Chicago, and Albany. The sites are connected via an ISDN modem from New York to Chicago and a T1 from Chicago to Albany.

Required result: Increase the connection speed between New York and Chicago.

Optional results: Add redundancy to the network; and multiplex all voice and data over a single WAN connection.

Proposed solution: Install an ATM link from New York to Chicago.

The proposed solution produces which of the following results?

A ○ The required result and both optional results

B ○ The required result and one of the optional results

C ○ The required result and none of the optional results

D ○ None of the results

36 Which layer of the OSI model handles error correction and flow control?

A ○ Network layer

B ○ Presentation layer

C ○ Transport layer

D ○ Application layer

37 Suppose that you are experiencing problems with the performance of your network servers. Which tool could you use to determine the amount and type of network traffic coming into your server?

A ○ Time domain reflector (TDR)

B ○ Digital volt meter (DVM)

C ○ Oscilloscope

D ○ Protocol analyzer

38 What kind of device is used to connect a NIC to a thicknet cable?

A ○ Network adapter

B ○ Transceiver

C ○ BNC barrel connector

D ○ Coaxial cable

39 Which statement best describes spread-spectrum radio broadcasts?

A ○ A single radio signal broadcast over a single frequency

B ○ A single radio signal broadcast over multiple frequencies

C ○ Multiple radio signals broadcast over a single frequency

D ○ Multiple radio signals broadcast over multiple frequencies

40 Suppose that you are designing a network for a new building. You generate a chart with the following information. The proposed plan will not meet Category 3 wiring standards for installation of a 10BaseT network. Which solution would be the most cost-effective for your new network?

Computer	Distance to hub
Joe	300 feet
Steve	200 feet
Anne	500 feet
Stacey	350 feet

A ○ Install Category 5 cables to all machines.

B ○ Install Category 3 cable to all machines; place a repeater between the hub and Anne and Stacey's machines.

C ○ Install Category 5 cable to all machines; place a repeater between the hub and Anne and Stacey's machines.

D ○ Replace all cabling with thinnet cables.

41 Which of the following is a characteristic of a token-ring network?

A ○ All computers have equal access to transmit data on the network.

B ○ All computers must arbitrate who can talk on the network next.

C ○ Servers are given a higher priority than workstations.

D ○ CSMA/CA is used to control traffic flow and communications.

42 Suppose that a critical server needs network transmissions protected from electromagnetic interference. Which cabling standard should you use?

A ○ Category 5 UTP

B ○ Category 3 STP

C ○ Fiber-optic

D ○ Thicknet

43 Suppose that you want to ensure the security of your servers by having a password policy. Which of the following will contribute to securing your passwords? (Choose all that apply.)

A ❏ Set a minimum password length.

B ❏ Lock out accounts if the wrong password is used.

C ❏ Do not allow users to change their passwords.

D ❏ Give everyone the same initial password.

44 To allow your sales force dial-in access to your Windows NT server, you would enable which service on the server?

A ○ Dial-Up Networking

B ○ RAS

C ○ UPS

D ○ Remote Boot

45 What are the two primary types of hubs?

A ○ Passive and FDDI

B ○ Active and regenerating

C ○ Passive and active

D ○ Regenerating and passive

46 Which of the following can be used to gather information about the machines on a network? (Choose all that apply.)

A ❏ SNMP

B ❏ SMS

C ❏ Protocol Analyzer

D ❏ Network Monitor

47 Suppose that you have just installed a network card in a new computer. The drivers supplied by the vendor do not recognize the card being installed. What is the most likely problem?

A ○ The card is not supported by the OS.

B ○ An IRQ conflict.

C ○ The wrong type of card for your network.

D ○ The network cable is not connected to the card.

48 Which protocol would you use to ensure that a network could be easily connected to the Internet and access all Internet resources?

A ○ AppleTalk

B ○ NetBEUI

C ○ TCP/IP

D ○ WWW

49 What types of connectors are used to connect two thinnet cables?

A ○ BNC barrel connector

B ○ Connector cable

C ○ Transceiver

D ○ RJ-45 connector

50 RG-58 (thinnet) cables require what device at each end of the cable?

A ○ 50-ohm terminator

B ○ 75-ohm terminator

C ○ Transceiver

D ○ BNC barrel connector

51 Suppose that you are developing a naming convention for the computers on your network. It is important that users be able to find each other and the servers easily. All user IDs on your network are between 8 and 12 characters. Which naming convention would satisfy this requirement best?

A ○ User machines: running series starting with computer1 and going to computer*xxx*. Servers: running series starting with server1 and running to server*xxx*.

B ○ A series of hexadecimal numbers starting at 000000 and going to FFFFFF with no differentiation between user machines and servers.

C ○ User machines: a combination of the user's full first and last names. Servers: labeled by function (that is, printserver, fileserver1, dbserver, and so on).

D ○ User machines: same as the user's logon name. Servers: labeled by function (that is, printserver, fileserver1, dbserver, and so on).

52 Which statement best describes a client/server environment?

A ○ Most processing is performed on the server, with each user machine accessing the server through a client application.

B ○ Most processing is performed on the client machine, with data stored on the server.

C ○ Processing is shared between the server and client, but all data is stored on the client.

D ○ All processing is performed on the server, but data is stored on the client machines.

53 Suppose a thinnet network is experiencing problems. When you test the cable, it generates a reading of 0 ohms. What is the best way to fix the problem?

A ○ Add terminators to the cables.

B ○ Add a grounded terminator to one end of the cable.

C ○ Replace the cable.

D ○ The problem must be elsewhere in the network.

Practice Exam 1 Answers

1 C. In a peer-to-peer network, each user must manage access to shared resources on his or her own machine. This is ideal for small companies in which little need exists for data sharing. *Objective: Compare a client/server network with a peer-to-peer network (Chapter 12).*

2 B. With share-level security, you create a share on each machine, and define a password with read or write permissions. Everyone uses the same password to access that share. *Objective: Compare user-level security with access permissions to a shared directory on a server (Chapter 12).*

3 B. The server-based model allows you to centralize data accessed by many users and allows for growth over time. *Objective: Compare a client/server network with a peer-to-peer network (Chapter 12).*

4 A. In a star topology, all computers connect to a central hub for network access. In a bus topology, all computers connect to a single wire (bus). In a ring topology, all computers directly connect to two other machines to form a ring. *Objective: Select the appropriate topology for various token-ring and Ethernet networks (Chapter 4).*

5 A. CSMA/CD is the method used to control communications on Ethernet networks. The NIC looks on the network first before sending out a packet. *Objective: Select the appropriate topology for various token-ring and Ethernet networks (Chapter 4).*

6 A. Ethernet is a common name for 10BaseT, 10Base2, and 10Base5. Fast Ethernet is also known as 100BaseT. *Objective: Select the appropriate topology for various token-ring and Ethernet networks (Chapter 4).*

7 A; D. Both AppleTalk and IPX are common network protocols. Telnet is an application that runs on TCP/IP. ARP is a method of address resolution. *Objective: Select the appropriate network and transport protocol or protocols for various token-ring and Ethernet networks. Protocol choices include: DLC, AppleTalk, IPX, TCP/IP, NFS, SMB (Chapter 3).*

8 B. Routers operate at the Network layer of the OSI model. *Objective: Define the communications devices that communicate at each level of the OSI model (Chapter 7).*

9 D. A bridge functions at the Data Link layer of the OSI model. *Objective: Define the communications devices that communicate at each level of the OSI model (Chapter 7).*

10 A. A gateway can perform protocol translation, allowing two networks running different protocols to communicate. *Objective: Define the communications devices that communicate at each level of the OSI model (Chapter 7).*

11 *B.* The current ISDN standard dictates two B channels running at 64K and one D channel running at 16K. *Objective: List the characteristics, requirements, and appropriate situations for WAN connection services. WAN connection services include X.25, ISDN, frame relay, and ATM (Chapter 6).*

12 *C.* A T1 offers a maximum transfer rate of 1.544 Mbps. *Objective: List the characteristics, requirements, and appropriate situations for WAN connection services. WAN connection services include X.25, ISDN, frame relay, and ATM (Chapter 6).*

13 *C.* ATM has the capability to carry voice, video, and data multiplexed on the same connection. This is one of the primary advantages of ATM in a WAN environment. *Objective: List the characteristics, requirements, and appropriate situations for WAN connection services. WAN connection services include X.25, ISDN, frame relay, and ATM (Chapter 6).*

14 *A.* Ethernet uses Category 5 UTP cable. The IEEE standard for Ethernet on twisted-pair cable (10BaseT) sets a maximum length of 100 meters. *Objective: Describe the characteristics and purpose of the media used in IEEE 802.3 and IEEE 802.5 standards (Chapter 4).*

15 *C.* A repeater can regenerate a signal, increasing the distance that the signal can travel. *Objective: Define the communications devices that communicate at each level of the OSI model (Chapter 4).*

16 *D.* 10BaseT Ethernet requires at least Category 3 cable, which is rated at 16 MHz or 16 Mbps. *Objective: Describe the characteristics and purpose of the media used in IEEE 802.3 and IEEE 802.5 standards (Chapter 4).*

17 *B.* Attenuation measures the signal loss as a signal travels down a cable. *Objective: Diagnose and resolve common connectivity problems with cards, cables, and related hardware (Chapter 11).*

18 *C.* Everyone else can communicate properly on the network. The most likely problem is that Joe's NIC is defective. *Objective: Diagnose and resolve common connectivity problems with cards, cables, and related hardware (Chapter 9).*

19 *D.* IRQ 2 is commonly the video card, IRQ 5 is commonly the LPT2 or sound card, and IRQ 7 is commonly LPT1. This leaves IRQ 10 available. *Objective: Given the manufacturer's documentation for the network adapter, install, configure, and resolve hardware conflicts for multiple adapters in a token-ring or Ethernet network (Chapter 8).*

20 *D.* A protocol analyzer enables you to capture and see into the packets on your network. *Objective: Diagnose and resolve common connectivity problems with cards, cables, and related hardware (Chapter 9).*

21 *C.* A time domain reflectometer (TDR) sends a signal down the cable and waits for it to be bounced back by a transceiver on the other end. A TDR can be used to diagnose a variety of Physical layer problems. *Objective: Diagnose and resolve common connectivity problems with cards, cables, and related hardware (Chapter 9).*

Practice Exam 1

22 *B.* An uninterruptible power supply (UPS) can protect against both power surges and power loss. *Objective: Choose a disaster recovery plan for various situations (Chapter 13).*

23 *C.* User Manager for Domains is the tool supplied with Windows NT Server to manage users and groups. *Objective: Choose an administrative plan to meet specified needs, including performance management, account management, and security (Chapter 13).*

24 *C.* RAID 5, striping with parity, protects against the loss of a single drive by storing parity information striped with the data. *Objective: Choose a disaster recovery plan for various situations (Chapter 13).*

25 *C.* With disk duplexing, you have two drive controllers, each with an independent set of disks. You then mirror the contents of one set to the other. *Objective: Choose a disaster recovery plan for various situations (Chapter 13).*

26 *A.* 10Base2 is commonly known as thinnet. 10Base5 is commonly known as thicknet. *Objective: Describe the characteristics and purpose of the media used in IEEE 802.3 and IEEE 802.5 standards (Chapter 4).*

27 *D.* Broadband transmissions are analog signals spread over a range of frequencies. *Objective: List the characteristics, requirements, and appropriate situations for WAN connection services. WAN connection services include X.25, ISDN, frame relay, and ATM (Chapter 6).*

28 *C.* Encryption protects data from unauthorized access by scrambling the data based on a password key. Without the password, the data cannot be accessed. *Objective: Choose a disaster recovery plan for various situations (Chapter 13).*

29 *B; C; D.* AppleTalk, TCP/IP, and IPX/SPX are all routable protocols. *Objective: Select the appropriate network and transport protocol or protocols for various token-ring and Ethernet networks. Protocol choices include DLC, AppleTalk, IPX, TCP/IP, NFS, and SMB (Chapter 3).*

30 *A.* The primary benefits of NetBEUI are that it is small, fast, and efficient. The fact that it is not routable makes it difficult to use on large LANs. *Objective: Select the appropriate network and transport protocol or protocols for various token-ring and Ethernet networks. Protocol choices include DLC, AppleTalk, IPX, TCP/IP, NFS, and SMB (Chapter 3).*

31 *A.* You have connected the two networks and isolated broadcast traffic with the router. *Objective: Select the appropriate topology for various token-ring and Ethernet networks (Chapter 4).*

32 *B.* By using a bridge to connect the two LANs, you have not isolated the broadcast traffic between them. *Objective: Define the communications devices that communicate at each level of the OSI model (Chapter 7).*

33 *D.* Routers do not allow broadcasts to travel between segments. *Objective: Define the communications devices that communicate at each level of the OSI model (Chapter 7).*

34 *B.* A brouter enables you to route some protocols, such as TCP/IP, while also allowing through broadcasts from other protocols, such as NetBEUI. *Objective: Define the communications devices that communicate at each level of the OSI model (Chapter 7).*

35 *C.* You have increased the performance but not the redundancy. A failure in Chicago will keep users in Albany from communicating with users in New York. Also, a T1 does not multiplex voice, video, and data as ATM does. *Objective: List the characteristics, requirements, and appropriate situations for WAN connection services. WAN connection services include X.25, ISDN, frame relay, and ATM (Chapter 6).*

36 *C.* Error correction and flow control between machines is the responsibility of the Transport layer in the OSI model. *Objective: Define the communications devices that communicate at each level of the OSI model (Chapter 7).*

37 *D.* A protocol analyzer enables you to gather statistics on network traffic and also look inside the packets going to and from your server. *Objective: Given the manufacturer's documentation for the network adapter, install, configure, and resolve hardware conflicts for multiple network adapters in a token-ring or Ethernet network (Chapter 9).*

38 *B.* A transceiver is required to connect a thicknet cable to a NIC. *Objective: Select the appropriate media for various situations. Media choices include twisted-pair cable, coaxial cable, fiber-optic cable, and wireless. Situational elements include cost, distance limitations, and number of nodes (Chapter 10).*

39 *B.* Spread-spectrum technology enables you to disperse a radio signal across many frequencies to improve performance. *Objective: Select the appropriate media for various situations. Media choices include twisted-pair cable, coaxial cable, fiber-optic cable, and wireless. Situational elements include cost, distance limitations, and number of nodes (Chapter 10).*

40 *B.* Because you are running only standard Ethernet, Category 3 cabling is adequate. You will need to add a repeater, however, to provide service to Anne and Stacey's machines because they exceed the maximum distance of 328 feet (100 meters). *Objective: Select the appropriate connectivity devices for various token-ring and Ethernet networks. Connectivity devices include repeaters, bridges, routers, brouters, and gateways (Chapter 7).*

41 *A.* On a token-ring network, a token is passed from machine to machine in sequential order. Each machine has an equal opportunity to communicate on the network. *Objective: Select the appropriate topology for various token-ring and Ethernet networks (Chapter 4).*

42 *C.* Fiber-optic cable is the only cable immune to electromagnetic interference. *Objective: Select the appropriate media for various situations. Media choices include twisted-pair cable, coaxial cable, fiber-optic cable, and wireless. Situational elements include cost, distance limitations, and number of nodes (Chapter 10).*

43 *A; B.* Setting a minimum password length makes the password more difficult to guess. Locking out accounts after a specified number of failed attempts keeps a hacker from being able to run a password cracker against the server. *Objective: Choose an administrative plan to meet specified needs including performance management, account management, and security (Chapter 13).*

44 *B.* RAS, Remote Access Service, gives remote users the ability to dial into your network. *Objective: Distinguish whether SLIP or PPP is used as the communications protocol for various situations (Chapter 5).*

45 *C.* Passive hubs provide basic connectivity between devices. Active hubs have management features that make them more robust and easier to monitor. *Objective: Select the appropriate connectivity devices for various token-ring and Ethernet networks. Connectivity devices include repeaters, bridges, routers, brouters, and gateways (Chapter 7).*

46 *A; B.* SNMP is an industry-standard method for collecting data about machines on the network. SMS is a Microsoft product suite that contains modules for inventory, screen control, and software distribution. *Objective: Select the appropriate hardware and software tools to monitor trends in the network (Chapter 13).*

47 *B.* IRQ conflicts are the most common source of problems when installing new hardware. *Objective: Diagnose and resolve common connectivity problems with cards, cables, and related hardware (Chapter 9).*

48 *C.* The standard protocol of the Internet is TCP/IP. *Objective: Select the appropriate network and transport protocol or protocols for various token-ring and Ethernet networks. Protocol choices include DLC, AppleTalk, IPX, TCP/IP, NFS, and SMB (Chapter 3).*

49 *A.* A BNC barrel connector is used to connect two thinnet cables. *Objective: Select the appropriate media for various situations. Media choices include twisted-pair cable, coaxial cable, fiber-optic cable, and wireless. Situational elements include cost, distance limitations, and number of nodes (Chapter 10).*

50 *A.* Each end of the thinnet cable must be terminated with a 50-ohm terminator. Only one end of the cable must be grounded. *Objective: Diagnose and resolve common connectivity problems with cards, cables, and related hardware (Chapter 11).*

51 *D.* Making computer names the same as the user's ID makes it easier to keep track of which computers belong to which users. This also ensures that you meet the 15-character limit on computer names. Servers should have easy-to-find names based on function. Watch out for the 15-character limit, though. *Objective: Implement a NetBIOS naming scheme for all computers on a given network (Chapter 12).*

52 *A.* In a client/server environment, all processing is performed on the server. Client computers generally access the server through an interface application. All data is stored on the server, where the processing occurs to improve performance. *Objective: Compare a client/server network with a peer-to-peer network (Chapter 12).*

53 *C.* The cable when tested should show a reading of infinity. This particular cable is bad and needs to be replaced. *Objective: Diagnose and resolve common connectivity problems with cards, cables, and related hardware (Chapter 9).*

Appendix B

Practice Exam 2

• •

▶ 75 minutes

▶ 44 correct answers to pass

▶ 56 questions

▶ No peeking!

• •

1 Specialized servers that provide communications between networks using different protocols are called _____.

A ○ Hubs

B ○ Repeaters

C ○ Gateways

D ○ Translators

2 Which of the following is not a characteristic of the bus network topology?

A ○ Bus networks are more difficult to reconfigure than the star topology.

B ○ The bus topology is considered passive.

C ○ A terminator at each end of the bus eliminates signal bounce.

D ○ Performance does not degrade as more computers are added to the bus.

3 Which type of network provides the highest degree of security and centralized administration?

A ○ Peer-to-peer

B ○ Server-based

C ○ Hybrid

D ○ Workgroup

4 The network topology in which several star hubs are linked with a linear trunk is known as a _____.

A ○ Bus

B ○ Star

C ○ Star ring

D ○ Star bus

5 Which of the following is an advantage of the ring topology?

A ○ Failure of one computer does not affect the entire network.
B ○ It is easy to troubleshoot.
C ○ Computers are given equal access to the network.
D ○ Changing the configuration of the network does not cause disruption of communications.

6 What is not true of the star topology?

A ○ Star networks are generally easy to reconfigure.
B ○ The start topology requires more cabling than other topologies.
C ○ If a computer goes down, the entire network goes down.
D ○ Signals travel through a hub to all other computers attached to the hub.

7 In Microsoft networking, a server-based network is recommended when the number of workstations exceeds _____.

A ○ 5
B ○ 10
C ○ 25
D ○ 50

8 Which network topology is the easiest to reconfigure and troubleshoot?

A ○ Mesh
B ○ Star
C ○ Star bus
D ○ Ring

9 What is the most common network media?

A ○ Fiber-optic
B ○ Copper
C ○ Radio
D ○ Air

10 What wireless method of network communications uses signaling over a range of frequencies and is relatively slow?

A ○ Scatter infrared
B ○ Laser
C ○ Narrow-band (single-frequency) radio
D ○ Spread-spectrum radio

11 Which of the following is true about the Physical layer of the OSI model?

A ○ Determines the route from the source to the destination computer
B ○ Transmits the raw bit stream over the physical medium
C ○ Manages traffic such as packet switching and routing
D ○ Serves as a window for applications to access network services

12 Which of the following is true about the Network layer of the OSI model?

A ○ Addresses and routes packets
B ○ Provides error-free transmission of frames
C ○ Provides flow control and error handling
D ○ Is where the redirector operates

13 Which layer of the OSI model ensures that packets are delivered error-free and in sequence?

A ○ Application
B ○ Presentation
C ○ Session
D ○ Transport

14 Which category of the IEEE 802 Project model defines Carrier-Sense Multiple Access with Collision Detection (Ethernet)?

A ○ 802.2
B ○ 802.3
C ○ 802.5
D ○ 802.12

15 Which layer of the OSI model is divided into the Medial Access Control and Logical Link Control sublayers?

A ○ Physical
B ○ Data Link
C ○ Network
D ○ Session

16 What is the role of the network adapter card driver?

A ○ Provides a standard protocol for communications between computers running the same operating system
B ○ Provides for communications between the network adapter card and the operating system of the computer
C ○ Provides for communications between different network media types
D ○ Provides a standard protocol for communications between computers running different operating systems

17 The TCP/IP protocol assures sequenced packet delivery. This type of communications session is known as _____.

    A ○ Connectionless
    B ○ Deterministic
    C ○ Connection-oriented
    D ○ Contention

18 The process of linking protocol stacks to the network device driver for the network interface card is known as _____.

    A ○ Addressing
    B ○ Multitasking
    C ○ Binding
    D ○ Stacking

19 The trailer of a packet contains error correction data known as the _____.

    A ○ SMB
    B ○ CRC
    C ○ ICMP
    D ○ DLC

20 Which of the following is not true regarding IPX/SPX?

    A ○ IPX/SPX is a protocol used by Novell in NetWare networks.
    B ○ IPX/SPX cannot be routed.
    C ○ NWLink is Microsoft's implementation of IPX/SPX.
    D ○ IPX/SPX is a fast and efficient choice for networks not requiring access to the Internet.

21 Suppose that you have been contracted to install a network for a small accounting firm consisting of six accountants. As many as five more staff members may be added within the next year. During peak times, two interns are hired to assist with administrative work. All accountants have stand-alone computers with personal passwords to secure their client's data. The accountants need to share client data among themselves, but must assure that it is secure from outsiders. They would like to purchase a single high-performance printer that everyone can use. What type of network would you recommend for this office?

    A ○ A workgroup with shared directories and a shared printer
    B ○ A hybrid network with each computer acting as a client/server
    C ○ A server-based system with a dedicated file-and-print server
    D ○ A peer-to-peer network with a dedicated file server

22 Which of the following is not true about Ethernet?

A ○ IEEE 802.3 specification
B ○ Uses CSMA/CD for traffic regulation
C ○ Uses thicknet, thinnet, or UTP cabling
D ○ Uses broadband signaling

23 The maximum segment length for 10BaseT is _____.

A ○ 100 meters (328 feet)
B ○ 185 meters (607 feet)
C ○ 500 meters (1,640 feet)
D ○ 925 meters (3,035 feet)

24 What type of cable can be run in the false ceilings of office buildings?

A ○ PVC
B ○ Category 3
C ○ Category 5
D ○ Plenum grade

25 You assign your newly hired assistant the task of setting up a new workstation attached to a 10Base2 network. After booting the computer, he cannot see any other computers on the network. He asks you to check his work, and you find that all drivers appear to be loaded correctly and all connections are secure at the workstation. Upon further inquiry, the assistant tells you he couldn't find a cable, so he borrowed one from the multimedia department. What is most likely wrong with the connection?

A ○ He has used UTP cabling.
B ○ He did not terminate the cable correctly.
C ○ He has used RG-59 cable.
D ○ He has selected the wrong IRQ for the network card.

26 What is the maximum number of computers per segment in a 10Base2 network?

A ○ 1024
B ○ 30
C ○ 100
D ○ 256

27 The redirector is software responsible for _____.

A ○ Managing users by controlling access and privileges
B ○ Controlling access to the processor
C ○ Accepting I/O requests and forwarding them to the appropriate network service
D ○ Allowing resource sharing and controlling access to those resources

28 Your current network runs NetBEUI and has grown tremendously over the past year. You decide to segment the network with a router. After installing the router, you can't see workstations on either side of the router. What is the best solution to this problem?

A ○ Reconfigure NetBEUI at each workstation to enable routing.

B ○ Replace the cabling on both sides of the router.

C ○ Reconfigure the router to forward NetBEUI packets.

D ○ Add the TCP/IP or IPX/SPX protocol to all workstations on both sides of the router.

29 Category 5 UTP cabling consists of _____.

A ○ Four twisted pairs of copper wire capable of transmission rates up to 100 Mbps using RJ-11 connectors

B ○ Four twisted pairs of copper wire capable of transmission rates up to 100 Mbps using RJ-45 connectors

C ○ Two twisted pairs of copper wire capable of transmission rates up to 10 Mbps using RJ-11 connectors

D ○ Two twisted pairs of copper wire capable of transmission rates up to 10 Mbps using RJ-45 connectors

30 Which of the following is not a characteristic of fiber-optic cabling?

A ○ It is excellent for high speed data transmission.

B ○ It is immune to electrical interference.

C ○ It requires two fibers, one to send and one to receive.

D ○ It is easy to install.

31 Crosstalk is _____.

A ○ A communications protocol used by older Macintosh computers

B ○ Signal overflow from an adjacent wire

C ○ The gradual weakening of a signal as it travels farther from its source

D ○ The communications between equivalent layers of the OSI model

32 Which dial-up protocol supports compression and allows for dynamic allocation of IP addresses?

A ○ CSLIP

B ○ SLIP

C ○ PPP

D ○ DHCP

33 After configuring your network card to use IRQ 4, you can't access the network. What is the most likely problem?

A ○ A hardware conflict exists between your network card and COM1.

B ○ A hardware conflict exists between your network card and COM2.

C ○ A hardware conflict exists between your network card and the floppy drive controller.

D ○ A hardware conflict exists between your network card and your IDE controller.

34 You have connected a new Windows 95 computer to your network using the IPX/SPX protocol, but you cannot see the network nor can the new computer be seen from the network. You have checked all your cabling, connections, and drivers and they are okay. What is the most likely cause of this problem?

A ○ You have entered an incorrect IP address at the computer.

B ○ You have specified the wrong frame type for this network.

C ○ IPX/SPX is not routable, so packets cannot be forwarded to the correct destination.

D ○ IPX/SPX cannot be used in a Microsoft network.

35 In the summertime, your location experiences brief power outages due to lightning storms. Last summer one of these outages took out a file server by damaging the hard disk. Only some of the data could be recovered from tape backup, and management was not pleased. You have decided to implement disaster recovery measures.

Required result: Implement a hardware solution to safeguard your file servers from power outages.

Optional results: Enable quick recovery from a disk failure and increase overall computer performance.

Proposed solution: Install a UPS system on the file server. Add a second hard disk to the file server and enable disk mirroring.

The proposed solution produces which of the following results?

A ○ The required result only

B ○ The required result and one optional result

C ○ The required result and both optional results

D ○ None of the results

36 Suppose that you have recently installed a SQL server backend on your server and have noticed that your server's disk I/O has slowed. You would also like to protect your mission-critical server from power transients. You decide to implement upgrades and disaster recovery measures.

Required result: Implement a RAID solution to safeguard the data on your server.

Optional results: Implement a hardware solution to safeguard your file servers from power outages and increase overall disk performance.

Proposed solution: Install additional hard disks on the computer and enable disk striping. Install a UPS system on the file server.

The proposed solution produces which of the following results?

A ○ The required result only

B ○ The required result and only one optional result

C ○ The required result and both optional results

D ○ The required result is not produced

37 You suspect a cable may be bad in your 10Base2 network. What inexpensive tool should you use to check the continuity of the cable?

A ○ Time domain reflectometer (TDR)

B ○ Protocol analyzer

C ○ Oscilloscope

D ○ Digital volt meter (DVM)

38 An incremental backup _____.

A ○ Backs up all files and marks them as being backed up

B ○ Backs up only files that have changed since the last backup and marks them as backed up

C ○ Backs up only files that have changed since the last backup but does not mark them as backed up

D ○ Backs up selected files but does not mark them as backed up

39 Which of the following is not true regarding modems?

A ○ Convert analog signals to digital for transmittal over phone lines

B ○ Asynchronous is the most common method of connectivity

C ○ Data is transmitted serially with start and stop bits surrounding data

D ○ V. 42 is a hardware implementation of error control

40 A bridge operates at the _____.

A ○ Network layer and can switch and route packets across multiple networks

B ○ Physical layer to regenerate attenuated signals

C ○ Data Link layer and can link networks of unlike media types

D ○ Session layer and can work with only routable protocols

41 T1 service provides _____.

A ○ On-demand switched digital dial-up service at 56 Kbps

B ○ 6 to 45 Mbps over leased lines

C ○ 1.544 Mbps over leased lines

D ○ 100 Mbps over fiber-optic lines

42 Which of the following network topologies uses token passing and fiber-optic cabling to transmit data at 100 Mbps over a distance of 100 kilometers?

A ○ X.25

B ○ Frame relay

C ○ ATM

D ○ FDDI

43 Suppose that you suspect that the processor may be causing a bottleneck on your Windows NT server. What troubleshooting tool would you use to analyze the problem?

A ○ Performance Monitor

B ○ Network Monitor

C ○ SNMP

D ○ Server Manager

44 Suppose that your company has three locations around the country, each with its own network. Your manager wants to improve communications and productivity by creating a single networked domain from the three independent sites.

Required result: Provide network connectivity between the three sites with centralized administration of the network.

Optional results: Provide connectivity of at least 1 Mbps, and the network must continue to operate even if one link fails.

Proposed solution: Use two T1 lines between the three sites and implement a Windows NT Server as a PDC at one of the sites.

The proposed solution produces which of the following results?

A ○ The required result and both of the optional results

B ○ The required result and one of the optional results

C ○ The required result only

D ○ None of the results

45 Which of the following is not true regarding asynchronous transfer mode (ATM)?

A ○ Can accommodate voice, data, or video signals

B ○ Transmits data in variable-length cells

C ○ Can transmit at speeds between 155 Mbps and 622 Mbps

D ○ Can be used with existing media types

46 What routing method uses distance vector to determine hop counts?

A ○ RIP
B ○ NLSP
C ○ OSPF
D ○ SNMP

47 What method of disk fault tolerance uses a separate controller on a mirrored disk?

A ○ Disk striping
B ○ Sector sparing
C ○ Disk duplexing
D ○ Striping with parity

48 Which of the following is the correct UNC command to specify the location of the shared folder Data on a computer named Server1?

A ○ /Server1/Data
B ○ //Server1/Data
C ○ \\Server1\Data
D ○ \\Data\Server1

49 What device sends sonar-like pulses along a cable to find the location of faults in the cable?

A ○ Protocol analyzer
B ○ Oscilloscope
C ○ Time domain reflectometer
D ○ Digital volt meter

50 A segment of your 10Base2 network has gone down, and you suspect a cable is at fault. You remove the cable from the network and then measure the resistance of the terminator and the cable between the core and the shield with an ohmmeter. The terminator reads 50 ohms and the cable reads 0 ohms. What do you conclude?

A ○ The cable is fine and can be returned to service.
B ○ The cable has a short in it and should be replaced.
C ○ You are using the wrong type of terminator.
D ○ You cannot check the cable using this method.

51 Your NetBEUI network has been experiencing broadcast storms even though you have a brouter in place on the network. What can you do to eliminate this problem?

A ○ Turn off bridging at the brouter and use TCP/IP in place of NetBEUI.
B ○ Replace the brouter with a router.
C ○ Replace the brouter with a bridge and use TCP/IP in place of NetBEUI.
D ○ Segment the network with another brouter.

52 What is NDIS?

A ○ A directory service system found in Novell NetWare networks

B ○ A network management protocol that uses agents to monitor network components

C ○ A specification developed by Novell and Apple to allow multiple network drivers to be bound to multiple transports

D ○ A specification developed by Microsoft to allow multiple network drivers to be bound to multiple transports

53 Which of the following tools can capture and decode packets and provide detailed analysis of network behavior in real time?

A ○ Performance Monitor

B ○ Protocol analyzer

C ○ Network Monitor

D ○ Time domain reflectometer

54 Which of the following is a packet-switching WAN protocol with extensive error checking, was developed for the mainframe environment, and is relatively slow?

A ○ ATM

B ○ SONET

C ○ ISDN

D ○ X.25

55 Which of the following is true about a NetBIOS name?

A ○ Each computer must have a unique name and the name cannot duplicate the name of a domain.

B ○ It can be up to 15 characters in length.

C ○ It is the name used in UNC names.

D ○ It can be up to 16 characters in length.

56 RAID level 1 is a disk fault tolerance method also known by what other name?

A ○ Disk striping

B ○ Disk striping with parity

C ○ Disk mirroring

D ○ Block interleaving

Practice Exam 2 Answers

1 *C.* A gateway translates communication protocols. For example, an NT workstation computer can access a NetWare server through Gateway Services for NetWare running on an NT server computer. *Objective: Select the appropriate connectivity devices for various token-ring and Ethernet networks. Connectivity devices include repeaters, bridges, routers, brouters, and gateways (Chapter 7).*

2 *D.* Performance degrades on bus networks as more computers are added to the bus. *Objective: Identify and resolve network performance problems (Chapter 13).*

3 *B.* Server-based networks offer user-level security that can be carefully controlled, whereas peer-to-peer networks offer share-level security that is more difficult to administer. *Objective: Compare a client/server network with a peer-to-peer network (Chapter 12).*

4 *D.* A star bus consists of hubs (the star) connected with a trunk (the bus). *Objective: Select the appropriate network topology for various token-ring and Ethernet networks (Chapter 4).*

5 *C.* Ring networks, such as token ring, use deterministic methods of network access, such as token passing. This gives all computers equal access to the network. *Objective: Select the appropriate network topology for various token-ring and Ethernet networks (Chapter 4).*

6 *C.* If a computer goes down in a star network, the rest of the network is unaffected. If a hub goes down in a star network, all computers on that hub lose communication. *Objective: Select the appropriate network topology for various token-ring and Ethernet networks (Chapter 4).*

7 *B.* It is generally recommended that you use a centralized server-based network for networks exceeding 10 users. *Objective: Compare a client/server network with a peer-to-peer network (Chapter 12).*

8 *B.* Star networks are easy to reconfigure by simply changing plugs at the hub. This also makes them easy to troubleshoot. *Objective: Select the appropriate network topology for various token-ring and Ethernet networks (Chapter 4).*

9 *B.* Copper is still the most commonly used network media. *Objective: Select the appropriate media for various situations. Media choices include twisted-pair cable, coaxial cable, fiber-optic cable, and wireless. Situational elements include cost, distance limitations, and number of nodes (Chapter 10).*

10 *D.* Spread-spectrum radio has a typical speed of 250 Kbps broadcast over a range of frequencies. *Objective: Select the appropriate media for various situations. Media choices include twisted-pair cable, coaxial cable, fiber-optic cable, and wireless. Situational elements include cost, distance limitations, and number of nodes (Chapter 10).*

11 *B.* The Physical layer is the lowest layer of the OSI model. It is responsible for sending the bits over the wire. *Objective: Define the communications devices that communicate at each level of the OSI model (Chapter 3).*

12 *A.* The Network layer is responsible for addressing and routing packets. Hint: remember that routers operate at the Network Layer of the OSI model. *Objective: Define the communications devices that communicate at each level of the OSI model (Chapter 3).*

13 *D.* The Transport layer is responsible for delivering messages error-free, in sequence, with no loss or duplication. *Objective: Define the communications devices that communicate at each level of the OSI model (Chapter 3).*

14 *B.* IEEE 802.3 defines LAN standards for Ethernet. Hint: Know what 802.5 defines also. *Objective: Describe the characteristics and purpose of the media used in IEEE 802.3 and IEEE 802.5 standards (Chapter 4).*

15 *B.* The IEEE enhanced the Data Link layer by defining the MAC and LLC sublayers. *Objective: Describe the characteristics and purpose of the media used in IEEE 802.3 and IEEE 802.5 standards (Chapter 4).*

16 *B.* The network adapter card driver is specific to the operating system running on the computer and enables the operating system to communicate with the card. *Objective: Given the manufacturer's documentation for the network adapter, install, configure, and resolve hardware conflicts for multiple adapters in a token-ring or Ethernet network (Chapter 8).*

17 *C.* Connection-oriented protocols, such as TCP/IP, are reliable and assure packet delivery. *Objective: Compare the implications of using connection-oriented communications with connectionless communications (Chapter 3).*

18 *C.* Binding establishes a communications link between a protocol and a network adapter driver. This process allows more than one protocol to be bound to the network card. *Objective: Given the manufacturer's documentation for the network adapter, install, configure, and resolve hardware conflicts for multiple adapters in a token-ring or Ethernet network (Chapter 8).*

19 *B.* The cyclical redundancy check (CRC) is added to the trailer for error checking. *Compare the implications of using connection-oriented communications with connectionless communications (Chapter 3).*

20 *B.* IPX/SPX is a routable protocol. IPX/SPX is easier than TCP/IP to administer, and unlike NetBEUI, it can be routed. *Objective: Select the appropriate network and transport protocol or protocols for various token-ring and Ethernet networks. Protocol choices include DLC, AppleTalk, IPX, TCP/IP, NFS, and SMB (Chapter 3).*

21 *C.* A server-based network would be the best choice to allow centralized administration and high security. *Objective: Compare a client/server network with a peer-to-peer network (Chapter 12).*

22 *D.* Ethernet uses baseband digital signaling. *Objective: Select the appropriate topology for various token-ring and Ethernet networks (Chapter 10).*

23 *A.* Remember that both UTP and STP can run 100 meters, and both are easy to use. STP, however has low interference and is more expensive. *Objective: Select the appropriate media for various situations. Media choices include twisted-pair cable, coaxial cable, fiber-optic cable, and wireless. Situational elements include cost, distance limitations, and number of nodes (Chapter 10).*

24 *D.* Plenum grade cable does not contain PVC, which can produce toxic fumes when burned. *Objective: Select the appropriate media for various situations. Media choices include twisted-pair cable, coaxial cable, fiber-optic cable, and wireless. Situational elements include cost, distance limitations, and number of nodes (Chapter 10).*

25 *C.* Because he borrowed the cable from the multimedia department, he most likely installed RG-59 75-ohm video cable, which will not work. *Objective: Select the appropriate media for various situations. Media choices include twisted-pair cable, coaxial cable, fiber-optic cable, and wireless. Situational elements include cost, distance limitations, and number of nodes (Chapter 10).*

26 *B.* Thirty computers can be added to a 10Base2 segment. Hint: Also know the 5-4-3 rule. You can connect five segments using four repeaters with three of the segments populated. *Objective: Select the appropriate media for various situations. Media choices include twisted-pair cable, coaxial cable, fiber-optic cable, and wireless. Situational elements include cost, distance limitations, and number of nodes (Chapter 10).*

27 *C.* The redirector is client software that handles network I/O requests. *Objective: Select the appropriate connectivity devices for various token-ring and Ethernet networks. Connectivity devices include repeaters, bridges, routers, brouters, and gateways (Chapter 7).*

28 *D.* NetBEUI is not a routable protocol and cannot be configured. A routable protocol, such as IPX/SPX or TCP/IP, must be used with a router. *Objective: Select the appropriate network and transport protocol or protocols for various token-ring and Ethernet networks. Protocol choices include DLC, AppleTalk, IPX, TCP/IP, NFS, and SMB (Chapter 3).*

29 *B.* Category 5 cabling is capable of 100 Mbps. Hint: Remember that RJ-11 telephone connectors have only four connections and RJ-45 connectors have eight. *Objective: Select the appropriate media for various situations. Media choices include twisted-pair cable, coaxial cable, fiber-optic cable, and wireless. Situational elements include cost, distance limitations, and number of nodes (Chapter 10).*

30 *D.* Fiber-optic cable requires precision connections and is typically difficult to install. *Objective: Select the appropriate media for various situations. Media choices include twisted-pair cable, coaxial cable, fiber-optic cable, and wireless. Situational elements include cost, distance limitations, and number of nodes (Chapter 10).*

31 *B.* Crosstalk is interference from adjacent wires. *Objective: Diagnose and resolve common connectivity problems with cards, cables, and related hardware (Chapter 10).*

32 *C.* PPP, or Point-to-Point Protocol, is a newer protocol that supports compression and IP address negotiation. *Objective: Distinguish whether SLIP or PPP is used as the communications protocol for various situations (Chapter 5).*

33 *A.* IRQ 4 is usually assigned to COM1. Hint: An easy way to remember default COM port IRQ assignments is COM(1)+IRQ(4)=5 and COM(2)+IRQ(3)=5. *Objective: Given the manufacturer's documentation for the network adapter, install, configure, and resolve hardware conflicts for multiple adapters in a token-ring or Ethernet network (Chapter 8).*

34 *B.* IPX/SPX networks can use four different frame types. Newer network cards will often auto-detect the frame type, but older ones will not. *Objective: Identify common errors associated with components required for communications (Chapter 9).*

35 *B.* A UPS will safeguard against power outages, and disk mirroring will provide fault tolerance, but mirroring will actually degrade performance slightly. *Objective: Choose a disaster recovery plan for various situations (Chapter 13).*

36 *D.* This solution does not produce the required result because disk striping does not provide fault tolerance. Disk striping with parity will provide the necessary fault tolerance and increase disk performance. *Objective: Choose a disaster recovery plan for various situations (Chapter 13).*

37 *D.* A DVM is used for measuring resistance. *Objective: Diagnose and resolve common connectivity problems with cards, cables, and related hardware (Chapter 9).*

38 *B.* An incremental backup backs up and marks files that have changed since the last backup. These backups are quicker to perform but slower to restore than differential backups. *Objective: Choose a disaster recovery plan for various situations (Chapter 13).*

39 *A.* Modems convert the digital signals of your computer to analog signals for telephone transmission. *Objective: Compare the implications of using connection-oriented communications with connectionless communications (Chapter 3).*

40 *C.* Bridges operate at the Data Link layer and can link unlike media types. Routers operate at the Network layer, and repeaters operate at the Physical layer. *Objective: Select the appropriate connectivity devices for various token-ring and Ethernet networks. Connectivity devices include repeaters, bridges, routers, brouters, and gateways (Chapter 7).*

41 *C.* T1 service provides 1.544 Mbps service. *Objective: Select the appropriate media for various situations. Media choices include twisted-pair cable, coaxial cable, fiber-optic cable, and wireless. Situational elements include cost, distance limitations, and number of nodes (Chapter 10).*

42 *D.* Fiber Distributed Data Interface (FDDI) is a topology useful for MANs (metropolitan area networks). *Objective: Select the appropriate media for various situations. Media choices include twisted-pair cable, coaxial cable, fiber-optic cable, and wireless. Situational elements include cost, distance limitations, and number of nodes (Chapter 10).*

43 *A.* Performance Monitor has a number of counters that can be activated to monitor computer performance. *Objective: Select the appropriate hardware and software tools to monitor trends in the network (Chapter 13).*

44 *B.* The proposed solution does not provide fault tolerance. A better choice would be to implement a third T1 link. *Objective: Choose an administrative plan to meet specified needs including performance management, account management, and security (Chapter 13).*

45 *B.* ATM transmits data in fixed 53-byte cells. *Objective: List the characteristics, requirements, and appropriate situations for WAN connection services. WAN connection services include X.25, ISDN, frame relay, and ATM (Chapter 6).*

46 *A.* RIP (Routing Information Protocol) determines hop counts. *Objective: Select the appropriate connectivity devices for various token-ring and Ethernet networks. Connectivity devices include repeaters, bridges, routers, brouters, and gateways (Chapter 7).*

47 *C.* Disk duplexing uses a separate controller to provide additional disk fault tolerance. *Objective: Choose an administrative plan to meet specified needs, including performance management, account management, and security (Chapter 13).*

48 *C.* UNC naming conventions follow the pattern *Computer_Name**Share_Name*. *Objective: Implement a NetBIOS naming scheme for all computers on a given network (Chapter 12).*

49 *C.* The time domain reflectometer is useful for finding the location of a cable fault. *Objective: Diagnose and resolve common connectivity problems with cards, cables, and related hardware. (Chapter 9).*

50 *B.* If the resistance is 0 ohms, continuity exists between the core and the shield that will render the cable useless. The resistivity should be infinite. *Objective: Identify common errors associated with components required for communications (Chapter 15).*

51 *A.* Bridging transmits broadcasts across the brouter. Turning off bridging will eliminate storms, but NetBEUI will not pass the router. A routable protocol such as TCP/IP must then be installed. *Objective: Resolve broadcast storms (Chapter 7).*

52 *D.* NDIS is a Microsoft specification that allows multiple transport protocols to be bound to a network adapter card. *Objective: Explain the purpose of NDIS and Novell ODI networks (Chapter 3).*

53 *B.* A protocol analyzer can perform real-time analysis of network behavior. *Objective: Identify and resolve network performance problems (Chapter 13).*

54 *B.* X.25 is an older protocol that is slow but virtually error-free. *Objective: Select the appropriate network and transport protocol or protocols for various token-ring and Ethernet networks. Protocol choices include DLC, AppleTalk, IPX, TCP/IP, NFS, and SMB (Chapter 3).*

55 *B.* NetBIOS names cannot exceed 15 characters. *Objective: Implement a NetBIOS naming scheme for all computers on a given network (Chapter 12).*

56 *C.* RAID level 1 is disk mirroring. Drives are paired, and each byte of information is written to both disks. *Objective: Choose a disaster recovery plan for various situations (Chapter 13).*

Appendix C

Microsoft Certification Programs

• •

• •

Microsoft offers a number of certifications that you can earn to accelerate your career. These certifications are the most in-demand certifications in the industry today, owing in large part to the overwhelming acceptance of the Microsoft Windows NT operating system. The following certifications all require passing computer-based exams that thoroughly test your ability to implement and support the product.

Many exams apply to more than one Microsoft certification. This appendix includes advice on choosing exams for basic certification requirements that can apply also to advanced certification.

Microsoft Certified Professional (MCP)

On your way to your MCSE, you earn an additional acronym: MCP (Microsoft Certified Professional). Upon passing any qualifying exams, you achieve MCP status for that operating system.

Qualifying exams

Passing any *one* exam (except Networking Essentials) earns you MCP status. We recommend these exams while you work toward MCSE certification for Windows NT 4.0:

✔ Implementing and Supporting Microsoft Windows 95 (either Exam 70-064, active, or Exam 70-063, retired)

✔ Implementing and Supporting Microsoft Windows NT Server 4.0 (Exam 70-067)

✔ Implementing and Supporting Microsoft Windows NT Workstation 4.02 (Exam 70-073)

✔ Implementing and Supporting Microsoft Windows NT Server 4.0 in the Enerprise (Exam 70-068)

✔ Implementing and Supporting Microsoft Windows 98 (Exam 70-098)

Consider working on one of the preceding exams before taking other MCSE exams. MCP-qualifying exams are required for MCSE certification, so it makes sense to earn MCP status as soon as possible.

The Windows NT Server 4.0 exam (70-067) is required for MCP+I certification. If you're planning to try for MCP+I certification, consider taking the NT Server 4.0 exam to get started on the MCP+I requirements and earn MCP certification at the same time. (The MCP+I requirements are covered in this chapter.)

Microsoft plans to retire the Windows NT 3.51 exams when Windows NT 5.0 exams come out. The following exams qualify you for MCP status for six months after they are retired:

✔ Implementing and Supporting Microsoft Windows NT Workstation 3.51 (Exam 70-042)

✔ Implementing and Supporting Microsoft Windows NT Server 3.51 (Exam 70-043)

One other exam earns MCP status and counts toward MCSD certification for developers:

✔ Analyzing Requirements and Defining Solution Architectures (Exam 70-100)

Benefits

Johnny, tell our lucky MCPs about their fabulous prizes!

✔ Authorization to use the Microsoft Certified Professional logos on your resume and other promotional materials, such as business cards

✔ An official Microsoft Certified Professional certificate, suitable for flaunting, a wallet card, and a lapel pin

✔ Access to a private area on the Microsoft Web site for Microsoft Certified Professionals; here, you can find information on Microsoft products and technologies

✔ A free subscription to *Microsoft Certified Professional Magazine,* which has a lot of great information on Microsoft products, new exams, new certification products, book reviews, and more

✔ Invitations to Microsoft conferences and training events

Microsoft Cerified Trainers (MCT)

Microsoft Certified Trainers (MCTs) are certified, technically competent individuals who can deliver Microsoft Official Curriculum at Microsoft certified Technical Education Centers (CTECs). And they have another cool set of initials to add to their resumes.

Requirements

For the MCT designation, candidates must

✔ Pass the exam for the course they are teaching

✔ Prove their instruction presentation skills

You prove your presentation skills by attending approved instructional presentations from Microsoft or through instructor certification by any of the following vendors:

✔ Novell

✔ Lotus

✔ Santa Cruz Operation

✔ Banyan

✔ Cisco Systems

✔ Sun Microsystems

Benefits

Benefits for becoming a Microsoft Certified Trainer are like the benefits of becoming an MCP:

✔ Use of the Microsoft Certified Trainer logos on your resume and other promotional materials, such as business cards

- An official Microsoft Certified Trainer certificate

- Access to a private area on Microsoft's Web site for Microsoft Certified Trainers, where you can exchange information with other MCTs and course developers

- A free subscription to *Microsoft Certified Professional Magazine,* which can help you prepare for your courses

- Invitations to Microsoft conferences and training events

Microsoft Certified Professional+Internet (MCP+Internet)

The Microsoft Certified Professional+Internet (MCP+I) certification documents your ability to plan, configure, and troubleshoot Windows NT Server systems for intranets and the Internet.

You can achieve MCP+I certification while you work toward MCSE status. All MCP+I requirements count toward MCSE certification for Windows NT 4.0. The Windows NT Server 4.0 exam (70-067) also qualifies you for MCP status, so consider taking it first.

Qualifying exams

MCP+I certification requires an exam for each of the three subjects listed in Table C-1. Your only option is your choice of Internet Information Server versions.

Table C-1	MCP+I Exams	
Subject	**Newest Exams**	**Older Exams**
Internet Information Server	Implementing and Supporting Microsoft Internet Information Server 4.0 (Exam 70-087)	Implementing and Supporting Microsoft Internet Information Server 3.0 and Microsoft Index Server 1.1 (Exam 70-077)
TCP/IP	Internetworking with Microsoft TCP/IP on Microsoft Windows NT 4.0 (Exam 70-059)	
Windows NT Server	Implementing and Supporting Microsoft Windows NT Server 4.0 (Exam 70-067)	

Consider taking the IIS 4.0 exam (70-087) for the Internet Information Server requirement of MCP+I certification because IIS 4.0 is the most recent version. When Microsoft decides that IIS 3.0 is obsolete, you may have to pass the IIS 4.0 exam to maintain your certification.

Benefits

In addition to receiving all the benefits listed for becoming an MCP, upon attaining the MCP+Internet certification, you can market yourself with an MCP+Internet logo and add another certificate to your wall.

Microsoft Certified Systems Engineer (MCSE)

Microsoft Certified Systems Engineer (MCSE) is one of the most respected certifications in the industry. The dominance of the Windows NT operating system in the market has created great demand for MCSEs skilled in planning, implementing, and troubleshooting Windows NT and the BackOffice suite of products.

Windows NT 4.0 certification requirements

To become a Microsoft Certified Systems Engineer for Windows NT 4.0, you are required to pass *six* Microsoft exams:

- Four core exams
- Two elective exams

Core exams

The MCSE core exam requirements for Windows NT 4.0 cover *four* subjects, listed in Table C-2. You must pass an exam for each subject. Your only option is your choice of desktop operating system.

Always try to take the newest exam for a subject. When Microsoft retires the older exam, you may have to pass a newer exam to maintain your certification.

Table C-2	MCSE Windows NT 4.0 Core Exams	
Subject	*Newest Exams*	*Older Exams*
Desktop operating system	Microsoft Windows NT Workstation 4.0 (Exam 70-073) Implementing and Supporting Microsoft Windows 98 (Exam 70-098)	Implementing and Supporting Microsoft Windows 95 (Exam 70-064)
Network basics	Networking Essentials (Exam 70-058) or approved equivalent certification	
Windows NT Server (basic)	Implementing and Supporting Microsoft Windows NT Server 4.0 (Exam 70-067)	
Windows NT Server (advanced)	Implementing and Supporting Microsoft Windows NT Server 4.0 in the Enterprise (Exam 70-068)	

Microsoft recognizes that other certification programs cover the requirements of the Networking Essentials exam. After you pass any of the MCSE exams, Microsoft will give you credit for Networking Essentials if you have proof for any of these certifications:

- Novell CNE, Master CNE, or CNI
- Banyan CBS or CBE
- Sun Certified Network Administrator for Solaris 2.5 or 2.6

Elective exams

MCSE certification requires you to pass elective exams for *two* of the subjects listed in Table C-3. *Retired exams* aren't available, but they count toward certification if you passed them when they were current.

Make sure that your MCSE elective exams cover two different subjects in Table C-3. If you take two exams for the same subject, only one exam counts toward your MCSE requirements.

Table C-3	MCSE Elective Exams		
Subject	*Newest Exams*	*Older Exams*	*Retired Exams*
Exchange Server	Implementing and Supporting Microsoft Exchange Server 5.5 (Exam 70-081)	Implementing and Supporting Microsoft Exchange Server 5 (Exam 70-076)	
Internet Explorer	Implementing and Supporting Microsoft Internet Explorer 4.0 by Using the Internet Explorer Administration Kit (Exam 70-079)		
Internet Information Server	Implementing and Supporting Microsoft Internet Information Server 4.0 (Exam 70-087)	Implementing and Supporting Microsoft Internet Information Server 3.0 and Microsoft Index Server 1.1 (Exam 70-077)	
Proxy Server	Implementing and Supporting Microsoft Proxy Server 2.0 (Exam 70-088)	Implementing and Supporting Microsoft Proxy Server 1.0 (Exam 70-078)	
Site Server	Implementing and Supporting Web Sites using Site Server 3.0 (Exam 70-056)		
SNA Server	Implementing and Supporting Microsoft SNA Server 4.0 (Exam 70-085)	Implementing and Supporting Microsoft SNA Server 3.0 (Exam 70-013)	
SQL Server administration	System Administration for Microsoft SQL Server 7.0 (Exam 70-028)	System Administration for Microsoft SQL Server 6.5 (Exam 70-026)	

(continued)

Table C-3 *(continued)*

Subject	Newest Exams	Older Exams	Retired Exams
SQL Server data warehouses	Designing and Implementing Data Warehouses with Microsoft SQL Server 7.0 (Exam 70-019)		
SQL Server implementation	Implementing a Database Design on Microsoft SQL Server 7.0 (Exam 70-029)	Implementing a Database Design on Microsoft SQL Server 6.5 (Exam 70-027)	Microsoft SQL Server 4.2 Database Implementation (Exam 70-021)
Systems Management Server	Implementing and Supporting Microsoft Systems Management Server 2.0 (Exam 70-086)	Implementing and Supporting Microsoft Systems Management Server 1.2 (Exam 70-018)	
TCP/IP	Internetworking with Microsoft TCP/IP on Microsoft Windows NT 4.0 (Exam 70-059)	Internetworking Microsoft TCP/IP on Microsoft Windows NT (3.5-3.51) (Exam 70-053)	

Some of the MCSE elective exams are *core* requirements for MCSE+Internet (MCSE+I) certification. If you're interested in that level of certification, consider fulfilling your MCSE elective requirements from these MCSE+I core requirements:

- ✔ Internetworking with Microsoft TCP/IP on Microsoft Windows NT 4.0 (Exam 70-059)

- ✔ Implementing and Supporting Microsoft Internet Explorer 4.0 by Using the Internet Explorer Administration Kit (Exam 70-079)

- ✔ Implementing and Supporting Microsoft Internet Information Server 4.0 (Exam 70-087) *or* Implementing and Supporting Microsoft Internet Information Server 3.0 and Microsoft Index Server 1.1 (Exam 70-077) (only *one* Internet Information Server exam counts toward your MCSE or MCSE+I certification)

Many of the MCSE elective exams *do not count* toward MCSE+I certification. When you select an MCSE exam, check whether it applies to MCSE+I. If it doesn't apply, consider selecting another exam. (MCSE+I requirements are covered in this Appendix.)

Windows NT 3.51 certification requirements

Microsoft plans to retire the Windows NT 3.51 exams after releasing the Windows NT 5.0 exams. Until then, you can earn an MCSE for Windows NT 3.51. The certification remains valid for a year after the exams are retired. At the end of that year, be prepared to requalify for a current version of Windows NT.

Table C-4 lists the required core subjects for MCSE certification on the Windows NT 3.51 track. You must pass an exam for each subject. (As with NT 4.0, the only NT 3.51 core option is your choice of desktop operating system.)

Table C-4	MCSE Windows NT 3.51 Core Exams	
Subject	*Newest Exams*	*Older Exams*
Desktop operating system	Implementing and Supporting Microsoft Windows 98 (Exam 70-098)	Implementing and Supporting Microsoft Windows 95 (Exam 70-064)
Network basics	Networking Essentials (Exam 70-058) or approved equivalent certification	

(continued)

Table C-4 *(continued)*

Subject	Newest Exams	Older Exams
Windows NT Workstation	Implementing and Supporting Microsoft Windows NT Workstation 3.51 (Exam 70-042)	
Windows NT Server	Implementing and Supporting Microsoft Windows NT Server 3.51 (Exam 70-043)	

MCSE for Windows NT 3.51 also requires two electives, as described for Windows NT 4.0 certification.

Don't bother with NT 3.51 certification. Microsoft intends to decertify the NT 3.51 exams, and they don't count toward MCSE+I. Unless you just need *one* NT 3.51 exam to finish your MCSE requirements on the NT 3.51 track, spend your time on NT 4.0.

Benefits

In addition to receiving all the benefits of becoming an MCP, upon attaining the MCSE certification, you enjoy these benefits:

- Marketing yourself with an MCSE logo
- Yet another certificate for your accomplishments
- One-year subscription to Microsoft TechNet Plus

MCSE+Internet

The designation MCSE+Internet is known as MCSE+I. This designates Microsoft Certified Systems Engineers who have extensive qualifications for Internet system management, including

- Web sites
- Browsers

🖝 Commerce applications

🖝 Intranets

MCSE+I requirements

Nine exams are necessary for MCSE+I certification:

🖝 Seven core exams

🖝 Two elective exams

The following sections show how they add up.

Core exams

The MCSE+I core exam requirements for Windows NT 4.0 cover *seven* subjects, listed in Table C-5. You must pass an exam for each subject. Your only options are your choice of desktop operating system and version of Internet Information Server.

Table C-5	MCSE+I Core Exams	
Subject	*Newest Exams*	*Older Exams*
Desktop operating system	Microsoft Windows NT Workstation 4.0 (Exam 70-073) Implementing and Supporting Microsoft Windows 98 (Exam 70-098)	Implementing and Supporting Microsoft Windows 95 (Exam 70-064)
Internet Explorer	Implementing and Supporting Microsoft Internet Explorer 4.0 by Using the Internet Explorer Administration Kit (Exam 70-079)	
Internet Information Server	Implementing and Supporting Microsoft Internet Information Server 4.0 (Exam 70-087)	Implementing and Supporting Microsoft Internet Information Server 3.0 and Microsoft Index Server 1.1 (Exam 70-077)

(continued)

Table C-5 *(continued)*

Subject	Newest Exams	Older Exams
Network basics	Networking Essentials (Exam 70-058) or approved equivalent certification	
TCP/IP	Internetworking with Microsoft TCP/IP on Microsoft Windows NT 4.0 (Exam 70-059)	
Windows NT Server (basic)	Implementing and Supporting Microsoft Windows NT Server 4.0 (Exam 70-067)	
Windows NT Server (advanced)	Implementing and Supporting Microsoft Windows NT Server 4.0 in the Enterprise (Exam 70-068)	

Elective exams

MCSE+I certification requires you to pass elective exams for *two* of the subjects listed in Table C-6.

Make sure your MCSE+I elective exams cover two different subjects in Table C-6. If you take two exams for the same subject, only one exam counts toward MCSE+I certification.

Table C-6   MCSE+I Elective Exams

Subject	Newest Exams	Older Exams
Exchange Server	Implementing and Supporting Microsoft Exchange Server 5.5 (Exam 70-081)	Implementing and Supporting Microsoft Exchange Server 5 (Exam 70-076)
Proxy Server	Implementing and Supporting Microsoft Proxy Server 2.0 (Exam 70-088)	Implementing and Supporting Microsoft Proxy Server 1.0 (Exam 70-078)
Site Server	Implementing and Supporting Web Sites using Site Server 3.0 (Exam 70-056)	
SNA Server	Implementing and Supporting Microsoft SNA Server 4.0 (Exam 70-085)	

Subject	Newest Exams	Older Exams
SQL Server administration	Administering Microsoft SQL Server 7.0 (Exam 70-028)	System Administration for Microsoft SQL Server 6.5 (Exam 70-026)
SQL Server implementation	Designing and Implementing Databases with Microsoft SQL Server 7.0 (Exam 70-029)	Implementing a Database Design on Microsoft SQL Server 6.5 (Exam 70-027)

Benefits

In addition to receiving all the benefits listed for becoming an MCSE, upon attaining the MCSE+Internet certification, you can also market yourself with an MCSE+Internet logo and receive another certificate for your accomplishments.

Online References

To find out more about the Microsoft's certification programs, check out Microsoft's Training and Certification Web site:

```
www.Microsoft.com/Train_Cert/
```

Make it a practice to visit this site regularly: It's the definitive source for updated information about the Microsoft Certified Professional program. Microsoft updates and retires exams often enough that you need to make an effort to stay on top of the changes, and this Web site is your best center for the latest information on certifications and exams.

Appendix D
About the CD

• •

You can find the following on the *MCSE Networking Essentials For Dummies,* 2nd Edition CD-ROM:

- ✔ The QuickLearn game, a fun way to study for the test
- ✔ Practice and Self-Assessment tests, to make sure that you're ready for the real thing
- ✔ Practice test demos from Specialized Solutions, Super Software, and Transcender
- ✔ A bonus chapter about Computerized Adaptive Testing
- ✔ A Links file to help you find resources on the Web

System Requirements

You need to make sure that your computer meets the following minimum system requirements. If your computer doesn't match up to most of these requirements, you may have problems using the contents of the CD.

- ✔ A PC with a 486 or faster processor
- ✔ Microsoft Windows 95 or later
- ✔ At least 16MB of total RAM installed on your computer
- ✔ A CD-ROM drive — double-speed (2x) or faster
- ✔ A sound card
- ✔ A monitor capable of displaying at least 256 colors or grayscale
- ✔ A modem with a speed of at least 14,400 bps

Important note: To play the QuickLearn game, you must have a 166 or faster computer running Windows 95 or 98 with SVGA graphics. You must also have Microsoft DirectX 5.0 or later installed. If you do not have DirectX, you can install it from the CD. Simply run D:\Directx\dxinstall.exe. Unfortunately, DirectX 5.0 does not run on Windows NT 4.0, so you cannot play the QuickLearn Game on a Windows NT 4.0 or earlier machine.

Using the CD

To install the items from the CD to your hard drive, follow these steps:

1. **Insert the CD into your computer's CD-ROM drive.**

2. **Click Start⇨Run.**

3. **In the dialog box that appears, type** D:\SETUP.EXE.

   Replace *D* with the proper drive letter if your CD-ROM drive uses a different letter.

4. **Click OK.**

   A License Agreement window appears.

5. **Read the license agreement, nod your head, and then click the Accept button if you want to use the CD. After you click Accept, you'll never be bothered by the License Agreement window again.**

   The CD interface Welcome screen appears. The interface is a little program that shows you what's on the CD and coordinates installing the programs and running the demos. The interface basically enables you to click a button or two to make things happen.

6. **Click anywhere on the Welcome screen to enter the interface.**

   Now you're getting to the action. The next screen lists categories for the software on the CD.

7. **To view the items within a category, simply click the category's name.**

   A list of programs in the category appears.

8. **For more information about a program, click the program's name.**

   Be sure to read the information that appears. Sometimes a program has its own system requirements or requires you to do a few tricks on your computer before you can install or run the program. This screen tells you what you need to do, if necessary.

9. **If you don't want to install the program, click the Go Back button to return to the preceding screen.**

   You can always return to the preceding screen by clicking the Go Back button. This feature enables you to browse the different categories and products and decide what you want to install.

10. **To install a program, click the appropriate Install button.**

    The CD interface drops to the background while the CD installs the program you chose.

11. **To install other items, repeat Steps 7 through 10.**

12. **When you finish installing programs, click the Quit button to close the interface.**

    You can eject the CD now. Carefully place it back in the plastic jacket of the book for safekeeping.

To run some of the programs on the *MCSE Networking Essentials For Dummies,* 2nd Edition CD, you will need to keep the CD in your CD-ROM drive.

What You'll Find

This section offers a summary of the software on the *MCSE Networking Essentials For Dummies,* 2nd Edition CD.

Dummies test prep tools

This CD contains questions related to Networking Essentials. Most of the questions are Networking Essentials topics that you can expect to be on the test. We also include some questions on other Networking Essentials topics that may or may not be on the current test or covered in the book, but that you will need to perform your job.

QuickLearn Game

The QuickLearn Game is the *...For Dummies* way of making studying for the Certification exam fun. Well, okay, less painful. OutPost is a DirectX, high-resolution, fast-paced arcade game.

Answer questions to defuse dimensional disrupters and save the universe from a rift in space-time. (The questions come from the same set of questions that the Self-Assessment and Practice Test use, but isn't this way more fun?) Missing a few questions on the real exam almost never results in a rip in the fabric of the universe, so just think how easy it'll be when you get there!

Please note: QUIKLERN.EXE on the CD is simply a self-extractor, to simplify the process of copying the game files to your computer. It does not create any shortcuts on your computer's desktop or Start menu.

Note: Don't forget, you need to have DirectX 5.0 or later installed to play the QuickLearn game; it does not run on Windows NT 4.0.

Practice Test

The Practice test is designed to help you get comfortable with the MCSE testing situation and pinpoint your strengths and weaknesses on the topic. You can accept the default setting of 60 questions in 60 minutes, or you can customize the settings. You can choose the number of questions, the amount of time, and even decide which objectives you want to focus on.

After you answer the questions, the Practice test gives you plenty of feedback. You can find out which questions you answered correctly and incorrectly and get statistics on how you did, broken down by objective. Then you can review the questions — all of them, all the ones you missed, all the ones you marked, or a combination of the ones you marked and the ones you missed.

Self-Assessment Test

The Self-Assessment test is designed to simulate the actual MCSE testing situation. You must answer 60 questions in 60 minutes. After you answer all the questions, you find out your score and whether you pass or fail — but that's all the feedback you get. If you can pass the Self-Assessment test regularly, you're ready to tackle the real thing.

Links Page

I've also created a Links Page, a handy starting place for accessing the huge amounts of information on the Internet about the MCSE tests. You can find the page at D:\Links.htm.

Bonus Chapter: Computerized Adaptive Testing For Dummies

This special CD chapter describes computerized adaptive testing (CAT) — how it works, and how it differs from both computerized testing in general and other types of tests. The chapter also discusses the many advantages of CATs and includes a FAQ about certification CATs specifically. There is even a section where test takers discuss their reactions to the CATs they have survived. A final section discusses the use of simulations in performance-based testing and shows you how such tests are superior to multiple-choice and other types of questioning for certification exams. This chapter is in PDF format, and you need Adobe Acrobat Reader to view it. If you don't already have Acrobat Reader, you can install it from the CD.

Screen Saver

A spiffy little screen saver that the ...*For Dummies* team created. Maybe, like sleeping with the book under your pillow, this screen saver can help you learn subliminally! Screen shots of test questions fill your screen, so when your computer is not doing anything else, it can still be quizzing you!

Commercial demos

MCSEprep Exam Simulator, from Super Software, Inc.

This demo, designed to help you prepare for the MCSE Networking Essentials exam, gives you five practice questions — just enough to get a taste. Get lots more by ordering the software. Learn more by visiting the Web site `www.mcseprep.com`.

QuickCert, from Specialized Solutions

This package, from Specialized Solutions, offers QuickCert practice tests for several Certification exams. Run the QuickCert IDG Demo to choose the practice test you want to work on. For more information about QuickCert, visit the Specialized Solutions Web site at `www.specializedsolutions.com`.

Networking Essentials Demo, from Specialized Solutions

This is a demo of some of the training aids you get from Specialized Solutions self-study courses. A practice quiz, video training, simulations, and an electronic dictionary give you a taste of the training module for Networking Essentials.

Transcender NetCert demo, from Transcender Corporation

Here is a demo of Transcender's Networking Essentials exam simulation. You can get a taste of Transcender's other products through the Certification Sampler, also on the CD. To find out more about what Transcender has to offer, check out its Web site at `www.transcender.com`.

Transcender NetFlash, from Transcender Corporation

Another demo from the good folks at Transcender, this one is designed to help you learn the fundamental concepts and terminology behind Networking Essentials. You provide short answer-type explanations to questions presented in a flash card format and grade yourself as you go.

Transcender Certification Sampler, from Transcender Corporation

Transcender's demo tests are some of the most popular practice tests available. The Certification Sampler offers demos of many of the exams that Transcender offers.

SimDemo, from Sylvan Prometric

This demo shows you two simulation questions and lets you work through them, to help you get comfortable with this question format.

Computer Adaptive Testing Demonstration, from Galton Technologies

This little program is designed to demonstrate how computer adaptive testing (CAT) works. When you start the Math CAT test, you are presented with a series of math problems. If you remember lots of high school algebra, you'll be done with this test pretty quickly. If you hadn't planned on ever solving for *x* again, it may take you a little longer. Either way, this program is a good way to see just what CAT is all about.

If You Have Problems (of the CD Kind)

I tried my best to compile programs that work on most computers with the minimum system requirements. Alas, your computer may differ, and some programs may not work properly for some reason.

The two most likely problems are that your computer doesn't have enough memory (RAM) for the programs you want to use, or that you have other programs running that are affecting the installation or running of a program. If you get error messages such as `Not enough memory` or `Setup cannot continue,` try one or more of the following actions and then try using the software again:

- ✓ **Turn off any antivirus software you have on your computer.** Installers sometimes mimic virus activity and may make your computer incorrectly believe that it is being infected by a virus.

- ✓ **Close all running programs.** The more programs you're running, the less memory is available to other programs. Installers also typically update files and programs; if you keep other programs running, installation may not work properly.

- ✓ **In Windows, close the CD interface and run demos or installations directly from Windows Explorer.** The interface itself can tie up system memory or even conflict with certain kinds of interactive demos. Use Windows Explorer to browse the files on the CD and launch installers or demos.

- ✓ **Have your local computer store add more RAM to your computer.** This step is, admittedly, drastic and somewhat expensive. If you have a Windows 95 PC with a PowerPC chip, however, adding more memory can really help the speed of your computer and enable more programs to run at the same time.

If you still have trouble installing the items from the CD, please call the IDG Books Worldwide Customer Service phone number at 800-762-2974 (outside the U.S.: 317-596-5430).

Index

Notes

Notes

Notes

Notes

Notes

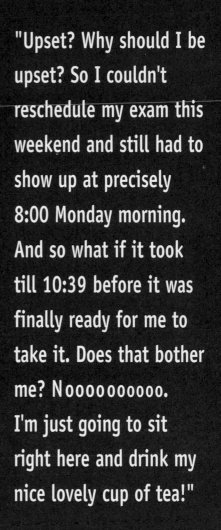

"Upset? Why should I be upset? So I couldn't reschedule my exam this weekend and still had to show up at precisely 8:00 Monday morning. And so what if it took till 10:39 before it was finally ready for me to take it. Does that bother me? Noooooooooo. I'm just going to sit right here and drink my nice lovely cup of tea!"

Hint: Now is not a good time to tell him he should have tested at a VUE Authorized Testing Center.

With VUE's real-time web-interface you can register or reschedule your exam 24 hours / 7days a week, not just when someone happens to be answering the phone. Also, all VUE Testing Centers are tied into our powerful registration system, so you can register and pay at the site, and be taking your exam minutes later. And if you want to take another crack at an exam that you just 'sub-optimized', a VUE testing center should have your exam ready in less than five minutes.

Also, VUE is the only testing network that live-links your records directly with Microsoft and Novell's certification databases; you can test at any VUE Testing Center with the assurance and confidence that your results will get where they need to go.

To register for a Microsoft exam call toll free 888-837-8616 (USA & CAN), to register on the Web or to obtain a complete list of world-wide toll free phone numbers go to www.vue.com/ms

When it really matters, test with VUE.

Microsoft Certified
Professional
Exam Provider

VUE®
VIRTUAL UNIVERSITY ENTERPRISES

a division of NCS®

For more information, go to
w w w . v u e . c o m

©1998 NCS, Inc. All rights reserved.

IDG Books Worldwide, Inc., End-User License Agreement

READ THIS. You should carefully read these terms and conditions before opening the software packet(s) included with this book ("Book"). This is a license agreement ("Agreement") between you and IDG Books Worldwide, Inc. ("IDGB"). By opening the accompanying software packet(s), you acknowledge that you have read and accept the following terms and conditions. If you do not agree and do not want to be bound by such terms and conditions, promptly return the Book and the unopened software packet(s) to the place you obtained them for a full refund.

1. **License Grant.** IDGB grants to you (either an individual or entity) a nonexclusive license to use one copy of the enclosed software program(s) (collectively, the "Software") solely for your own personal or business purposes on a single computer (whether a standard computer or a workstation component of a multiuser network). The Software is in use on a computer when it is loaded into temporary memory (RAM) or installed into permanent memory (hard disk, CD-ROM, or other storage device). IDGB reserves all rights not expressly granted herein.

2. **Ownership.** IDGB is the owner of all right, title, and interest, including copyright, in and to the compilation of the Software recorded on the disk(s) or CD-ROM ("Software Media"). Copyright to the individual programs recorded on the Software Media is owned by the author or other authorized copyright owner of each program. Ownership of the Software and all proprietary rights relating thereto remain with IDGB and its licensers.

3. **Restrictions on Use and Transfer.**

   (a) You may only (i) make one copy of the Software for backup or archival purposes, or (ii) transfer the Software to a single hard disk, provided that you keep the original for backup or archival purposes. You may not (i) rent or lease the Software, (ii) copy or reproduce the Software through a LAN or other network system or through any computer subscriber system or bulletin-board system, or (iii) modify, adapt, or create derivative works based on the Software.

   (b) You may not reverse engineer, decompile, or disassemble the Software. You may transfer the Software and user documentation on a permanent basis, provided that the transferee agrees to accept the terms and conditions of this Agreement and you retain no copies. If the Software is an update or has been updated, any transfer must include the most recent update and all prior versions.

4. **Restrictions on Use of Individual Programs.** You must follow the individual requirements and restrictions detailed for each individual program in Appendix D of this Book. These limitations are also contained in the individual license agreements recorded on the Software Media. These limitations may include a requirement that after using the program for a specified period of time, the user must pay a registration fee or discontinue use. By opening the Software packet(s), you will be agreeing to abide by the licenses and restrictions for these individual programs that are detailed in Appendix D and on the Software Media. None of the material on this Software Media or listed in this Book may ever be redistributed, in original or modified form, for commercial purposes.

5. **Limited Warranty.**

   (a) IDGB warrants that the Software and Software Media are free from defects in materials and workmanship under normal use for a period of sixty (60) days from the date of purchase of this Book. If IDGB receives notification within the warranty period of defects in materials or workmanship, IDGB will replace the defective Software Media.

   (b) **IDGB AND THE AUTHOR OF THE BOOK DISCLAIM ALL OTHER WARRANTIES, EXPRESS OR IMPLIED, INCLUDING WITHOUT LIMITATION IMPLIED WARRANTIES OF MER- CHANTABILITY AND FITNESS FOR A PARTICULAR PURPOSE, WITH RESPECT TO THE SOFTWARE, THE PROGRAMS, THE SOURCE CODE CONTAINED THEREIN, AND/OR THE TECHNIQUES DESCRIBED IN THIS BOOK. IDGB DOES NOT WARRANT THAT THE FUNCTIONS CONTAINED IN THE SOFTWARE WILL MEET YOUR REQUIREMENTS OR THAT THE OPERATION OF THE SOFTWARE WILL BE ERROR FREE.**

   (c) This limited warranty gives you specific legal rights, and you may have other rights that vary from jurisdiction to jurisdiction.

6. **Remedies.**

   (a) IDGB's entire liability and your exclusive remedy for defects in materials and workmanship shall be limited to replacement of the Software Media, which may be returned to IDGB with a copy of your receipt at the following address: Software Media Fulfillment Department, Attn.: *MCSE Networking Essentials For Dummies, 2nd Edition* IDG Books Worldwide, Inc., 7260 Shadeland Station, Ste. 100, Indianapolis, IN 46256, or call 800-762-2974. Please allow three to four weeks for delivery. This Limited Warranty is void if failure of the Software Media has resulted from accident, abuse, or misapplication. Any replacement Software Media will be warranted for the remainder of the original warranty period or thirty (30) days, whichever is longer.

   (b) In no event shall IDGB or the author be liable for any damages whatsoever (including without limitation damages for loss of business profits, business interruption, loss of business information, or any other pecuniary loss) arising from the use of or inability to use the Book or the Software, even if IDGB has been advised of the possibility of such damages.

   (c) Because some jurisdictions do not allow the exclusion or limitation of liability for conse- quential or incidental damages, the above limitation or exclusion may not apply to you.

7. **U.S. Government Restricted Rights.** Use, duplication, or disclosure of the Software by the U.S. Government is subject to restrictions stated in paragraph (c)(1)(ii) of the Rights in Technical Data and Computer Software clause of DFARS 252.227-7013, and in subparagraphs (a) through (d) of the Commercial Computer–Restricted Rights clause at FAR 52.227-19, and in similar clauses in the NASA FAR supplement, when applicable.

8. **General.** This Agreement constitutes the entire understanding of the parties and revokes and supersedes all prior agreements, oral or written, between them and may not be modified or amended except in a writing signed by both parties hereto that specifically refers to this Agreement. This Agreement shall take precedence over any other documents that may be in conflict herewith. If any one or more provisions contained in this Agreement are held by any court or tribunal to be invalid, illegal, or otherwise unenforceable, each and every other provision shall remain in full force and effect.

Installation Instructions

To install the items from the CD to your hard drive with Microsoft Windows, follow these steps:

1. **Insert the CD into your computer's CD-ROM drive.**

2. **Click Start⇨Run.**

3. **In the dialog box that appears, type** D:\SETUP.EXE.

   Replace *D* with the proper drive letter if your CD-ROM drive uses a different letter.

4. **Click OK. Read the license agreement, nod your head, and then click the Accept button if you want to use the CD. After you click Accept, you'll never be bothered by the License Agreement window again.**

5. **Click anywhere on the Welcome screen to enter the interface.**

6. **To view the items within a category, just click the category's name.**

7. **For more information about a program, click the program's name.**

8. **If you don't want to install the program, click the Go Back button to return to the preceding screen.**

9. **To install a program, click the appropriate Install button.**

10. **To install other items, repeat Steps 6 through 9.**

11. **When you finish installing programs, click the Quit button to close the interface.**

    You can eject the CD now. Carefully place it back in the plastic jacket for safekeeping.

To run some of the programs on the *MCSE Networking Essentials For Dummies,* 2nd Edition CD, keep the CD in your CD-ROM drive.

For details about the contents of the CD-ROM and instructions for installing the software from the CD-ROM, see Appendix D in this book.

Discover Dummies™ Online!

The *Dummies* Web Site is your fun and friendly online resource for the latest information about ...*For Dummies®* books on all your favorite topics. From cars to computers, wine to Windows, and investing to the Internet, we've got a shelf full of ...*For Dummies* books waiting for you!

Ten Fun and Useful Things You Can Do at www.dummies.com

1. Register this book and win!
2. Find and buy the ...*For Dummies* books you want online.
3. Get ten great *Dummies Tips™* every week.
4. Chat with your favorite ...*For Dummies* authors.
5. Subscribe free to *The Dummies Dispatch™* newsletter.
6. Enter our sweepstakes and win cool stuff.
7. Send a free cartoon postcard to a friend.
8. Download free software.
9. Sample a book before you buy.
10. Talk to us. Make comments, ask questions, and get answers!

Jump online to these ten fun and useful things at
http://www.dummies.com/10useful

For other technology titles from IDG Books Worldwide, go to
www.idgbooks.com

Not online yet? It's easy to get started with *The Internet For Dummies®*, 5th Edition, or *Dummies 101®: The Internet For Windows® 98*, available at local retailers everywhere.

Find other ...*For Dummies* books on these topics:
Business • Careers • Databases • Food & Beverages • Games • Gardening • Graphics • Hardware
Health & Fitness • Internet and the World Wide Web • Networking • Office Suites
Operating Systems • Personal Finance • Pets • Programming • Recreation • Sports
Spreadsheets • Teacher Resources • Test Prep • Word Processing

IDG BOOKS WORLDWIDE BOOK REGISTRATION

Register This Book and Win!

We want to hear from you!

Visit **http://my2cents.dummies.com** to register this book and tell us how you liked it!

- Get entered in our monthly prize giveaway.

- Give us feedback about this book — tell us what you like best, what you like least, or maybe what you'd like to ask the author and us to change!

- Let us know any other *...For Dummies*® topics that interest you.

Your feedback helps us determine what books to publish, tells us what coverage to add as we revise our books, and lets us know whether we're meeting your needs as a *...For Dummies* reader. You're our most valuable resource, and what you have to say is important to us!

Not on the Web yet? It's easy to get started with *Dummies 101*®: *The Internet For Windows*® *98* or *The Internet For Dummies*®, 5th Edition, at local retailers everywhere.

Or let us know what you think by sending us a letter at the following address:

...For Dummies Book Registration
Dummies Press
7260 Shadeland Station, Suite 100
Indianapolis, IN 46256-3917
Fax 317-596-5498

...FOR DUMMIES™

BESTSELLING BOOK SERIES